*Intergenerational
Linkages*

Vern L. Bengtson, PhD, is the AARP/University Professor of Gerontology and Sociology at the Andrus Gerontology Center of the University of Southern California and Past President of the Gerontological Society of America. He directs the 23-year Longitudinal Study of Three-Generation Families at the University of Southern California. Among his most recent publications is *The Changing Contract Across Generations.*

Robert A. Harootyan, MS, MA, is Senior Research Associate in the Forecasting and Environmental Scanning Department at the American Association of Retired Persons (AARP) and was Director of the former New Roles in Society Program at AARP. Prior to joining AARP, he was a Senior Analyst at the Office of Technology Assessment, U.S. Congress, where he directed the OTA studies of *Technology and Aging in America* and *Life-Sustaining Technologies and the Elderly.* He has held faculty positions at Cornell University, the State University of New York at Oswego, and the University of Southern California. Mr. Harootyan's current research focuses on demographic aspects of aging, technological advances in residential environments, intergenerational relationships, and forecasts of health and mortality trends in the older population.

Intergenerational Linkages

Hidden Connections in American Society

Vern L. Bengtson
Robert A. Harootyan

Contributors

Karl Kronebusch
Leora Lawton
Mark Schlesinger
Merril Silverstein
Robert E. Vorek

Springer Publishing Company

Copyright © 1994 by Springer Publishing Company, Inc. and the American Association of Retired Persons.

Springer Publishing Company, Inc.
536 Broadway
New York, NY 10012-3955

American Association of Retired Persons
601 E. Street, NW
Washington, DC 20049

94 95 96 97 98 / 5 4 3 2 1

Library of Congress Cataloging-in-Publication-Data

Intergenerational linkages: hidden connections in American society
   Vern L. Bengtson and Robert A. Harootyan, editors
      p.   cm.
   Includes bibliographical references and index.
   ISBN 0-8261-8670-X
   1. Parent and adult child—United States.   2. Intergenerational relations—United States.   3. Family—United States—Psychological aspects.   I. Bengtson, Vern L.   II. Harootyan, Robert A.
HQ755.86.I58   1994
306.874—dc20   94-29230
                                                                          CIP

Printed in the United States of America

Contents

Contributors   *vii*

Foreword   *ix*

Preface   *xvii*

Acknowledgments   *xix*

1   Intergenerational Linkages: The Context of the Study   1
Robert A. Harootyan and Vern L. Bengtson

2   Solidarity Between Generations in Families   19
Leora Lawton, Merril Silverstein, and Vern L. Bengtson

3   Types of Relations Between Parents and Adult Children   43
Merril Silverstein, Leora Lawton, and Vern L. Bengtson

4   Volunteering, Helping, and Gift Giving in Families
and Communities   77
Robert A. Harootyan and Robert E. Vorek

5   Intergenerational Transfers   112
Karl Kronebusch and Mark Schlesinger

6   Intergenerational Tensions and Conflict: Attitudes and
Perceptions About Social Justice and Age-Related Needs   152
Mark Schlesinger and Karl Kronebusch

7   The Sources of Intergenerational Burdens and Tensions   185
Mark Schlesinger and Karl Kronebusch

8 Generational Linkages and Implications for Public Policy   210
   Vern L. Bengtson and Robert A. Harootyan

Appendix A   *235*
Appendix B   *241*
Appendix C   *252*
Appendix D   *265*
Appendix E   *278*
Appendix F   *287*
Appendix G   *295*

References   *309*

Index   *323*

Contributors

W. Andrew Achenbaum, PhD, is Professor of History at the University of Michigan, Ann Arbor, and Deputy Director of the Institute of Gerontology there. Among his many publications is *Social Security: Visions and Revisions.*

Karl Kronebusch, PhD, is Assistant Professor in the Department of Political Science and in the Robert M. La Follette Institute of Public Affairs at the University of Wisconsin, Madison. His research interests concern health policy, social policy, and the politics of health and social policy decision making. He worked for a number of years at the Office of Technology Assessment of the U.S. Congress.

Leora Lawton, PhD, is Research Analyst at Bellcore in Morristown, New Jersey, and a Research Associate at the Andrus Gerontology Center at the University of Southern California. She is also Adjunct Assistant Professor of Sociology at Montclair State College, New Jersey, and at the John Jay College of Criminal Justice, City University of New York. Her research focuses on intergenerational relations, specifically as a function of parental divorce.

Mark Schlesinger, PhD, is Associate Professor of Public Health and Fellow at the Institution for Social and Policy Studies, Yale University, and Visiting Associate Professor at the Institute for Health, Health Care Policy, and Aging Research at Rutgers University. He was previously on the faculty at the Kennedy School of Government and Harvard Medical School. Dr. Schlesinger has been a consultant to a variety of state and federal agencies, including the Departments of Elder Affairs in Massachusetts and New York, the Department of Mental Health in Massachusetts, the General Accounting Office, Office of Technology Assessment, Department of Veterans Affairs, National Institution on

Drug Abuse, and the National Institute of Mental Health. A recent publication edited with L. Eisenberg is *Children in a Changing Health System.*

Merril Silverstein, PhD, is the Hanson Family Trust Assistant Professor of Gerontology and Assistant Professor of Sociology at the Andrus Gerontology Center of the University of Southern California. His research addresses such issues as changes in parent–child relations over the adult life course, the consequences of intergenerational social support on physical and mental health of older parents, and the role health and social factors play in the decision of older people to migrate into planned retirement communities. In collaboration with the Chinese Academy of Social Sciences, he is studying the impact of economic modernization on intergenerational relations within the Chinese family.

Robert E. Vorek, PhD, an anthropologist, is Senior Research Associate in the Evaluation Research Services Department at the American Association of Retired Persons (AARP). He has taught at the University of Maryland and American University, and has conducted ethnographic fieldwork in the Republic of Ireland. As a Senior Research Analyst with Applied Systems Institute, Dr. Vorek conducted research projects for the Education Services, the U.S. Department of Education, the U.S. Department of Agriculture, the Federal Aviation Administration, and the Governor's Office of Job Training in Michigan. He recently served as principal author on a report on "Environmental Issues and an Aging Population."

Foreword

Historians, literary critics, political scientists, and sociologists have long been trying to figure out the "hidden connections" that enable this diverse society of ours to hang together, despite the many and obvious differences between groups that constitute it. Gerontologists are relative newcomers to this endeavor. This volume reports data from a nationwide study concerning differences and linkages across age groups in American society today. It provides convincing evidence that there are hidden connections between young and older Americans that may not be reflected in the mass media or current political discussions.

Frederick Jackson Turner attributed distinctive features of American life to the legacy of our "frontier" mentality. Pioneers had to band together at the margins of civilization, pooling resources in times of danger and sharing responsibilities for governing themselves. "The existence of an area of free land, its continuous recession, and the advance of American settlement westward, explain American development," Turner hypothesized. "So long as free land exists, the opportunity for a competency exists, and economic power secures political power. But the democracy born of free land . . . has its dangers as well as its benefits."[1] Note how both positive and negative traits in the American character were attributed to the availability of free land as an "escape valve" in the United States. Turner thought that he was writing at the end of an era of American history: According to the U.S. Census Bureau, the "frontier" had closed. Yet the features of the American experience that Turner cited as pivotal—energy, innovation, a desire for self-rule—surely remain as central in our nation's temperament as they did a century ago. Building metropolises at home and an empire overseas became the new frontier for the 20th century, once there was less virgin territory to settle.

By the time I was an undergraduate, Turner's essays were still required reading, but his frontier thesis had largely been discredited by subsequent events. In its place was David Potter's interpretation of the centripetal and centrifugal forces that interacted in the New World. Americans, Potter contended, were a "people of plenty." More than was true anywhere else on earth, economic abundance provided the necessary wherewithal to enable most individuals to achieve their dreams. The freedom to set goals and to try to attain them was itself an ideal nurtured in Americans from birth.

> Economic abundance is a factor whose presence and whose force may be clearly and precisely recognized in the most personal and intimate phases of the development of the personality in the child. Yet, at the same time, the presence and the force of this factor are recognizable with equal certainty in the whole broad, general range of American experience, American ideals, and American institutions. At both levels, it has exercised a pervasive influence in the shaping of the American character.[2]

Like Turner, Potter focused on a single factor which he believed was sufficient to explain the making of United States society, past and present.

Louis Hartz, a professor of government at Harvard, was also struck by the unique manner in which United States society developed. According to Hartz's "fragment" thesis, the process of colonization took place just as "liberalism," with its emphasis on capitalism, democracy, and individuals, was the regnant ideology in Western Europe. Thus the United States became the quintessential liberal society, spared the ills of feudalism and socialism. "America represents the liberal mechanism of Europe functioning without the European social antagonisms, but the truth is, it is only through these antagonisms that we recognize the mechanism."[3] Comparative cross-national and transhistorical analyses facilitated the discovery of hidden connections. Hartz fully appreciated the ambivalence engendered by being a "fragment," for it was evident in the country's historical development:

> The liberal society analyst is destined in two ways to be a less pleasing scholar than the Progressive: he finds national weaknesses and he can offer no absolute assurance on the basis of the past that they will be remedied. He tends to criticize and then shrug his shoulders, which is no way to become popular, especially in an age like our own.[4]

Potter and Hartz had many admirers and some detractors in the 1960s. Since then, their style of writing history has been eclipsed by

Marxist and neoconservative interpretations, as well as by the so-called "new" social history (with its emphases on African-American history, women's history, gender studies, urban history, labor history, youth studies, history of education, and old-age history, etc.). A few recent studies in this "grand" synthetic tradition—Christopher Lasch's *Culture of Narcissism* in 1977 and *Habits of the Heart* in 1985 by Robert Bellah and associates come to mind—attempted to construct an argument about what united and divided Americans around a small cluster of themata.[5] None of these works, however, enjoyed the following, or is likely to have the enduring impact, of Alexis de Tocqueville's magisterial interpretation of American culture. *Democracy in America* (written and revised 1835–1840) remains the *classicus locus* for starting an analysis of any aspect of American culture, including its integrative and conflict-ridden hidden connections.[6]

L'individualisme, de Tocqueville hypothesized, is the dominant quality of the American culture. "Individualism" is not a synonym either for individuality (which has positive connotations) or for selfishness (which does not). By the term de Tocqueville meant a distinctive personality trait manifested only in societies that embraced a democratic form of government and in which there was, compared to class-ridden Europe, relative equality of condition. Individualism was a mixed blessing. De Tocqueville was convinced that most American white, male property owners in Jacksonian America truly were self-reliant, just as Ralph Waldo Emerson was celebrating in speeches and essays. Yet, because generational relations were attenuated in the United States, the French aristocrat also perceived that most citizens did not pay much attention to tradition. Nor did they evince much concern for their progeny. Americans truly seized the moment. As a result, their economy, their polity, and their comity were atomistic. Any manifestation of an "American" collective will, it seemed to follow, would be no more enduring than the ephemeral fancies of various segments of a multicultural populace. Yet the messiness of American "reality" intruded on the elegance of the French man's logic: in his travels, de Tocqueville in fact did observe many instances in which Americans from all sorts of backgrounds and conditions supported one another.

"When an American asks for the co-operation of his fellow citizens, it is seldom refused; and I have often seen it afforded spontaneously, and with great goodwill," de Tocqueville observed. "If an accident happens on the highway, everybody hastens to help the sufferer; if some great and sudden calamity befalls a family, the purses of a thousand strangers are at once willingly opened and small but numerous donations pour in to relieve their distress."[7] Like Turner, Potter, and Hartz, de Tocqueville was quick to note the difference between the United States and other civilized countries. Elsewhere, the wretched are friendless. Americans, in contrast, may appear "always cold and often coarse in their manners," but United States citizens do not refuse to help those in need. This humanitarian impulse, de Tocqueville believed, did not contradict the pervasive spirit of individualism. Indeed, it arose from the same source. "Equality of condition, while it makes men feel their independence, shows them their own weakness: they are free, but exposed to a thousand accidents; and experience soon teaches them that although they do not habitually require the assistance of others, a time almost always comes when they cannot do without it."[8] Thus, Americans realized that it was in their ultimate self-interest to join voluntarily with others to help others.

Conditions in the United States, according to de Tocqueville, provided "hidden connections" in the social fabric. Democratic egalitarianism induced a sense of solidarity among those who might independently go their separate ways. "The more equal social conditions become, the more do men display this reciprocal disposition to oblige each other. In democracies no great benefits are conferred . . . but all men are ready to be of service to one another."[9] American historians recently have questioned whether the United States during the 1830s and 1840s was really as homogeneous as de Tocqueville assumed. It now seems likely that there was as much inequality in terms of income as any period in our national experience, with the possible exception of the Reagan years, which were appalling for their maldistribution of wealth. That said, *Democracy in America* remains an insightful text today concerning the ties that bind us together.

Whereas de Tocqueville, Turner, Potter, and Hartz all deduced from a central organizing theme their respective insights about the forces that kept the United States together and that split the country apart, Vern Bengtson, Robert Harootyan, and their colleagues adopt an inductive approach characteristic of contemporary social science methodology in *Intergenerational Linkages: Hidden Connections in American Society*. Their analysis rests on telephone interviews with a nationally representative sample of 1,500 subjects between the ages of 15 and 90. One focus of the research design was on generational relations among kin. Hence, several chapters deal with the structure of generational bonds among family members, with specific emphasis on intergenerational transfers and assistance. A second focus concerns the range of images and beliefs that various age groups have about themselves and others. Yet a third concern of the volume is to examine attitudes among young, middle-aged, and elderly respondents as a way of gauging contemporary intergenerational tensions and burdens.

Intergenerational Linkages confirms, or at least reinforces, things that those who are familiar with contemporary research on aging already knew. Among other things, this volume effectively challenges a central premise of the generational-equity debate: that Phillip Longman's baby boom generation was *Born to Pay*.[10] The thesis proposed by the authors in this volume calls into question both the rhetorical and the empirical bases for claiming that the interests of the old are pitted against the young. They find strong ties across generations. The authors acknowledge inequities between groups, but claim that the gaps fall along gender, socioeconomic, and age lines; the United States is not riddled with intergenerational rivalries.

This research breaks new ground. The socioeconomic accounting of cross-generational transfers in this volume offers the most persuasive reckoning of the value of "hidden" transfers across age cohorts that I have seen. If the authors are correct, the value of goods and services exchanged across generational lines is worth twice the amount of public transfers—and their figures are adjusted (rightly) to include items that Samuel Preston ignored in his famous essay a decade ago.[11] And while Bengtson, Harootyan, and their colleagues generally agree with Faye Lomax Cook and others whose surveys have documented strong support for the nation's social security system, they also show that this support is not unequivocal. The *perception* of inequity, they claim, is palpable among a sizeable minority of their respondents. If so, it means that opinions could quickly become volatile if another "crisis" besets the program. Indeed, even generational relations seem more complicated than one might expect in a volume of this sort.

The study also breaks new ground in analyses of family-level generational linkages. Given my own experiences and those of my acquaintances, I was not surprised when the authors stressed that, at one time or another, many relations between elders and their adult children were distant and ritualized. But I did not expect that the three biggest categories of relationships—tight-knit and helping, alienated and independent, and dispersed and independent—would add up to less than half of the total. This finding demonstrates one of the main points that the authors make—the enormous diversity among families in intergenerational styles.

The great virtue of *Intergenerational Linkages* is the authors' effort to link together, without distorting, trends across age groups operating at three different levels of societal reality: family, community, nation. The past masters in the search for "hidden connections"—de Tocqueville, Turner, Potter, and Hartz—all seized on a "Big Idea" (equality of condition, the frontier, abundance, and the part-becomes-the whole), and then directed readers' attention back and forth from the central theme to the various issues under scrutiny. Bengtson, Harootyan, and their associates, in contrast, talk about *family* relationships in terms of relationships and exchanges, *community* activities in terms of neighborhood involvement, and *nation* in terms of societal-level transfers. Especially in Chapter 4, where Harootyan and Vorek discuss volunteering (a subject that, oddly, rarely gets much attention in the social science literature), the analysis is enhanced by their multilevel foci.

This volume deserves a wide audience. More than most social science researchers who focus on aging, the contributors have gone beyond that "land of many islands of data with few bridges between them,"[12] as James Birren has metaphorically characterized the field of gerontology. By showing links among domains that are not contiguous and by illuminating connections hitherto "hidden" in most gerontology studies, they have made a genuine contribution to the literature.

W. ANDREW ACHENBAUM
University of Michigan

NOTES

[1]Frederick Jackson Turner, "The Significance of the Frontier in American History" (originally published 1893) in Frederick Jackson Turner, *The Frontier in American History* (New York: Holt, Rinehart & Winston, 1962), pp. 1, 32.

[2]David M. Potter, *People of Plenty: Economic Abundance and the American Character* (Chicago: University of Chicago Press, 1954), p. 208.

[3]Louis Hartz, *The Liberal Tradition in America* (New York: Harcourt, Brace & World, 1955), p. 16.

[4]Hartz, *Liberal Tradition*, p. 32.

[5]Christopher Lasch, *Culture of Narcissism* (New York: W. W. Norton, 1977); Robert Bellah, Richard Madsen, Ann Swidler, and Steven T. Tipton, *Habits of the Heart* (Berkeley: University of California Press, 1985).

[6]Alexis de Tocqueville, *Democracy in America* [Phillips Bradley trans.],

2 vols. (New York: Vintage Books, 1945).

[7]Alexis de Tocqueville, *Democracy in America* [Phillips Bradley trans.], 2 vols. (New York: Vintage Books, 1945), II: 185.

[8]Ibid.

[9]de Tocqueville, *Democracy in America,* p. 186.

[10]Phillip Longman, *Born to Pay* (Boston: Houghton Mifflin, 1987).

[11]Samuel H. Preston, "Children and Elderly in the U.S.," *Scientific American, Vol. 25* (December 1984): 44–49.

[12]James E. Birren, "My Perspective on Research on Aging," in *The Course of Later Life,* ed. Vern L. Bengtson and K. Warner Schaie (New York: Springer Publishing, 1989), p. 144.

Preface

The theoretical framework, research design, and data analysis that resulted in *Intergenerational Linkages: Hidden Connections in American Society* were the product of collaboration among the authors, who at the time of the study were researchers at three institutions: the University of Southern California's Andrus Gerontology Center, Harvard University's Kennedy School of Government, and the Forecasting and Environmental Scanning (FES) Department of the American Association of Retired Persons (AARP).

The idea for the study arose in discussion among FES researchers at AARP regarding the limited information about the full array of behaviors, attitudes, and values that could describe the relationships among generations in American society. Lamenting the dearth of such data, in contrast to readily available statistics on federal and other *government* outlays to specific age groups, the FES researchers decided to develop a national survey of all adults to obtain as much data as feasible.

The data on which the analyses are based were obtained through a telephone survey conducted by DataStat, Inc. of Ann Arbor, Michigan, in July and August, 1990, of a sample of 1,500 adults aged 18 to 90, representative of the noninstitutionalized United States population. The survey data allowed us to develop a broad understanding of the many linkages between generations in American society. Such linkages often are unrecognized or insufficiently appreciated by most Americans. Our results unveil this complex set of attitudes and behaviors—hidden connections—between different age groups in our society.

Acknowledgments

We wish to acknowledge several individuals for their contributions to the success of this project. First, thanks to Horace Deets, Executive Director of AARP, who endorsed our proposal for a nationwide survey on intergenerational exchanges and supported its implementation. Thanks also to Constance Swank, PhD, Director of AARP's Research Division, for her support and encouragement in the completion of this publication. Michael Berens, PhD, Senior Research Associate in the Division office, reviewed the manuscript and provided many useful suggestions. Martha Ramsey, Deputy Director of the Communications Division at AARP, was responsible for all arrangements with Springer Publishing Company.

We have been fortunate to work with an exceptional staff in the production of this volume. At the University of Southern California, Linda Hall assisted with chapter production and managed the coordination of tables and figures. Working with her, David Sharp painstakingly formatted and made revisions to the 64 tables for publication, and Christopher Hilgeman produced most of the 41 figures. At AARP, Wendy Cater and Annette Dixon provided valuable secretarial assistance in the preparation of Chapters 1, 4, and 8.

We reserve our greatest debt to Pauline Robinson, PhD, formerly UPS Foundation Research Professor of Gerontology at the University of Southern California, who served as managing editor for this volume. She provided substantive and editorial suggestions to the authors, reviewed all data cited in the text, and made significant changes that greatly improved the manuscript. She is the reason this volume has seen publication, and we are grateful for her unstinting efforts.

The opinions presented in this volume are those of the authors of the chapters and do not necessarily represent those of the American Association of Retired Persons.

CHAPTER 1

Intergenerational Linkages: The Context of the Study

Robert A. Harootyan and Vern L. Bengtson

Thomas Jefferson enunciated an American value that seems to have endured since the founding of the republic: It is the goal of each generation not to incur debts that would have to be repaid by future generations and to leave the next generation better-off than they themselves were (Randall, 1993). For more than two centuries this aspiration has, by and large, been met in America—the standard of living of each successive generation has generally been higher than that of the generation preceding it.

In recent years, however, there has been increasing concern that Jefferson's goals may not be realized in future American society, that the next generation may never be as well-off as their parents were. Is it true that recent economic circumstances have made this objective impossible to achieve? Is the rising national debt an inexorable burden to be faced by future generations? Do parents still feel it is their responsibility to ensure that their children's generation will have a better standard of living than their own?

Such questions about economic well-being across age groups are, in turn, based on even more fundamental questions about the generational social contract and about relationships across age cohorts (Laslett, 1992). Have family bonds changed so that extended families are less close than in previous generations? Do younger age groups still respect elders and seek to assure their well-being? Do older generations express a concern for younger generations and seek to assist them? Is the average American's stake in future generations limited to concerns for his or her own family, or is there also a concern for the well-being of the nation and future age cohorts as a whole?

These questions about age groups and their connections with each other have arisen as the complexity and diversity of American society have increased, as the roles and responsibilities of individuals have been redefined, as social institutions have been transformed, and as the population has rapidly aged. Family changes, altered work patterns, increases in educational opportunities, new government programs—each of these institutional changes in our society during the past five decades has led to new questions about generational attitudes and behaviors, especially those related to exchanges and reciprocities across age groups.

This volume presents findings from a nationwide survey regarding relationships and expectations across generations and age groups in contemporary American society. The study evolved from a desire to examine the array of connections and conflicts across age groups, to explore their impact on the daily lives of persons in various age groups, and to consider their implications for the future. We have sought to identify and measure these intergenerational linkages in American society—connections that, although often unacknowledged, can have significant implications for future age group relationships. We refer to these linkages as *hidden connections* because they are often unrecognized or unseen by most Americans.

THEMES OF THE INTERGENERATIONAL LINKAGES SURVEY

In 1989 we began planning a multidisciplinary investigation of the connections, exchanges, and conflicts across age groups in American society—"intergenerational linkages." The design of the research reflected six general goals:

1. To describe intergenerational attitudes, transfers, and support in a nationally representative sample of adult Americans.
2. To examine public opinion about intergenerational interaction and obligations, and to contrast them with possibly inaccurate media images of intergenerational relationships.
3. To determine the extent to which volunteering and informal assistance at the community and neighborhood levels are an

important component of intergenerational linkages and transfers.

4. To estimate the economic value of the intergenerational transfers that occur within families, communities, and the nation as a
whole, with particular focus on nonmonetary exchanges.

5. To examine the potential for emerging intergenerational tensions
based on allocations of societal resources, especially those tensions
related to whether "baby boomers" and succeeding generations are
likely to be less well-off than their parents' generation has been.

6. To identify policy-related issues in intergenerational relations—
based on demographic, economic, attitudinal, and institutional
changes now evident in our society—that will require governmental attention in the next two decades.

Moreover, we wanted to frame these research goals in the context
of three distinct but interrelated levels of social structure and age
group linkages: family, community, and nation. Previous research has
provided considerable information about intergenerational relationships within families (see Bengtson, Rosenthal, & Burton, 1990;
Brubaker, 1990; Elder, Rudkin, & Conger, in press; Rossi & Rossi, 1990).
Other recent analyses have focused on comparisons across age
cohorts at the national level (Easterlin, 1987; Kotlikoff, 1992; Russell,
1982). To date, however, little research has examined community-
based interactions across different age cohorts. Yet it is at the community level where many age group interactions take place, especially in
the context of formal and informal volunteer activities.

These three social-structural levels of age group relationships—
family, community, nation—have rarely been studied together. But
they need to be considered jointly if we are to see the many hidden
connections—and conflicts—that exist between age groups in
American society. Moreover, awareness of the types of intergenerational linkages that are prevalent today is important for anticipating
how American families, communities, and the nation as a whole will
respond to tomorrow's increasingly aging society.

THE GROWING POLICY DEBATE CONCERNING
INTERGENERATIONAL CONFLICT

In the mid-1980s the American public was confronted with a growing
debate concerning the equitable distribution of societal resources

between age groups. This issue has often been posed on the basis of generational or age-based population groups, and is usually spoken of in terms of *intergenerational equity* (Bengtson, Marti, & Roberts, 1991; Binney & Estes, 1988; Binstock, 1992; Kingson, 1988; Marshall, Cook, & Marshall, 1993; Quadagno, 1989).

INCOME INEQUALITY IN THE 1980S

The debate about intergenerational equity grew more vociferous during the late 1980s as the American public began to feel the effects of a burgeoning federal deficit and national debt, made worse by a recession that was felt beyond the nation's borders. Indeed, public perceptions of the economy and of the fate of the average American became less optimistic by the early 1990s. These public perceptions were quite accurate, as evidenced by various studies indicating that the wealthiest gained even more wealth at the expense of the middle or working class, including the poor, in the United States during the 1980s (Kennickell & Shack-Marquez, 1992; Mishel & Bernstein, 1992; U.S. Bureau of the Census, 1992c).

This divergence in economic well-being *in general* has been well documented in analyses of economic trends in the last decade, but assertions about the relative well-being of different *age groups* in America have been less well documented. In fact, the economic status of today's middle-class families has been largely maintained by the rapid growth of dual-income households. In 1960 only 30% of married-couple families included wives who were in the paid labor force. By 1990 this proportion almost doubled, reaching 58% (U.S. Bureau of the Census, 1992b). Studies have shown that the share of the nation's total income that is received by those in the highest quintile of the distribution would have been lower, and the share received by those in the lowest quintile higher, had not this change in wives' work patterns occurred (Ryscavage, Green, & Welniak, 1992).

Thus, as young adults struggled to maintain an increasingly fragile standard of living during the 1980s, many perceived that the average American's life was getting worse. During the past decade of growing economic insecurity and stagnation or decline of real income for the majority of American households, federal programs that primarily benefit older people grew larger and costlier. Income inequality among Americans had worsened at the same time that many older Americans' retirement incomes became more secure through annual cost of living increases in Social Security benefits and higher percentages of retirees who receive private pension payments. Thus, the general concern about increased income inequality as a whole was amplified in the late 1980s by those who drew attention to the improvement in the economic well-being of the older population relative to other age groups.

INTERGENERATIONAL EQUITY AND PUBLIC RESOURCES

Assessments of intergenerational equity are generally based on age-specific allocations of *public* resources, usually comparing public resources received by older people and younger people. Furthermore, these public resources are usually measured by *federal* government expenditures for different age groups such as the elderly population or those under age 18 (and their families). But the evolution of federal entitlement programs has focused on the population that traditionally was considered the most needy and most at risk *as a group*—the elderly. In the 1930s and even as recently as the 1960s, chronological age group definitions correlated well with need, and the elderly were a compelling case for inclusion among the "faultlessly poor" (Harootyan, 1981). As the major entitlement programs of Social Security and Medicare grew—especially in the 1970s and 1980s—federal expenditures devoted to older persons also grew in comparison to the share for any other age group.

Thus, federal domestic expenditures have become increasingly dominated by outlays to the older population. And data on federal outlays are often used as yardsticks for measuring the allocation of public resources across age groups—perhaps because these statistics are the most readily available indicators of age-based public expenditures (Kotlikoff, 1992). But public expenditures include *state and local government spending* as well. At those levels—state and local combined—total government spending on children and youth far outpaces spending on elders. While federal domestic expenditures are dominated by entitlement programs that primarily benefit persons aged 62 or 65 and older, state and local expenditures are dominated by spending for recreation and public education, which primarily benefit young people and their families. When all levels of government spending are included in the data on age-based public expenditures, the difference between the older and younger populations is basically eliminated (see Chapter 5).

But whether focused on federal outlays alone or on the combined outlays at all levels of government, the emphasis on public benefits targeted to specific age groups establishes an *a priori* perspective of age group or generational competition. When looking only at the distribution of federal resources, the issue becomes framed as older age groups receiving more than their "fair share" of our nation's resources. In contrast, when looking at nonfederal government expenses, younger age groups could be perceived as receiving more than their fair share of public resources. The dangers of such competitive orientations were noted almost two decades ago by researchers who warned of the increasing potential for generational animosity and competitive pressures in the policy arena (Foner, 1974; Hudson, 1978; Neugarten, 1979).

Since those early warnings in the 1970s, increased attention has been given to questions of intergenerational equity. But most of the observations about this issue remain grounded in data on federal outlays. Thus, as the federal poverty rate within the older population declined throughout the 1980s and reached parity with the general population after 1990, the inevitable contrasts were made with the increasing proportion of younger persons who were in households having incomes below the poverty level.

These age group comparisons have been made in studies using national demographic and economic data, which usually noted the growing economic advantage of the older population compared to the younger population (Preston, 1984). Other analyses yielded projections showing that today's younger population faces increased economic burdens and high lifetime costs for future entitlement benefits, burdens that will be far higher than those of today's older generation (Kotlikoff, 1992). The media have fostered similar views about the potential generational inequity in net benefits that today's younger generations are likely to experience over their lifetimes.

Thus, media reports and the statements of those who purport to be representatives of the young adult generation often state that not only are older people getting too much, but that such advantages are gained at the expense of children and young adults (Longman, 1986; Pearlstein, 1993; Smith, 1992). Taken together, these writings on generational *equity* have raised concerns about the potential for intergenerational *conflict* in American society.

INTERGENERATIONAL CONFLICT

Many of those who promote the notion of intergenerational *inequity* also claim that intergenerational *enmity* has grown notably during the last two decades. They assert that the growing economic well-being of the older population today compared to decades past has fueled a growing animosity of the young toward the old in American society (Longman, 1986). But available national survey data do not support such contentions (American Association of Retired Persons, 1987), nor do historical analyses suggest these concerns are unique today (Achenbaum, 1993). Moreover, it appears that the questions raised concerning generational equity have not, to date, led many Americans to abandon the positive connection that they feel with other age groups. A recent comprehensive review of available data on media reports concerning relationships across generations indicates little intergenerational anger, antagonism, or perceptions of major inequity (Marshall et al., 1993). The data reported in this volume carry that examination further.

This does not mean that Americans today are not concerned about the equitable distribution of societal resources across age groups. But their perceptions of what constitutes "societal resources" and "equity" are more comprehensive than generally assumed. How Americans define equity, and how they think about the distribution of resources, is more complex than is suggested in many portrayals of the debate concerning intergenerational equity. *Equity* has often been inaccurately equated with *equality* in these comparisons (Bengtson & Murray, in press). While age-related differences (i.e., inequalities) in receipt of societal benefits have been seen by some as unequal and thus unfair, such assertions neglect the broader or more subtle definitions of equity that include the values of justice and fairness, and that take into account assessments of differing needs, opportunities, circumstances, contributions, and responsibilities among age groups (Binstock, 1983; Daniels, 1989). Documenting and understanding the complexity of these perceptions, attitudes, and behaviors across many facets of intergenerational relationships is one of the primary goals of this study.

DEFINING SOCIETAL RESOURCES AND THEIR DISTRIBUTION ACROSS AGE GROUPS

The crux of the generational equity controversy concerns three issues: first, the way that societal resources are defined and perceived; second, the accounting of how these are distributed across age groups;

and third, whether this distribution is equitable in terms of societal needs and values. Unfortunately, the generational equity debate to date has reflected primarily the self-interests of different advocacy groups and has suffered from selective use of data and limited perspectives regarding "societal resources" and "equitable allocation" among age groups.

An example of how data related to the generational inequity thesis are improperly used is the often-cited statistic that "the 65 and older population currently consumes 29% of total federal government outlays" (U.S. House of Representatives, 1991). This statistic often stands alone as depicting the way societal resources are allocated and distributed across the generations. It is noteworthy that such statements emphasize what is "consumed" by the older population, as if such activity occurs in a vacuum, with no "production" component in the activities of older people. Thus, although the statistic is accurate in itself, its use often rests on a narrow view that federal outlays constitute an accurate portrayal of intergenerational exchanges within our society.

We propose on the basis of the analyses reflected in this volume an alternative perspective on the generational equity debate. First, it should be noted that these federal outlays have been consistently supported by American society in general, reflecting attitudes that strongly favor social insurance programs benefiting not only older people, but also those who are disabled and those who are dependents of persons covered by such programs.

Second, and more importantly, these governmental programs are only *part* of a larger fabric of both formal and informal connections and transfers that bind our society together by a series of mutual dependencies, which we call *intergenerational linkages.* These linkages have increased the ways in which young, middle-aged, and elderly persons can and do contribute to the welfare of others in their families and across their communities. It is important to measure the extent and depth of these connections, as well as to assess how the public *perceives* these linkages, to understand how changing socioeconomic conditions may affect intergenerational relations in the future.

Third, it is crucial to examine the intergenerational distribution of resources across time, and across the lifetimes of those growing up and growing old—not at just one point in time or at one point in the life course. Too little research has examined transfer flows down as well as up the generational ladder throughout the life course, especially nonpublic transfers. Nor has sufficient attention been paid to a range of reciprocal transfers and exchanges at different life course stages.

The research reported in this volume attempts to address these interrelated and complex components in order to provide a more complete picture of generational linkages in American society.

THREE SOCIAL CONTEXTS OF INTERGENERATIONAL LINKAGES

The conceptual design of this study has focused on three important contexts (or levels of social-structural analysis) of intergenerational linkages in American society. These, taken together, reflect how societal resources are allocated and transferred across age groups, and how the different generations contribute to one another in often unrecognized ways. The three components of intergenerational linkages that serve as the focus for the study are:

- family relationships and exchanges,
- community and neighborhood involvement, and
- national or societal-level transfers.

During this century, all three aspects of intergenerational linkages have become more complex as the roles of family, community, and government have changed. For example, in previous decades the family was the primary—or only—social resource available for the care of dependent age groups, and older persons were principally care receivers within an extended family structure. Today, with longer life expectancy and greater geographic dispersion of extended-family units, older persons are both care receivers and care givers, and over much longer periods of time than in previous eras. But in addition, caregiving to dependent older persons is likely to involve people outside the traditional extended-family structure—as in caregiving through community service and paid work.

Reviews of the social science literature have concluded that, even in the face of these changes in family structure, solidarity between generations is an enduring characteristic of families (Brubaker, 1990; Treas & Bengtson, 1987). Continuity, then, rather than discontinuity, has characterized the response of families to social change. Contemporary family structure is based on a larger number of living generations, but with fewer members in each generation—a phenomenon that has been labeled the *beanpole* family structure (see Bengtson et al., 1990).

These changes in family structure are only one part of the larger set of societal changes that have been occurring in the post-World War II era. The fact that extended families have retained their intergenerational bonds—even in the face of such significant changes as greater geographical dispersion, higher rates of divorce, increased prevalence of single-person households and single-parent families (U.S. Bureau of the Census, 1989)—attests to the strength of such ties. This study explores not only these types of family ties but also community and societal ties that characterize the full set of hidden connections—and possible stressors—across the generations in American society.

"GENERATIONS," "COHORTS," AND "AGE GROUPS"

The term *generation* is frequently employed in the discussion of conflicts and connections that have arisen between generations as the result of increased longevity, decreased fertility, and decreasing societal resources. But which generations? Indeed, what is meant by the term *generation*?

The term has been used in the mass media and even in the research literature in multiple ways, with the meaning frequently ambiguous and dependent on the context in which a particular writer uses it. The several meanings of the term can be seen in some recently published works by well-known scholars:

- Economist Lawrence Kotlikoff titled his volume *Generational Accounting* (1992); what he means by generation is a group of individuals who have in common nothing more or less than birth in a particular year or short interval of years.
- Paul Strauss and Neil Howe based their *Generations: The History of America's Future, 1584–2069* (1991) on what they vaguely define as a "cohort group . . . whose boundaries are fixed by peer personality" (p. 60), the characteristics of which vary in a 19-year cycle.
- Elizabeth Russell, in *The Baby Boom Generation and the Economy* (1982), refers to those born between 1946 and 1964 as a *generation*. This encompasses a 19-year span of births, and some baby

boomers have children who, by this definition, are also members of the baby boom generation.

- Alice and Peter Rossi titled their volume *Of Human Bonding: Parent-Child Relationships Across the Life Course* (1990). They use the term *generation* to refer solely to lineage position within the family.

At least four forms of age groupings must be distinguished in discourse about generational conflict or generational justice. In this volume, we have not restricted the terms *generation* or *intergenerational* to one single, comprehensive definition—since they are not so restricted in contemporary scientific discourse spanning the disciplines of demography, economics, sociology, and policy analysis. Instead, we try to make clear in the chapters to follow the specific social context of age group comparisons involved in each type of analysis. The different contexts indicate the meaning of generation as a*ge cohort, kinship lineage,* or *age group.*

GENERATIONAL RELATIONS ACROSS AGE COHORTS

When economists, policymakers, and media analysts today use the term *generation* they are most often referring to what in fact is an *age cohort:* a group of individuals sharing a common characteristic, in this case period of birth, which is usually defined arbitrarily as 10 years. The key assumption behind this grouping is that, as a result of their sharing a common historical point of time of birth, individuals in a birth cohort experience the same unfolding historical events at the same point of their development into adulthood, and thus have many other characteristics in common as they age. Hence, we use the term *age cohort* for this group of persons.

GENERATIONAL RELATIONS IN KINSHIP LINEAGES

A *lineage* refers to the descending rank of family members from great-grandparent to grandparent, parent to child, grandchild to great-grandchild. Generation in the sense of *kinship lineages* refers to a position in the succession of individuals born within a kinship unit. This type of generational relation describes interactions within the family unit by individuals related through "biological time" and thus to historical time (see Bengtson & Allen, 1993).

GENERATIONAL RELATIONS ACROSS OTHER AGE GROUPINGS

Other terms can be used to identify age groups that are not ordered in strictly birth cohort or family generation terms (for a more comprehensive discussion see Bengtson, Cutler, Mangen, & Marshall, 1985). *Historical generation* is a concept used by political scientists and social historians, following Karl Mannheim (1928/1952), to characterize age cohorts who may develop a sense of group consciousness or "identity" because they share some common experiences in history, and who become part of social movements based on age. *Age group* is a term often employed to differentiate the population into segments who share a common stage of life: for example, children/youth; adults; elders. These life course distinctions, however imprecise, have become the basis for evolving public policy legislation and "welfare" provisions in the United States since 1934. Similar to this approach, *policy age group* is a concept that we use in analyses of intergenerational transfers (Chapter 5). The three policy age groups that are used in our analyses are: children and teens under age 20; adults aged 20–59; and elders aged 60 and above. These reflect current policy distinctions between age groups viewed largely as "dependent" (i.e., least likely to be in the labor force) and those viewed as "self-sufficient" (i.e., most likely to be in the labor force). Most programs that are age-targeted use these or similar age groupings.

It is clear that there are several logically distinct meanings to the term *generation,* and that there is no one definition that will satisfy all scholars writing about age-based social interactions. In this volume, we use the most appropriate definition of *generation* for each chapter's substantive focus. In Chapters 2 and 3, the focus is on relations between kinship generations; in Chapters 5 through 7, on relations across age cohorts; Chapters 4 and 8 incorporate both meanings.

DESIGN OF THE INTERGENERATIONAL LINKAGES SURVEY

The purpose of this study has been to examine current relationships and expectations across cohorts and generations. One concern was to examine assertions about intergenerational equity, testing these against empirical data concerning attitudes and behaviors across cohorts and lineages. A second concern was to identify the many intergenerational transfers in contemporary society, measure them, and indicate some possible implications of these transfers.

The data and analyses presented in this volume are based on the 1990 American Association of Retired Persons Intergenerational Linkages Survey, a project developed by AARP's Forecasting and Environmental Scanning Department. The survey involved a random sample of 1,500 adults, aged 18–90, in the 48 contiguous states, who were interviewed by telephone in July and August of 1990. The average interview lasted 35 minutes. Because this was a random telephone survey, residents of institutions and group quarters (such as nursing homes, board and care homes, college dormitories, and prisons) were not part of the sample; only residents of individual households could be included in the sample.

In order to insure the representativeness of the sample, a statistical technique of weighting, described in Appendix A, was carried out. The data were first weighted to adjust for differences in probability of a respondent's selection within a household that was contacted. The sample was then poststratified and weighted on the basis of socio-demographic characteristics of the United States population at the time of the survey. The distribution of the sample before and after weighting, by age, gender, race/ethnicity, and socioeconomic status of respondent, is shown in Table 1.1. Further information about the sample, interview, and methods of analysis is provided in Appendix A.

The survey included ten major topic areas:

- Personal profile data on respondent
- Family background information
- Current family relationships
- Formal volunteer activity
- Informal assistance patterns
- Gift giving
- Housing assistance
- Inheritance and bequests
- Perceptions and opinions about younger and older people, as well as about programs targeted to these groups
- Perceptions and opinions about family and community responsibility.

These topics were chosen in order to secure data on individuals' cross-generational attitudes, perceptions, and behavior within families,

TABLE 1.1   Distribution of Sample Before and After Weighting, by Age, Gender, Race, Ethnicity, and Socioeconomic Status

Characteristic	Before Weighting	Weighted
Age		
18-49	1,066	980
50-64	224	279
65 +	210	240
Gender		
Male	591	716
Female	909	784
Race		
African American	123	137
Other	1,377	1,363
Ethnicity		
Hispanic	75	88
Other	1,425	1,412
Socioeconomic status[a]		
White-collar	1,043	952
Blue-collar	220	301

Note.   Numbers may not total 1,500 because of rounding.
[a]Information on occupation available for only 1,263 respondents.

communities, and the broader society. An abbreviated version of the survey instrument is reproduced in Appendix G.

Two additional aspects of the survey should be noted. First, to our knowledge nationally representative data have never been collected on *cross-generational* aspects of formal volunteering. From this survey we were able to develop specific measures of the extent to which one generation's volunteer activity benefits another generation (see Chapter 4). In doing so, we were also able to estimate the economic value of such volunteer activity and to show the dollar value of one generation's contributions to another. Similar economic estimates were developed for family and community-based patterns of informal assistance that individuals provide to one another in their daily lives (see Chapter 5). These estimates of the monetary value of private intergenerational transfers add considerable information to our knowledge of how the nation's resources are distributed among the generations.

Second, in the area of family ties, we have developed a typology of ten *family types* that may provide a new picture of intergenerational strengths and weaknesses in families (see Chapter 3). Some of these ten types are more prevalent than others, reflecting some interesting contrasts in family relationships in our society. For example, while high rates of family interaction and feelings of closeness appear prevalent, some family relationships in American society are very limited and emotionally distant. The typology helps us understand these differences and their relevance to family members' attitudes about generational differences.

OVERVIEW OF THIS VOLUME

In the chapters to follow we analyze intergenerational linkages in terms of perceptions and behaviors across age groups, as reported by a representative sample of American adults in 1990. We examine the concerns and exchanges respondents report at the level of family, community, and nation. Three overarching research questions have guided the design and analysis of the study:

1. What connections and conflicts are most evident across age groups and generations in America today, at the family, community, and societal levels of social-structural analysis?
2. How can these intergenerational linkages best be explained in terms of underlying dimensions—processes that might be "hidden" from current journalistic or politically targeted analyses, but made evident from concerted social science analysis?
3. What are the social, economic, and political implications of these connections in the context of growing public concerns about intergenerational equity and entitlement across age groups and generations?

In Chapter 2 we examine the survey data concerning intergenerational linkages within the family. We analyze relationships between adult children and parents, and between grandchildren and grandparents, in terms of six specific components of *family intergenerational solidarity*. We address questions such as: To what extent are aging parents and their adult children isolated or distant from each other? How strong are the bonds of obligation and support between them? What

accounts for differences among families in contact, emotional closeness, similarity of opinions, and exchanges of help? Do the two
generations share the same perception of solidarity between them?
The survey data reflect not only the complexity of contemporary family relationships, but some surprising anomalies in the family-related
attitudes, perceptions, and behaviors of different generations.

In Chapter 3 we continue to explore the "hidden connections"
across family generations by identifying and measuring the prevalence
of ten types of relationships between parents and adult children.
These types reflect the dimensions of solidarity described in Chapter
2, and with them we address questions about the distribution of and
explanation for parent-adult child relationships. Taking two of the ten
types as an example, are *tight-knit-helping* relationships more common
than *alienated-independent* relationships? Does this depend on the age
of the parent, the gender of the child, the marital status of either, their
race, or other factors? Results indicate how the interaction among
many of these factors influences the type of family relationship that
evolves over the life course.

Chapter 4 examines another important but principally hidden
aspect of intergenerational linkages in contemporary America: how
people volunteer their time and give assistance and gifts to others in
their communities. Volunteering, helping, and giving gifts are often
ignored in sociological surveys or econometric analyses concerning
interactions across age groups. To what extent are members of different generations involved in such activities? What kinds of activities are
they involved in, and which age groups benefit from their efforts?
What characteristics and factors help explain differences in volunteering and helping behaviors? How do these apply *within* as well as *across*
age groups? Survey findings reflect the complex interaction among values, family experiences and orientations, socioeconomic status, and
other aspects of social structure that influence the likelihood, type,
and extent of volunteer activity among adult Americans.

In Chapter 5 we address the issue of intergenerational transfers: the
flow of resources, public and private, from one age group to another.
Chapters 2, 3, and 4 note several forms of private transfers—social
support, shared housing, financial gifts for family members, volunteering on behalf of other members of the community. What is the total
economic value of these transfers? How does that value compare to
the value of public transfers between age groups—which are much
more frequently discussed? And what is the relative "generosity" of different age groups; are today's elders primarily the *recipients* of a vast

intergenerational transfer largesse, as suggested by many critics; or are they in fact primarily *donors* toward younger age groups? Which types of private transfers are most prevalent among the different generations? The analyses reported here not only yield an astonishingly high monetary value for these private transfers, but also indicate that each generation has particular patterns of giving and receiving. Many of these patterns are quite different from the impressions generated in the media concerning cross-generational exchanges.

Chapter 6 examines tensions and frictions between age groups in terms of attitudes about social justice and perceptions of age-related needs. We suggest a model to characterize the development of discord between age groups in society, involving three stages: (a) *stressors,* creating a perception of burden in terms of another age group's needs; (b) *tensions,* resulting from the judgment that these burdens are unfair; and (c) *frictions,* created when intergenerational tensions are attributed to the actions of the beneficiary group. How common are each of these forms of intergenerational discord? Do people view the distribution of resources across age groups as unfair? How do people of different ages or in different socioeconomic circumstances differ in their perceptions of the treatment of age groups or in their assessment of what constitutes fair treatment?

In Chapter 7 we explore further the sources of what we term *intergenerational dissonance,* the belief that certain age groups are not being treated in an equitable manner. To do this, we identify factors that lead some Americans—a small minority—to conclude that age-targeted government benefits are too burdensome or unfairly allocated among age groups. This allows us to examine several relevant questions. To what extent do the factors that actually shape intergenerational tensions match those that have been set forth in past writings about intergenerational equity? More specifically, to what extent are programs that are judged too costly also seen as unfair? How are intergenerational tensions affected by an individual's personal circumstances or family obligations? To what extent are reports of tensions or burdens influenced by perceptions about the needs of particular age groups or the fairness of the programs designed to meet those needs? We also explore the ways that tensions involving programs for elders are similar or dissimilar to those stemming from programs for children.

Chapter 8 provides a summary of the major research findings and suggests implications for current social, economic, and policy questions regarding the distribution of resources across age groups and generations. We reiterate that many of the intergenerational linkages discussed in earlier chapters are indeed hidden, since policy debates have not reflected the solidarity and exchanges between generations revealed in our data.

We further note that more informed public policy must address not only the *conflicts* but also the *connections* across age groups and generations at three levels of society: family, community, and nation. Without this broad perspective, we risk falling prey to superficial, overly simplified, and media-based perspectives on intergenerational relationships in the United States. Clearly, the hidden connections that link rather than separate the generations are more prevalent than many have assumed. By examining *both* the continuities and discontinuities across contemporary age groups and generations, we should be better able to anticipate and plan for social change in the years ahead.

CHAPTER 2

Solidarity Between Generations in Families

Leora Lawton, Merril Silverstein, and Vern L. Bengtson

$\mathbf{A}$ popular perception today is that family bonds have weakened over the past decades in the United States, and that family support to elderly persons in particular has been jeopardized. Weakened intergenerational linkages, it has been suggested, are the consequences of several trends—smaller families, high rates of divorce, geographic mobility, and social changes such as the increasing participation of women in the labor force.

At the same time there is much evidence to suggest that family bonds are not weaker than in earlier periods of American history (Shanas, 1979). In fact an entirely different picture has been suggested by contemporary surveys on intergenerational relations (Bengtson, Rosenthal, & Burton, 1990; Hagestad, 1987). Researchers find that intergenerational bonds among adult family members may be even more important than in earlier decades—in part because individuals live longer and thus can share more years and experiences with other generations.

In this chapter we focus on intergenerational linkages within the family as they are revealed by data from the 1990 AARP Intergenerational Linkages Survey. We address the following questions in our analyses:

- To what extent are aging parents and their adult children isolated from each other in America today?

19

- How frequent is the contact between adult family members in different generations?
- How close do parents and adult children feel toward each other? Is there a sense of estrangement?
- How similar are different family generations in their opinions?
- How much help is exchanged between family generations?
- How strong are the bonds of obligations and expectations between generations in the family?
- What accounts for differences in contact, closeness, similarity of opinions, expectations, and the exchange of help?

We use the term *solidarity* to describe the complex and sometimes contradictory linkages between parents and children, and between grandparents and grandchildren (see Bengtson & Schrader, 1981; Roberts, Richards, & Bengtson, 1991). We have found that intergenerational family solidarity is multidimensional, consisting of six distinct but interdependent dimensions:

1. *Structural:* living in the same home or in geographic proximity.
2. *Associational:* contact among family members.
3. *Affectual:* feelings of emotional closeness.
4. *Consensual:* sharing of opinions.
5. *Functional:* helping each other with everyday tasks.
6. *Normative:* feelings of responsibility for other generations.

We examine these six dimensions of family solidarity across intergenerational pairs of family members—child–mother, child–father, parent–child, grandchild–grandparent, and grandparent–grandchild—as reflected in the intergenerational survey data. Each pair represents a particular generation's perspective about the relationship, with the respondent listed as the first member of the pair. For example, the analysis of the grandchild–grandparent pair is based on information from the grandchild, and the analysis of the grandparent–grandchild pair is from the point of view of the grandparent.

We then consider what might account for family differences on each of these dimensions of solidarity. To do this we examine individual, family, and social structural characteristics that might affect the extent of solidarity in each intergenerational pair. Two *individual characteristics* of family members are their age and gender. The age of family members can affect the features of family solidarity in part because of the process of maturation and learning about each other, and in part because with age come changes in roles and responsibilities. Gender is important because women and men have different ways of socializing, and women tend to maintain social relations between family members more than men do (Aldous, 1987; Dewit, Wister, & Burch, 1988; Hagestad, 1986).

Family members' relationships with each other are also affected by *family characteristics*—the positions they hold within the family structure; for example, whether they are married, divorced, widowed, or never married, and whether the younger generations have their own children or not (Altergott, 1985). Adult children who are married and have children are likely to have a better understanding of their own parents, which might create greater harmony with the parent. Never married children generally have different needs and may rely more on parents than those who are more established in their own families. Children who are divorced may need additional help from parents, compared to married children.

The parents' marital status also needs to be considered. Widowed parents may rely more on children, whereas divorced parents may face weakened ties between them and their children (Cooney & Uhlenberg, 1990; Lawton, 1990a, 1990b).

We are not necessarily positing a *causal* relationship between such family characteristics and family solidarity, because our data do not allow this conclusion. With characteristics such as marital status and childbearing the direction of causality can work in either direction, or both characteristics and solidarity may be due to a third factor.

Social structural characteristics represent a third level of influence on family intergenerational linkages. One important social structural factor to examine is race, since other research has shown that African American women take on centralized family roles more than women in other families (Mindel, 1983; Stack, 1974). Consequently, we might expect to find more solidarity in African American families than in other families in the survey. Since we control for income and educational attainment in one kind of statistical analysis, the effect of race is not due simply to lower income and education. This is important because these two socioeconomic factors in and of themselves may well affect family solidarity.

This chapter presents data from the survey on six aspects of family solidarity: proximity, contact, emotional closeness, similarity of opinions, giving help, and responsibility. Data on these dimensions are analyzed for five different intergenerational pairs of family members, taking into account individual, family, and social structural factors that facilitate or hamper family solidarity. (In analyses of the child–parent pair, only children with a living mother or father, as appropriate, are included; only parents with a child 18 or older are included. Grandchildren were asked questions about the grandparent with whom they currently have the most contact, and grandparents were asked questions about their oldest grandchild 18 or older.)

We identify the factors that most influence solidarity by methods known as *multiple regression* and *logistic regression,* which allow us to take all the factors into consideration at the same time. (For a description of the regression methods and for the statistical results of these analyses see Appendix B.)

We look first at data on solidarity between adult children and their parents, and then at solidarity between grandchildren and grandparents.

RELATIONSHIPS BETWEEN ADULT CHILDREN AND PARENTS

Six dimensions of solidarity between adult children and their parents are analyzed in this section, beginning with structural solidarity, the two aspects of which are living in the same household and living within an hour's driving time.

STRUCTURAL SOLIDARITY: LIVING TOGETHER OR LIVING NEAR EACH OTHER

The first question to ask about family relations is whether adults of different generations share living space, live nearby, or live farther away. Being geographically distant certainly does not mean that affection is low, but living in close proximity does make sharing experiences and helping more feasible. More face-to-face contact, communication, and opportunities to help each other may strengthen other aspects of solidarity, providing the "opportunity structure" for interaction (Mangen, Bengtson, & Landry, 1988).

Coresidence

Living under the same roof, as an adult, with another adult of a different generation is rare in contemporary American society, except that it is common for young adults to be living with their parents: of the 18–24 year olds in our sample, 59% live with their mothers and 46% with their fathers (Table 2.1). More adult children at all ages live with their mothers than with their fathers.

As in most surveys, we cannot tell from these survey data which of the pair who co-reside is the householder, so we cannot tell if the parent has moved in with the child, or vice-versa, or simply if the child has not left the home yet. Parents in the survey were asked if their *oldest* adult child lived with them. Only 12%—and only 5% of those 65 and older—said that their oldest adult child lived with them.

Are there some circumstances that lead to a higher frequency of house sharing? Individual, family, and social structural characteristics do encourage or discourage living together, perhaps indirectly—by creating situations that are more or less conducive to coresidence.

TABLE 2.1 Structural Solidarity: Coresidence Between Generations, by Selected Characteristics (Asked of Adult Child)

Characteristic	Percent living with mother	*Number (Total N = 963)*	Percent living with father	*Number (Total N = 754)*
Age of child				
18-24	59	227	46	215
25-34	14	325	11	279
35-49	5	284	3	221
50 +	10	128	4	39
Marital status of parent[a]				
Married	52	108	53	108
Unmarried	42	55	18	40
Remarried	34	38	10	42
Marital status of child				
Married	3	549	2	424
Separated	22	28	18	19
Divorced	12	78	12	48
Never married	58	290	45	261
Race				
African American	34	86	26	65
Other	20	877	18	689

[a]Marital status of parent analyzed for children aged 18-24 only.

We have seen that children are more likely to live with mothers than with fathers in almost every age group (Table 2.1). Furthermore, when a mother is no longer married (because of separation, divorce, or widowhood), the likelihood of coresidence with children is not a great deal less (42%) than when she is married (52%) unless she remarries (the data on marital status are for children 18–24 only—see Table 2.1). If she remarries, an adult child is less likely to live with her (34%). But when a father is no longer married, the likelihood of coresidence is much less; an adult child is far less likely to co-reside with that unmarried father (18%), and even less likely should the father remarry (10%).

The marital status of the adult child, as we would expect, also affects the likelihood of living with the parent; never married children are much more likely (58%) than married children (3%) to live with a mother (Table 2.1). Separated and divorced children, moreover, are also more likely than married children to live with the parent (22% and 12%, respectively).

Along with these individual and family characteristics of age and marital status, one social structural factor related to coresidence is race. In other research, mothers in African American families have been found to be a stronger force than in white families (Mindel, 1983). Consistent with that research is the fact that African Americans in the survey are more likely (34%) than others (20%) to be living with their mothers (Table 2.1).

Regression analysis reveals that of all the factors discussed, those with the greatest independent effect on living with parents are family structure variables, that is, the marital status of both the parents and children (Table B.1, in Appendix B).

Living Close to the Other Generation

Living *with* the older generation is not common among adults except for those children who have not yet left the home; but once they have gone, how far do they go? And what characteristics are associated with staying near versus going farther away? We can compare those who currently live more than an hour's travelling time away with those who live within an hour of the other generation. Living close to other family members means being able to visit and phone more often, and having access to resources that family can provide. Many of the survey respondents do live close to the older or younger generation. Over half at all ages live within an hour's drive of their mothers or fathers (Table 2.2).

TABLE 2.2 Structural Solidarity: Living Within One Hour of Parents, by Selected Characteristics (Asked of Adult Child)

Characteristic	Percent living within one hour from mother	Number (Total N = 789)	Percent living within one hour from father	Number (Total N = 616)
Age of child				
18-24	64	94	58	116
25-34	62	280	54	249
35-49	63	271	59	214
50 +	62	115	59	38
Marital status of parent				
Married	63	372	63	372
Unmarried	64	290	52	126
Remarried	54	97	44	118
Home ownership (child)				
Rent	54	295	46	266
Own home	68	494	65	350
Education of child				
Less than high school	70	125	55	96
High school	67	280	63	233
Some college	66	169	64	138
College graduate	48	186	41	149
Race				
African American	61	57	48	48
Other	63	702	58	567

Children are not quite so likely to live near parents who are not still married to each other. Owning one's own home increases the likelihood of living near a parent. A higher level of education decreases that likelihood (Table 2.2).

Being African American is a factor in increasing the likelihood of parent and child living together, but—once children are out of the house—race does not affect living near parents (see regression equation, Table B.2).

ASSOCIATIONAL SOLIDARITY: FREQUENCY OF CONTACT

How often do adults have contact with family members in other generations? Is it true that family contacts between generations are becoming infrequent in our fast changing society?

Contrary to some popular perceptions, it appears from this survey that there is a great deal of contact between adult children and parents (Table 2.3). That contact is greater with mothers than with fathers, however. For example, 69% of all respondents report contact with their mothers at least once a week, and 20% report contact every day. Somewhat fewer, 56%, report at least weekly contact with fathers and 12% report daily contact. Parents report comparable frequency of contact with their oldest child.

With regression analysis, the pattern of factors affecting associational solidarity turns out to be similar to that found with structural solidarity (coresidence), and family structure is again important (Table B.3). Two characteristics having the most independent effect on *lowering* contact with parents are: the father having remarried or being widowed or divorced, and the mother having remarried. Home ownership by the children *increases* contact. Being a daughter versus a son increases contact with the mother, but has no effect on contact with the father. Level of education has the effect of decreasing the amount of association (with the mother), just as it decreases the likelihood of living near the parent. The independent effect of race depends on whether the parent or child was reporting—with parents' reports, regression analysis shows that being African American increases contact, although that effect did not show up with children's reports.

AFFECTUAL SOLIDARITY: FEELINGS OF CLOSENESS

Do parents and adult children tend to feel somewhat estranged from each other in our society today? Not according to the survey. When

TABLE 2.3 Associational Solidarity: Frequency of Contact, by Selected Characteristics (Asked of Adult Child and Parent)

| | Percent reporting contact with | | |
| | Mother | Father | Oldest child |
Characteristic	(N = 760)	(N = 618)	(N = 572)
Asked of adult child			
Daily	20	12	
Weekly or more often	69	56	
Asked of parent			
Daily			16
Weekly or more often			58

adult children were asked how close they feel to other members of their family, almost three quarters (72%) of the respondents stated that they feel very close to their mother, and very few (3%) feel not at all close (Table 2.4). This pattern of feeling very close to the mother holds for all age groups as well. The relationship between children and their fathers is somewhat more distant—more than half (55%) feel very close, but 11% feel not at all close to the father.

By now it should not be a surprise that adult children report that their relationship with fathers who are no longer married is not so close as it is when the parents are still married to each other (Table 2.4). The marital status of the mother, again, does not make a sizeable difference in feelings of closeness.

The pattern of feelings of closeness holds at all age groups, with feelings of closeness to mother more prevalent than closeness to father (Table 2.4). Closeness to mother does not vary by age; closeness to father appears to vary by age but the difference is not significant in the multivariate analysis (Table B.4).

African Americans report a closer relationship with their mothers (88%) than do others (70%), and again this effect does not hold with the child–father relationship (Table 2.4).

Turning to the parents' perspective, they also describe harmonious relationships with children. When they were asked how close they felt to their oldest child, they reported that generally their relationships are quite harmonious—81% state that they feel very close. Only a very few (4%) say that the relationship is not at all close with their children (Table 2.4).

CONSENSUAL SOLIDARITY: SIMILARITY OF OPINIONS

How similar are family members in their orientations and attitudes? Or a more important question is, how similar in opinions do they *feel* they are to the other generation? Such feelings reflect the potential for intergenerational tension or disagreement. A certain amount of difference in opinion may be healthy for families, allowing for growth and creativity. If there is too much divergence in perspective and not enough unity, then the social unit—the family—will not function well.

Adult children were asked how similar they thought their opinions were generally to those of their mother, father, and grandparents; parents were asked about similarity of opinions to those of their oldest child. Overall, about 50–70% of respondents feel that their opinions are "similar" or "very similar" to their parents (Table 2.5). Adult children

TABLE 2.4 Affectual Solidarity: Feelings of Closeness (Asked of Adult Child and Parent)

	Mother	Number (Total N = 963)	Father	Number (Total N = 754)	Oldest child	Number (Total N = 653)
	Percent feeling close to					
Very close	72		55		81	
Somewhat close	25		33		15	
Not at all close	3		11		4	
Characteristic			Percent feeling very close			
Marital status of parent						
Married	74	493	67	493		
Unmarried	70	352	32	138		
Remarried	70	118	35	123		
Age of child						
18–24	70	227	48	215		
25–34	74	325	57	279		
35–49	70	284	57	221		
50 +	74	128	69	39		
Race						
African American	88	86	57	65		
Other	70	877	55	689		

feel that their opinions are generally similar to those of both of their parents. Despite talk of the generation gap, most people do think similarly across generations within the family.

What seems to account for perceived intergenerational similarity, or dissimilarity? There is very little variation in consensual solidarity by race, age, and most other factors. Perceived similarity to fathers' opinions is lower when the father is unmarried or remarried (Table 2.5). More variation would probably have been found if the question had asked about similarity of opinions on specific topics, such as politics, religious practices, and gender roles.

Nevertheless, the multivariate analysis does reveal the effect of certain factors on overall similarity of opinions (Table B.5). A pattern of consensual solidarity that is similar in other dimensions of solidarity is that unmarried or remarried fathers are associated with more dissonance than married fathers (Table B.5). This effect of marital status is not seen in the mother–child relationship.

The marital status of the child does not affect consensus when the child is the respondent, but when parents were asked about the similarity of their opinions with those of their oldest child, whether the child was married was the most important factor, in regression analysis results (Table B.5). Married children are perceived as being more similar in opinions than unmarried children, with all other factors held constant.

FUNCTIONAL SOLIDARITY: HELPING EACH OTHER

The exchange of help between parents and adult children is the fifth dimension of intergenerational solidarity within the family. Such

TABLE 2.5 Consensual Solidarity: Similarity of Opinions, by Parent's Marital Status (Asked of Adult Child)

Characteristic	Percent stating opinion very or somewhat similar to mother	Number (Total N = 963)	Percent stating opinion very or somewhat similar to father	Number (Total N = 754)
Marital status of parent				
Married	68	493	65	493
Unmarried	67	352	48	138
Remarried	70	118	50	123

assistance, often at a cost of great time and energy, is motivated by positive sentiment as well as by obligations felt toward members of another generation. One generation can serve as a resource to another generation for help with everyday activities, such as housekeeping and transportation. In this section we examine flows of noneconomic assistance in both directions between adult children and their parents who do not live with each other.

To measure intergenerational assistance, respondents were asked if they provide free help to neighbors, friends, and family members, and if so to whom. *Help* in this survey is limited to hands-on assistance such as running errands, helping with repairs, and babysitting. Next, respondents were asked if they *receive* free help from neighbors, friends, and family members, and from whom. Only help between adult children and parents is considered here. Parents are included in the analysis only if they mention at least one adult child in giving or receiving help. Similarly, adult children are included only if they mention a father or mother in giving or receiving help.

Overall, there are modest levels of assistance between parents and adult children, with no more than 35% in any category of child or parent reporting the giving or getting of help (Table 2.6). Slightly more than 1 in 3 adult children help their mothers (35%), but only slightly more than 1 in 4 help their fathers (28%). Similarly, children are more likely to receive help from mothers (29%) than from fathers (25%). Children are less likely to receive help from either parent than they are to give help to them.

TABLE 2.6   Functional Solidarity: Helping Behavior of Adult Children and Parents (Asked of Adult Child and Parent)

	Percent
Adult child's perspective:	
With mother (N = 760)	
Child gives help to mother	35
Child gets help from mother	29
With father (N = 616)	
Child gives help to father	28
Child gets help from father	25
Parent's perspective:	
With child (N = 570)	
Parent gives help to child	30
Parent gets help from child	24

Turning to the perspective of the parents, 30% report giving help to adult children, and 24% report getting help from them, an apparent contradiction in statements about who gives and receives more. Taken together, these patterns indicate that more respondents consider themselves providers than receivers, but that in any case the level of transfers is relatively low.

That one fourth to one third of adults give assistance to a parent or adult child can be interpreted as a demonstration of intergenerational solidarity when we take into account the circumstances of the family members responding. First, it is likely that many parents and adult children are willing to assist each other, but are not faced with a current need for help. Second, geographic distance between many parents and children may inhibit their ability, but not their willingness, to exchange help with each other. From the child's perspective, the rates of assistance are not as low when help from mothers and help from fathers are considered together. Almost 4 in 10 adult children report receiving assistance from at least one parent.

We use logistic regression to examine the factors that have an effect on transfers of assistance between adult children and their mothers and fathers, and between parents and their adult children, after all other factors have been taken into account. It should be noted that our findings are adjusted for frequency of contact between parents and children in order to identify factors affecting helping behavior apart from the effects of opportunity and availability.

The Adult Child's Perspective

Information from adult children's reports about the exchange of help between them and their parents is examined first for giving help to parents and then for receiving help from them. (The regression equation for giving help to parents is found in Table B.6.)

Giving Help to Parents

Adult children who are African American are less likely (23%) than others (36%) to provide assistance to their mothers (Table 2.7). Although African American adult children are also less likely to provide help to their fathers, this result does not hold when other factors are taken into account in the regression equation (Table B.6). The low rate of helping mothers within African American families is consistent with the results of other investigators (e.g., Eggebeen & Hogan, 1990) who

TABLE 2.7 Functional Solidarity: Assistance to Parents, by Selected Characteristics (Asked of Adult Child)

Child's characteristic	Percent providing assistance to mother	Number (Total N = 760)	Percent providing assistance to father	Number (Total N = 616)
Gender				
Sons	33	362	35	295
Daughters	36	397	21	321
Race				
African American	23	57	15	48
Other	36	702	29	567
Labor force				
Works for pay	37	599	31	499
Does not work for pay	25	160	15	117

speculate that social and economic barriers faced by African Americans inhibit informal exchanges.

There is little difference between sons and daughters in providing help to mothers. Sons, however, are more likely (35%) than daughters (21%) to provide help to their fathers (Table 2.7). The help from sons to fathers may reflect activities that traditionally divide along gender lines, such as home and car repair.

Labor force participation has a surprising effect on giving assistance. Adult children working for pay are more likely than those not working for pay to provide assistance to both mothers and fathers (Table 2.7). Financial resources and the social stability gained through employment may thus be a more important spur to giving help to parents than the discretionary time gained from not working.

Receiving Help from Parents

Younger adult children are obviously more likely than older adult children to receive assistance from mothers and from fathers. Children 18–24 are much more likely (49%) than those in older age groups to get help from their mothers, and also more likely (33%) than those who are older to get help from their fathers (Table 2.8). Being younger is associated with receiving parental assistance for two probable reasons: Younger adult children may need more help because they are less likely than older children to be established, and older children tend to have older parents who are less likely to have the physical resources to provide help.

TABLE 2.8   Functional Solidarity: Assistance from Parents, by Selected Characteristics (Asked of Adult Child)

Characteristic	Percent receiving assistance from mother	Number (Total N = 760)	Percent receiving assistance from father	Number (Total N = 616)
Age				
18-24	49	94	33	116
25-34	37	280	29	249
35-44	28	211	20	177
45-54	7	100	6	57
55 +	5	75	10	17
Age of youngest child				
No children	30	193	27	209
< 10 years	41	307	29	278
10-17 years	25	107	19	70
18 + years	4	153	7	58

Having a young child is associated with receiving help from mothers. About 2 out of 5 adult children with offspring under 10 years of age (41%) receive help from their mothers, compared to only 1 in 4 with teenage offspring (25%), and only 4% with adult offspring (Table 2.8). Since the offspring of adult children are the grandchildren, it seems likely that many of these grandmothers are helping their adult children by providing child care or babysitting assistance.

The Parent's Perspective

Turning to reports of giving and receiving help from the parent's perspective, many of the same patterns appear as when the child is reporting. (The regression equations are found in Table B.7.)

Giving Help to Children

Not surprisingly, mothers are more likely (36%) than fathers (21%) to provide assistance. This finding is consistent with literature showing that mothers are more involved than fathers in supportive services to family members (Brody, 1985; Troll, 1988). African American parents are less likely providers of help to adult children (only 9%) than other parents (31%) (Table 2.9).

Getting Help from Children

The probability of receiving assistance from an adult child rises

TABLE 2.9   Functional Solidarity: Assistance to Adult Child, by Selected Characteristics (Asked of Parent)

Parent's characteristics	Percent giving assistance	Number
Gender		
Father	21	262
Mother	36	309
Race		
African American	9	45
Other	31	525

steadily with the age of the parent. Parents 65 and older are much more likely (30%) than parents under 45 (12%) to receive help. Divorced, separated, and widowed parents are more likely to receive help from adult children (30%) than married parents (22%) (Table 2.10).

The income of the parent is shown to be positively related to receiving support from an adult child (Table B.7). It may be that the adult children of lower income parents are less able to provide help, suggesting that less affluent parents are disadvantaged in social as well as economic resources.

TABLE 2.10   Functional Solidarity: Assistance from Adult Child, by Selected Characteristics (Asked of Parent)

Parent's characteristics	Percent receiving assistance	Number
Age		
< 45	12	67
45-54	18	132
55-64	27	165
65 +	30	206
Total N		570
Marital status		
Married	22	425
Divorced/separated	30	66
Widowed	30	75
Total N		566

NORMATIVE SOLIDARITY: RESPONSIBILITY FOR OTHER GENERATIONS

How much should one generation be responsible for the welfare of another? How one answers this question reveals feelings of what we refer to as *intergenerational normative solidarity,* expectations of responsibility by one generation for another. Unlike other dimensions of intergenerational solidarity discussed previously, normative solidarity represents an *ideal* of what should be and not necessarily what occurs in practice. Thus, one's norms of intergenerational obligation may or may not be reflected in behavior within one's family.

Norms of intergenerational family responsibility are measured using agreement with five statements from the survey (Table 2.11). Each statement is evaluated on a five point scale ranging from strongly disagree (1) to strongly agree (5). Items 1–4 show responsibility of parents for their adult children and Item 5 indicates responsibility of adult children toward their parents. Items 1–4 are combined to form a single index of parental responsibility (as explained in Appendix B). Since normative solidarity is a generalized set of expectations, the analysis in this section includes all survey respondents, not just those with living parents or adult children.

TABLE 2.11   Norms of Intergenerational Responsibility

		Parent's responsibility for adult children				Adult children's responsibility for parents
		Item 1	Item 2	Item 3	Item 4	Item 5[a]
		%	%	%	%	%
Strongly disagree	1	13	27	14	14	23
	2	16	17	13	13	12
	3	36	21	30	28	23
	4	16	13	19	20	19
Strongly agree	5	20	23	24	24	24
	(N)	(1480)	(1487)	(1491)	(1490)	(1488)

Item 1: Parents whose adult children have financial problems should assist them with housing costs.
Item 2: Parents should save money or property to leave as an inheritance for their children.
Item 3: Parents should assist adult children in paying for health care, if those children cannot do it themselves.
Item 4: Parents should assist adult children with their child care if needed.
Item 5: Grown children should not be expected to support their parents.

Note.   Percentages may not total to 100% because of rounding.
[a]Disagreement with Item 5 indicates stronger responsibility.

The distribution of responses to each item is shown in Table 2.11. Overall, about 1 in 5 respondents feel very strongly that the generations should be responsible for each other—on the part of both parents and adult children. Opinions are strongest with regard to the obligation of parents to provide child care assistance to adult children (24%, Item 4). Still, fewer than half of all respondents express agreement or strong agreement with any given statement about intergenerational responsibility. Later in this section, we will examine whether intergenerational norms influence intergenerational family behavior.

Parents' Obligations to Children

Table 2.12 shows agreement with statements about intergenerational responsibility, both by parents for children and by children for parents. First, we consider the extent to which respondents feel that parents are obligated to their adult children (regression equation found in Table B.8). Never married respondents more strongly endorse norms of parental responsibility than the married. One explanation for this is that the never married, because they have not formed families of their own, have a greater *personal* stake in the resources of their parents.

Self-interest gives way to altruism, however, for those who are themselves parents. Parents of adult children agree more with norms of parental responsibility (30%) than do the childless (19%) (Table 2.12).

Age is also related to endorsement of parental obligation, but the relationship is not a simple one. From early to middle adulthood there is little age difference, with not more than one in four agreeing with the norms, but in old age the commitment rises to 39% for those 65 to 74 (Table 2.12). This finding refutes some popular accounts of the elderly as "greedy geezers" who are unconcerned with the welfare of the younger generation.

Those with less than a high school education express stronger endorsement of parental obligation (40%) than do respondents with more years of education (17–21%) (Table 2.12). The less educated, because they tend to have the fewest economic resources, may view parents as sources of needed assistance.

Adult Children's Obligations to Parents

When we turn to responsibility of adult children toward their parents, a different picture unfolds (regression equation in Table B.8). Educational level and parental status, again, shape norms of responsi-

TABLE 2.12 Normative Solidarity: Agreement with Norms of Intergenerational Responsibility, by Selected Characteristics

Characteristic	Percent strongly agreeing with norm of responsibility for children	Number	Percent strongly agreeing with norm of responsibility for parents	Number
Age				
18-24	23	237	49	237
25-34	16	350	54	351
35-44	22	289	46	290
45-54	22	183	39	184
55-64	25	187	26	192
65-74	39	162	27	164
75 +	38	63	32	69
Total N		1,471		1,487
Marital Status				
Married	24	922	40	931
Divorced/separated	20	149	40	151
Widowed	34	87	31	89
Never married	24	313	54	317
Total N		1,471		1,488
Education				
Less than high school	40	346	32	353
High school grad	21	579	41	586
Some college	15	277	50	277
College grad	17	269	50	269
Total N		1,471		1,485
Parental status				
No adult child	19	843	52	845
Has adult child	30	628	30	642
Total N		1,471		1,487

Note. Scales used to measure responsibility for parents and responsibility for children are computed using different methods and should not be compared.

bility but show a different trend than that reported in the previous section. The less educated endorse weaker norms of obligation for parents than do the more highly educated. Less than one third of those who have not finished high school endorse this norm, compared to one half of college graduates (Table 2.12). This finding may reflect the greater financial capability among those with high education to actually fulfill the responsibility of supporting older parents.

Parents of adult children endorse norms of children's responsibility less often (30%) than the childless (52%) (Table 2.12). It is reasonable to speculate that such expectations are softened by the tendency of parents to avoid being a burden on their own children (Seelbach & Sauer, 1977). If this is the case, altruism for the well-being of their own children, rather than self-interest, shapes parents' attitudes toward children's responsibility. Taken together with evidence in the previous section, it appears that parents, hoping for the best future for their children, minimize their expectations of support from them, while maximizing their responsibility of support to them.

Relation of Intergenerational Norms to Other Dimensions of Solidarity

Are general attitudes expressed about intergenerational responsibility related to the solidarity that people experience with family members in other generations? In order to investigate the link between societal norms on the one hand and solidarity within families on the other, we examine the statistical relationship between normative solidarity and the measures of other dimensions of solidarity: distance, contact, affection, consensus, and exchange of help between the generations.

The results of the analysis indicate that norms of intergenerational responsibility are only weakly related to the quality of intergenerational relations within families, suggesting that beliefs and practices are largely, although not completely, independent. Nevertheless, there is some evidence that adherence to norms of intergenerational responsibility is associated with personal family experiences. Feeling that parents should be responsible for their adult children is related to (a) greater closeness to the oldest child, (b) living nearer to both parents, and (c) more frequent interaction with mothers (Table B.9). Feeling that adult children should be responsible for their parents is related to greater closeness to and consensus with mothers, as well as a greater propensity to get help from mothers. Although these correlations are modest in size, they suggest that abstract beliefs about intergenerational obligations may color and be colored by the nature of cross-generational family relations.

RELATIONSHIPS BETWEEN GRANDPARENTS AND GRANDCHILDREN

Information from the survey about relationships between grandparents and grandchildren allows us to observe intergenerational linkages across two generations. We can view these linkages along four of the same dimensions as the child–parent relations, namely: structural, associational, affectual, and consensual solidarity. (The dimensions of normative and functional solidarity could not be discussed for the grandparent–grandchild pair because the direction of the flow of functional help was not precise and because analysis by pairs was not possible with norms.) The analysis is limited because of the small numbers in the sample in certain categories. In this sample, many of the respondents (particularly those who are older) do not have living grandparents, and many of the older respondents are not old enough to have adult grandchildren (at least 18 years old). Only 179 respondents have adult grandchildren, and 502 respondents have at least one living grandparent.

STRUCTURAL SOLIDARITY: LIVING CLOSE TO THE OTHER GENERATION

The first aspect of structural solidarity, as with children and parents, is living together. Only 3% of those who have living grandparents live with them. The second aspect of structural solidarity is living within an hour, and here one half (54%) of the grandchildren live within an hour's distance of at least one of their grandparents.

The regression analysis indicates that a higher level of education of grandchildren decreases their likelihood of living within an hour of a grandparent (Table B.2). This result is similar to the effect of education on living farther away from parents.

ASSOCIATIONAL SOLIDARITY: FREQUENCY OF CONTACT

Contact with a grandparent at least once a week is reported by 26% of adult grandchildren. Contact is defined as a visit or a telephone call. The most important feature in determining contact between adult children and their grandparents (with regression analysis) is how much influence the grandparents had in their childhood (Table B.3).

AFFECTUAL SOLIDARITY: FEELINGS OF CLOSENESS

Grandparents were asked about their relationship with their oldest adult grandchild. When asked how close they were, their answers were quite positive, with 73% answering "very close," 21% "somewhat close," and 6% "not at all close" (Table 2.13). Grandchildren were asked how close they felt to the grandparents they have the most contact with. Their answers were not as positive as the grandparents' answers, but still 44% say "very close," 41% say "somewhat close," and only 15% say "not at all close." These results differ by race, with 64% of African Americans but only 41% of others reporting that they feel very close to grandparents.

In the regression analysis of these data, the two factors with the greatest effect on feeling close to grandparents are race and the influence of grandparents in childhood (Table B.4). Being African American has a positive effect on closeness to grandparents, as in closeness to parents. The influence of grandparents in childhood also increases closeness to grandparents.

TABLE 2.13   Grandparent–Grandchild Solidarity (Asked of Grandparent and Grandchild)

Characteristic	Percent close to grandparents	Number (Total N = 502)	Percent close to grandchild	Number (Total N = 179)
Affectual solidarity				
Very close	44		73	
Somewhat close	41		21	
Not at all close	15		6	
	Percent feeling very close			
Race				
African American	64	60	75	17
Other	41	442	72	161
Consensual solidarity				
Very similar	10		20	
Somewhat similar	36		47	
Somewhat different	33		15	
Very different	20		17	
	Percent stating opinion very or somewhat similar			
Race				
African American	56	60	64	17
Other	45	442	68	161

CONSENSUAL SOLIDARITY: SIMILARITY OF OPINIONS

Almost half of the grandchildren feel that their opinions are similar to those of their grandparents, with 10% reporting "very similar," and 36% "somewhat similar." Again, results differ by race—56% of African Americans report being very or somewhat similar to grandparents in their opinions, compared to 45% of others (Table 2.13).

Factors that affect perceptions of similarity (in regression analysis) are the influence of the grandparents in childhood and being African American (Table B.5).

INTERGENERATIONAL SOLIDARITY: THE SUM OF ITS PARTS

This chapter has examined six dimensions of solidarity, portraying pairs of family members for whom intergenerational solidarity— "togetherness"—is high, and pairs for whom there is some kind of distance and dissonance between generations. In general, we found evidence of strong intergenerational ties in many families. In most parent and adult child pairs, the individuals live nearby, have frequent contact, feel that they are emotionally close, and believe that they have similar opinions. In many pairs, parents and adult children help each other with tasks. The connections between generations are thus stronger than might have been supposed.

There are several individual, family, and social structural characteristics that are key factors in family solidarity. One key factor is *gender:* Women exhibit higher solidarity in family relationships than do men, with mothers more likely than fathers to share a home, live nearby, have contact, have a close relationship, and give and receive help. *Marital status* of the parent is another factor: Intact marriages are associated with closer ties between adult children and fathers, especially in living together or nearby, feelings of closeness, and shared opinions. *Education:* Persons who have achieved higher levels of education may trade off some family solidarity, since they are more likely to be geographically distant from their parents and grandparents. *Race:* African Americans as adult children share a home with their mothers and feel close to them and to their grandparents more often than others, but solidarity in terms of living nearby, contact, or helping patterns is not found as often among African Americans.

From one fourth to one third of adult children help their mothers or fathers and receive help from them on everyday kinds of tasks such as running errands and babysitting. Mothers give and receive help more than fathers.

One of the six dimensions studied was *normative solidarity,* the only dimension tapped by questions about other generations in general, rather than family members. Age is related to attitudes of parental obligation toward adult children—after middle age and into old age the sense of obligation rises dramatically. This finding refutes some popular accounts of the elderly as "greedy geezers" who are unconcerned with the welfare of the younger generation. In point of fact, they are the age group who express the *most* support of parental responsibility toward youth.

Grandparents and grandchildren make up the only pairs in this survey for which we can look at the quality of the relationship in the past. It is not surprising that the influence of the grandparent in an individual's childhood is associated with more frequent contact, emotional closeness, and shared opinions in the child's adult years. This finding suggests that to the extent that a generation "invests" in the next generation the return may be a strong family bond.

Solidarity is a complex matter, and the information we have gathered needs to be interpreted with care. For example, a shared living space does not signify a close relationship per se, and in fact may increase tension (Aquilino & Supple, 1991; Suitor & Pillemer, 1988). Frequent phone calls and visits may be due to the poor health of a family member as much as to affection, and such contact may be a source of stress when the quality of the relationship is poor. Similarly, members of a geographically dispersed family may feel very affectionate toward each other, and may actually find that a little distance alleviates a lot of tension.

Furthermore, each of these dimensions affects the others. Emotional closeness may influence family members to live closer to each other, whereas tension may lead to being father away. On the other hand, being nearby may make it easier for closeness to develop, but living 3,000 miles away prevents everyday kinds of mutual assistance. Chapter 3 explores further the complexity of solidarity and the interrelationships of the dimensions of solidarity analyzed in this chapter.

CHAPTER 3

Types of Relations Between Parents and Adult Children

Merril Silverstein, Leora Lawton, and Vern L. Bengtson

Intergenerational relations within families represent complex social bonds, which are sometimes surprising when we delve into their complexity. Family members are linked by multiple kinds of solidarity, which have been discussed in Chapter 2, but since they are linked *concurrently* by these aspects of solidarity, they may be high on some dimensions and low on others. Like the threads of a rope, the more numerous and the stronger the separate ties that bind the generations, the greater the total strength of the attachment.

In order to understand these complex and sometimes contradictory family linkages in all their detail, it is necessary to *simultaneously* consider the multiple aspects of the intergenerational bond—the topic of this chapter. In order to do this we develop a typology of intergenerational relations and identify the circumstances in which we find families with stronger or weaker intergenerational relationships. Specifically, we will address the following research questions:

- What are the fundamental components of solidarity in intergenerational family connections?
- How can we use these components to describe diverse types of multifaceted intergenerational family connections?
- Which individual and family characteristics distinguish those individuals who are linked to others by certain types of family connections?

43

TYPES OF FAMILY RELATIONS

In this chapter we develop a system for classifying relations between adult children and parents into categories that uniquely describe the qualities of these multifaceted family linkages. The building blocks of our typology are the characteristics of intergenerational family relationships discussed in Chapter 2—geographic distance, frequency of contact, emotional closeness, consensus of opinion, giving help, and receiving help (as explained in Appendix C). These characteristics are used with data from the 1990 AARP Intergenerational Linkages Survey to summarize, first, each relationship between an adult child in the sample and a surviving parent, and, second, each relationship between a parent in the sample and the oldest adult child.

Adult children in the sample evaluated a total of 1696 relations with their parents, 954 (56%) of which were with their mothers and 742 (44%) with their fathers. Parents in the sample evaluated 623 relations with the oldest adult child.

Some of these pairs of parents and adult children lived together, but these coresident pairs are analyzed differently. Since relationships between adult family members of different generations who live together are usually characterized by almost daily contact and substantial exchanges of assistance, three of our measures of solidarity— frequency of contact, giving help, and receiving help—are not appropriate for coresidents. Therefore, we treat coresident family pairs as distinct types of family relations. Of the adult children, 204 shared a residence with their mothers and 138 shared a residence with their fathers. Of the parents in the survey, 93 lived with their oldest child. After developing a typology of family relations, based on our data, we examine how types of relations differ by individual and family characteristics, both for pairs who live apart and for pairs who live together.

FACTOR ANALYSIS OF COMPONENTS OF SOLIDARITY

We are able to summarize intergenerational relations by grouping them into a relatively small set of meaningful types based on whether they measure high or low on our six components of solidarity. In order to make this task manageable, it is necessary to simplify the many-sided nature of solidarity by combining, where appropriate, some of the components of solidarity—geographic distance, contact, emotional closeness, consensus, giving help, and getting help—into a smaller number of factors. We use a statistical tool, *factor analysis,* which allows us to identify whether some components are similar enough to each other to be merged into a single common measure. (See Appendix C for a discussion of factor analysis and for procedures followed in this study.)

After we establish that the six components of solidarity can be represented by a small set of underlying factors, we ask whether parents and adult children evaluate relations with each other by thinking of the components of solidarity in terms of the *same* underlying factors. This second question requires that the analysis be performed both for parents' evaluations of their relations with their adult children *and* for children's evaluations of their relations with their parents.

The results of the factor analyses show that in both parents' and children's evaluations six components of intergenerational solidarity can be effectively reduced to the same three underlying factors of *opportunity, closeness,* and *helping behavior* (Table 3.1). Also, factor analyses performed separately for child-father and child-mother relations gave the same results, allowing them to be pooled, as in the discussion that follows. Thus, the complexity of the analysis can be substantially reduced with little loss of information by combining the six components into three composite factors—opportunity, closeness, and helping behavior—and we can use the same three factors to describe intergenerational relations regardless of whether the child or parent is reporting on the relationship.

Even more confidence is gained from analyzing grandparents' and grandchildren's views. Adult grandchildren evaluated 516 relations with grandparents, and grandparents evaluated 130 relations with grandchildren. Factor analysis was performed on these reports as well (Table 3.1). Two underlying factors (opportunity and closeness) emerge for the reports of both grandparents and grandchildren, and both in turn match those discovered within parent–child relations. (Helping behavior occurs too infrequently in grandparent–grandchild relations to be analyzed.) The emergence of the same two constructs—opportunity and closeness—improves our confidence in the validity of a basic underlying way of thinking about intergenerational relations. That the components of solidarity generally dovetail in similar ways for grandparents, parents, children, and grandchildren suggests that the features of intergenerational linkages have a common meaning across generational perspectives.

Factor analysis has reduced the six indicators measuring the components of solidarity into three factors. The first factor relates to the

TABLE 3.1 Factor Structure of Intergenerational Linkages for Those Living Apart: Rotated Factor Pattern[a]

Linkage	Child with mother	Child with father	Child with parent	Parent with child	Grandchild with grandparent	Grandparent with grandchild
Opportunity factor						
Distance	.892	.974	.938	.942	.903	.833
Contact	.819	.738	.774	.771	.839	.841
Closeness factor						
Emotional closeness	.778	.799	.783	.785	.778	.730
Consensus	.858	.911	.896	.780	.870	.873
Helping behavior factor						
Gives help	.689	.830	.760	.775	[b]	[b]
Gets help	.891	.854	.873	.822	[b]	[b]
N	751	604	1355	530	516	130
% variance explained	71.8	77.8	74.9	69.9	77.2	71.3

[a]Common factor analysis performed with oblique (procrustes) rotation. Factor loadings below .40 are not shown.
[b]Too few individuals engaged in helping behavior for analysis.

opportunity for meaningful interaction between the parent and child, and comprises geographic distance and frequency of contact. The second factor relates to feelings of *closeness* toward a parent or child, and comprises emotional closeness and consensus, the perceived similarity of opinion with the member of the other generation. The third factor relates to *helping behavior* between parent and child, and comprises informal assistance provided to and received from a parent or child. Each factor is represented by a summary index that measures whether the intergenerational relationship is relatively high or low on the components of solidarity that the construct describes. These three underlying factors are then combined to form types, which are used to characterize the general nature of each linkage.

A TYPOLOGY OF FAMILY RELATIONS

In order to group relationships into types, each intergenerational relationship is measured on each of the three solidarity indexes (opportunity, closeness, and helping behavior). Relationships are considered high on a given index if they rank above or equal to the average score of the index, and are considered low if they rank below the average score.

Joint consideration of the three dichotomies (high or low on each index) yields eight possible types of child–parent relations. Two additional types need to be added to describe adult children who live with their parents, because it was inappropriate to ask them about geographic proximity, contact, or giving or getting help, as discussed above. The two additional types of relations, in which the child coresides with the parent, are therefore based on reports of either high or low closeness with the parent. The resulting ten possible types were then labeled to characterize the high or low scores on the solidarity indexes. They are summarized below:

1. *Tight-knit-helping:* high on opportunity, high on closeness, high on helping behavior. In this type of relationship parents and children are engaged on all three dimensions of intergenerational solidarity.

2. *Ritualized-helping:* high on opportunity, low on closeness, high on helping behavior. Contact and support persist in spite of a lack of closeness.

3. *Dispersed-helping:* low on opportunity, high on closeness, high

on helping behavior. This type of relationship is characterized by intimacy *and* functional exchange, but the parties have little opportunity for regular contact.

4. *Alienated-helping:* low on opportunity, low on closeness, high on helping behavior. In this type of relationship only helping behavior is high. We might assume that functional assistance is provided or received on the basis of a sense of obligation to the other generation.

5. *Tight-knit-independent:* high on opportunity, high on closeness, low on helping behavior. While help is not exchanged, children and parents in relations of this type have opportunities for inter-action and feel close. This type of relationship is most similar to what has been referred to as the "modified-extended" family form. Perhaps the potential for interaction and support exists, and help would be given should the need arise.

6. *Ritualized-independent:* high on opportunity, low on closeness, low on helping behavior. In this type of relationship, opportuni-ty for interaction is not accompanied by feelings of intimacy or patterns of assistance.

7. *Dispersed-independent:* low on opportunity, high on closeness, low on helping behavior. This type of relationship is emotionally intimate but maintained at a distance.

8. *Alienated-independent:* low on opportunity, low on closeness, low on helping behavior. This type of relationship is low on all three dimensions and represents the relative isolation of the child from the parent.

9. *Coresident and Close:* parent and child live together and are close.

10. *Coresident and Less Close:* parent and child live together but are not close.

It should be kept in mind that the division of child-parent relations into types is based on an arbitrary criterion (i.e., being higher or lower than the average score on each dimension). Therefore, the labels attached to each type should be interpreted in a relative, rather than in an absolute manner.

The next step is to view the distribution of types of relations, both from the perspective of the adult child as respondent and from the perspective of the parent as respondent, in order to understand which types are more or less common.

In addition to viewing how the types of family relationships are distributed, the ten types can be used to see if the individuals describing their varying family relationships are different on characteristics such as gender, marital status, age, race, and education. We can carry out this analysis of child–parent relations from the perspective of either the child or the parent. Neither perspective can be claimed to represent the "true" nature of the relationship, and each represents an equally valid perception of the parent–child bond. Whether one is the parent or child does color how one perceives the relationship (Rossi & Rossi, 1990). We therefore consider it important to examine responses from both perspectives, first from the perspective of the adult child and then from the perspective of the parent.

CHILD–PARENT RELATIONS: THE ADULT CHILD'S PERSPECTIVE

Based on responses of the adult child, child–parent relationships are classified into the ten types. As shown in Figure 3.1, the most frequently occurring type is the tight-knit-helping (16%), followed by the alienated-independent (13%). Thus, for the first eight types of relationships between child and parent (excluding pairs living together), over one third of the pairs (36%) are either *high* on all three dimensions or *low* on all three. The dispersed-helping and the alienated-helping types, representing the most paradoxical combinations of attributes, occur least frequently. In the last two types the intergenerational pairs who live together are almost equally divided between the more and the less intimately connected, based on their standing on the closeness dimension.

Are certain types of relations found more often in connection with various characteristics of parents and their adult children? To answer this question we focus on the core individual and family characteristics of gender, marital status, parental status, age, race, and education as they relate to type of family relations, and find that in fact all of these characteristics are associated in some way with types of relations. (For the figures that show the types of relations by characteristics, Tables C.3-C.15 in Appendix C present the actual percentages.) Because relations between parents and adult children who live apart are qualitatively distinct from relations of those who live together, we treat separately in our analysis the eight types of relations where

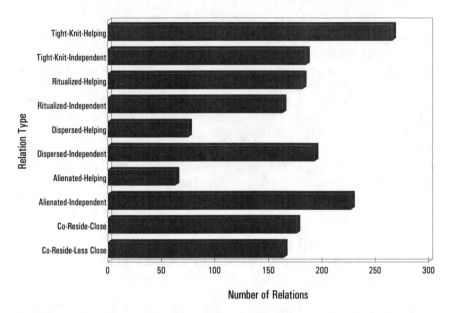

Figure 3.1 Distribution of child–parent relation types from child's perspective.
N = 1696. (Types do not total 1696 because of rounding of weighted numbers.)

parent and child live apart from the two types where they co-reside.
(See Appendix C for information on the regression analysis technique
that was used.)

GENDER: MOTHERS AND FATHERS

Adult children have quite different kinds of relationships with their
mothers than with their fathers. This finding becomes apparent when
we divide child–parent bonds into child–mother relations and child–
father relations and then compare them on distribution of intergenerational types. As seen in Figure 3.2, relations with mothers are more
likely (23%) than relations with fathers (16%) to be of the *tight-knit-helping* type, which is defined as high on all three dimensions of solidarity.
At the other end of the spectrum, relations with mothers are far less
likely (12%) than relations with fathers (22%) to be characterized as
alienated-independent, which is defined as low on all three dimensions.

Among adult children who live with parents, a similar pattern can
be seen. Relations with mothers are somewhat more likely to be close

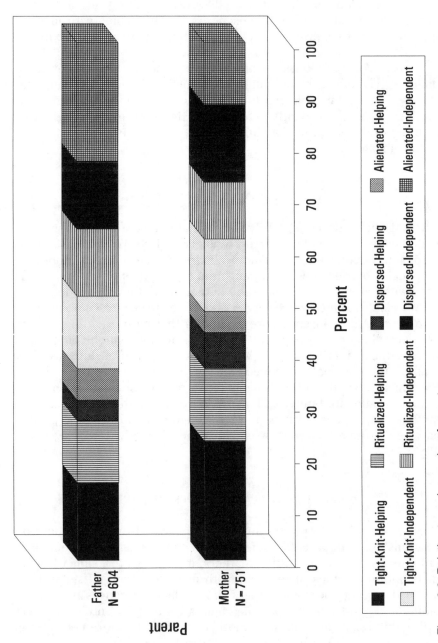

Figure 3.2 Relation types by gender of parent.

(57%) than relations with fathers (45%) (Table 3.2). Adult children's perceptions of differences in closeness of relationships with mother and father are thus present whether the children live with the parents or not.

This analysis of intergenerational linkages clearly shows that adult children have stronger overall relationships with mothers than with fathers. That adult children have more connecting links with their mothers affirms the relative strength of the matriarchal role as the intergenerational glue that bonds the generations in the modern American family.

GENDER: SONS AND DAUGHTERS

Other studies have consistently shown that daughters have more intimate ties to their families than do sons (Troll, 1987; Wright, 1985). Our results, however, fail to confirm this difference: We find only minor discrepancies between sons and daughters in the types of relations they have with parents, and this is true whether or not they co-reside.

We also examined same-gender and opposite-gender combinations of parents and children. Figure 3.3 shows that more than one fourth (26%) of all daughter–mother relationships are tight-knit-helping (high on all three solidarity factors). Mother–daughter relationships are also unlikely to be alienated-independent (low on all three factors) (13%). By contrast, one fifth of both daughter–father and son–father relationships are alienated-independent. This evidence affirms the unique strength and intimacy of the mother–daughter bond that is typically ascribed to the role of women as "kin-keepers" (Brody, 1985; Hagestad, 1986).

MARITAL STATUS AND GENDER OF PARENT

The survey results reported in Chapter 2 showed that the quality of relationships with parents is affected less by the single status of mothers than by the single status of fathers. In this chapter, similarly, the distribution of types of relations with married, divorced/separated, and widowed mothers and fathers shows clear differences by marital status and gender of the parent (Figures 3.4 and 3.5 and Table 3.2). Adult children's relations with mothers tend to be more consistent, regardless of the mothers' marital status. In contrast, relations with

TABLE 3.2 Closeness of Child–Parent Relations as Reported by Adult Child, by Personal Characteristics (Coresiding Pairs)

Characteristic	Percent high on closeness	Total N
Gender of parent		
Mother	57	204
Father	45	138
Gender of parent and child		
Son-father	51	82
Daughter-father	36	56
Son-mother	58	106
Daughter-mother	55	97
Marital status of mother		
Married	52	121
Divorced/separated	70	45
Widowed	56	101
Marital status of father		
Married	42	121
Divorced/separated	71	12
Widowed	[a]	
Age of child		
18-24	50	232
25-44	60	89
45 +	39	21
Marital status of child		
Married	48	27
Divorced/separated	50	25
Never married	52	286
Parental status of child		
Has no children	54	272
Has children	44	70
Race of child		
Other	50	296
African American	65	46
Education of child		
Less than high school	46	51
High school grad	55	165
Some college	52	100
College grad	46	26

[a]Too few widowed for analysis.

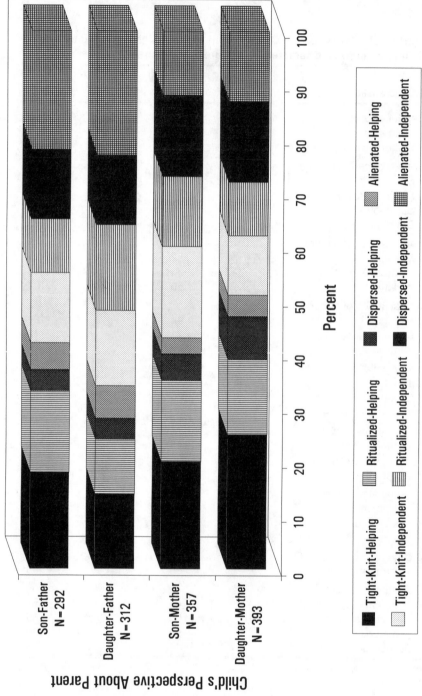

Figure 3.3 Relation types by gender of child and parent.

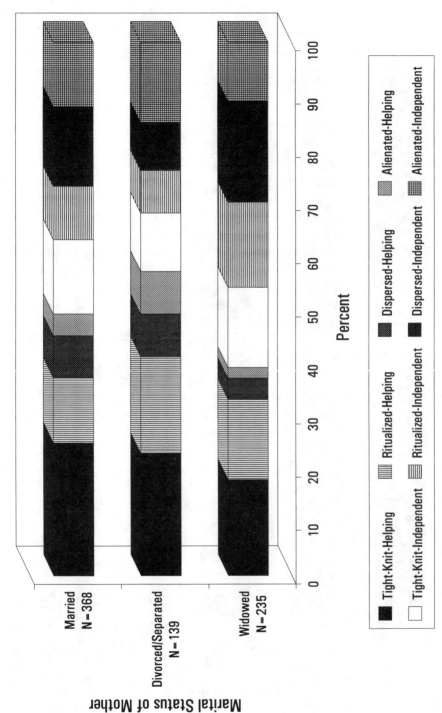

Figure 3.4 Relation types by marital status of mother.

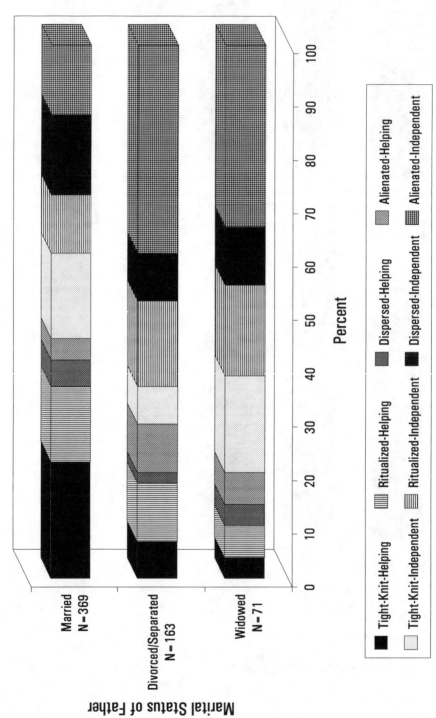

Figure 3.5 Relation types by marital status of father.

fathers are more variable, depending on the fathers' marital status. The proportion of relations that are tight-knit-helping is generally greatest (22%) when the father is married, and least when the father is divorced or separated (7%) and widowed (4%). It is especially striking that few linkages to divorced/separated and widowed fathers are of the strongest type (tight-knit-helping) (7% and 4%) *and* many linkages are of the weakest type (alienated-independent) (39% and 34%).

These results suggest that many fathers who are not married—as a result of divorce, separation, or widowhood—may tend to disengage from their offspring; or conversely, that weaker ties with children may be followed by divorce or separation. Since divorced fathers rarely get custody, they have fewer opportunities for interaction and the development of solidarity with their children. Adult children who live with their fathers, on the other hand, are more likely to feel close to a divorced (71%) than to a married father (42%) (Table 3.2).

There is a higher proportion of alienated relations (alienated-helping and alienated-independent) with widowed fathers (40%) than with widowed mothers (13%) (Figures 3.4 and 3.5). One explanation for the weaker ties with widowed fathers is that widowers, by virtue of their rarity, may occupy a "deviant" social position in the family toward which rules of behavior and obligations are more ambiguous than they are toward widowed mothers (Blau, 1961).

AGE OF ADULT CHILD

The nature of the parent–child relationship changes over the child's life course, reflecting the developmental needs of the linked generations as they pass through time. Young adults are quite different from middle-aged and older adults in their relations with parents. Young adult children, faced with a set of demands typical of their life stage, may need their parents' emotional and practical support. Somewhat later in life, having entered more established roles, adult children may become more socially distanced from their parents. Finally, middle-aged and older children may again become close to their very old parents due to the social support needs of those parents, many of whom are likely to be frail (Bengtson & Kuypers, 1985).

We examined whether the age of adult children in this study appears to influence the nature of their relations with parents, and found that it does. The distribution of child–parent types for three age groups is shown in Figure 3.6. The younger adult children (ages 18–24)

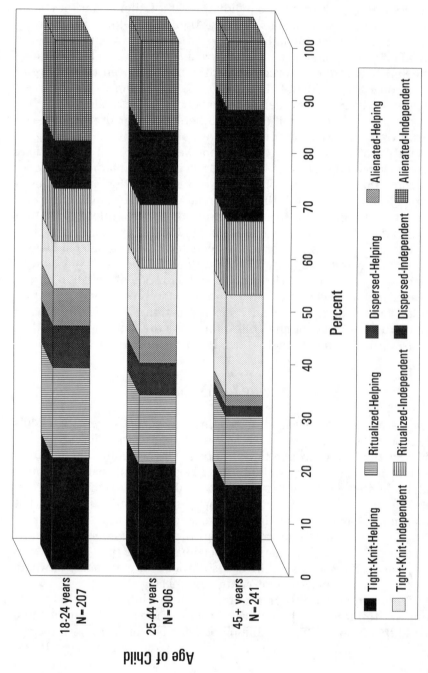

Figure 3.6 Relation types by age of child.

are more likely than older children (45+) to be linked on all or none of the dimensions of solidarity (tight-knit-helping and alienated-independent types). This suggests that intergenerational relations are less extreme with advancing age (i.e., less likely to be high or low on all three factors of our solidarity types). The most salient aspect of age is with regard to helping behavior (i.e., help provided to and received from a parent or child). One half of young adult children (18–24) are engaged in functional exchanges with parents (52%); among adult children aged 25–44 that proportion drops to 45%, and drops again to one third (33%) at age 45 and older. Contrary to what might have been expected, then, given concerns over elder caregiving, the functional helping linkage between the adult generations is strongest relatively early in the family life cycle.

Moreover, the dispersed-independent type of linkage is especially prevalent among the oldest adult children (21%), who are thus less likely than younger adult children to live near parents and to exchange help, but who nevertheless feel emotionally close.

Among adult children who reside with a parent, the youngest and oldest adult children are the least likely to feel close to their parents (Table 3.2). Coresidence at these ages may be associated with dependence of children on parents among the youngest adult children and dependence of parents on children among the oldest. In both instances intergenerational coresidence may sometimes involve negotiations over autonomy and power and thus create tension in the relationship.

MARITAL AND PARENTAL STATUS OF ADULT CHILD

Whether adult children are married and have children of their own might also be expected to affect their relationships with their parents. Insofar as they alter family roles and responsibilities, marriage and progeny do shape the nature of the intergenerational bond in our data. Figure 3.7 shows types of linkages for married, divorced/separated, and never married children. Linkages of married adult children to parents are most likely to be high on all dimensions of solidarity (tight-knit-helping, 21%), as well as least likely to be low on all dimensions (alienated-independent, 14%). Linkages of the never married are relatively weak, with fewer never married in the two tight-knit types than married or divorced/separated. (Among those living with parents, children's marital status does not affect feelings of closeness, as shown in Table 3.2.)

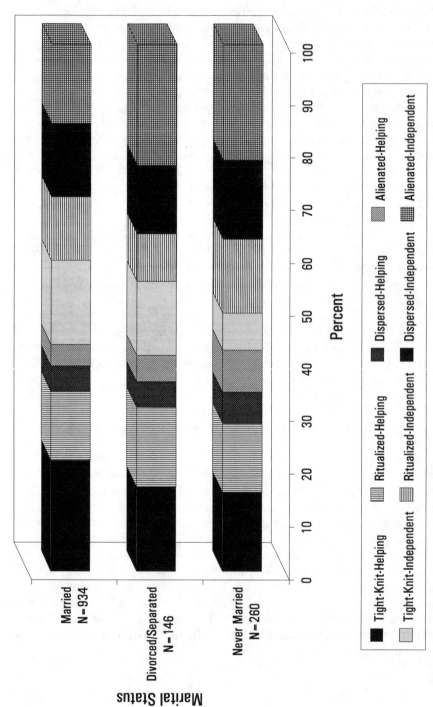

Figure 3.7 Relation types by marital status of child.

Having children is also associated with stronger linkages to a parent, as shown in Figure 3.8. Those with children are more likely (36%) than those without children (26%) to report tight-knit relationships with their parents, and less likely to feel alienated from them, (19% compared to 28%). (On the other hand, the effect is opposite for adult children who live with a parent and have children of their own, as in Table 3.2.) Thus, for adult children who do not live with parents, both being married and having children appear to strengthen the bond with the parental generation. The spouse and offspring of the adult child may provide an added link to the parent indirectly, because of an increase in shared activities.

RACE OF ADULT CHILD

The distribution of relational types for African Americans and others is shown in Figure 3.9 and Table 3.2. (We do not analyze Hispanics as a separate group because there are too few of them in the sample—88, 6% of the sample—to permit a meaningful assessment of types.) African American adult children are more likely (25%) than other adult children (13%) to report dispersed-independent relationships, and are no more likely than others to have tight-knit-helping relationships. For those who live with a parent, however, African Americans are more likely (65%) than others (50%) to feel close to that parent (Table 3.2). Together these findings affirm the closeness between generations traditionally ascribed to the African American family (Jackson, 1980) but raise some doubts about the functional exchanges of intergenerational family members who live apart.

EDUCATION OF ADULT CHILD

Differences in types of relations by education are shown in Figure 3.10. Adult children who have graduated from college are least likely to describe relations with parents as tight-knit-helping (13%). Since level of education is related to both occupation and norms of parent–child obligation (as described in Chapter 2), this finding can be attributed to either or both of these aspects of education. The more highly educated are not only more geographically mobile, and thus have less face-to-face contact with kin, but also tend to have social networks that are more varied and less dominated by kin (Fischer, 1982).

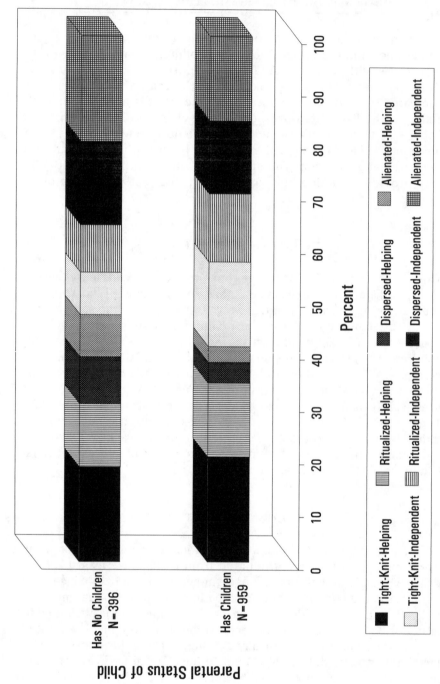

Figure 3.8 Relation types by parental status of child.

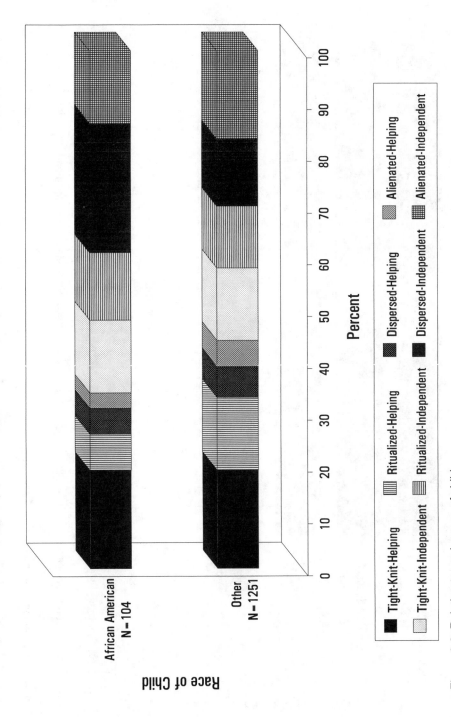

Figure 3.9 Relation types by race of child.

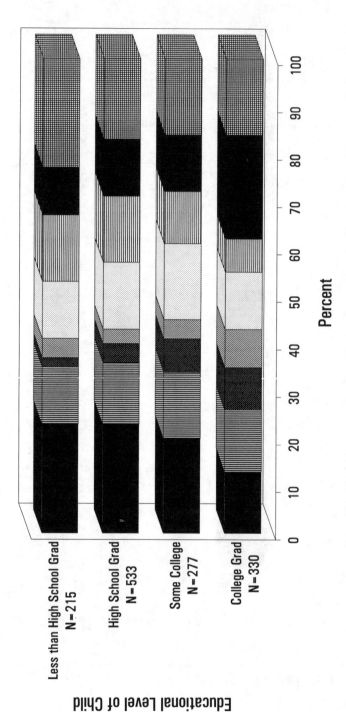

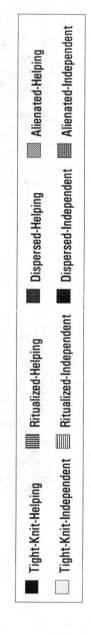

Figure 3.10 Relation types by education of child.

The least educated group (some high school or less) is overrepresented in the alienated-independent type of relationship (23%), suggesting that those who are on the lowest rung of the socioeconomic ladder may experience greater intergenerational strain as a consequence of their material need.

There is not a clear pattern of educational difference and closeness for adult children who live with parents, as shown in Table 3.2.

PARENT–CHILD RELATIONS: THE PARENT'S PERSPECTIVE

We now turn to the *parent's* perspective on family relations, acknowledging again that reports about parent–child relations may be shaped by whether the parent or child is doing the reporting. Parents were asked to describe their relations with the oldest adult child. Using the same method as before, we categorize the parent's report on the basis of the three dimensions of intergenerational solidarity (opportunity, closeness, and helping behavior).

The distribution of the ten types of parent–child relations from the parent's perspective is shown in Figure 3.11. The most common type is the tight-knit-helping (19%), followed by the tight-knit-independent (15%) and the dispersed-independent (15%). Since the pattern is similar to that of relationship types from the child's perspective (in Figure 3.1), whether the perspective is the parent's or child's in fact makes little difference to the relationship typology. Because the number of parents who live with an oldest adult child is relatively small, the following discussion will be restricted to parents and children who live apart.

Which characteristics of parents and adult children are tied to the nature of the intergenerational linkage when the parent describes the relationship? As with the analysis of relations from the child's perspective, the characteristics of gender, age, race, and education are associated with the type of relationship a parent has with an adult child; but in the case of the parent's perspective, marital status is not associated with type of relationship.

GENDER: MOTHERS AND FATHERS

The gender of the parent again plays a major role in shaping the types

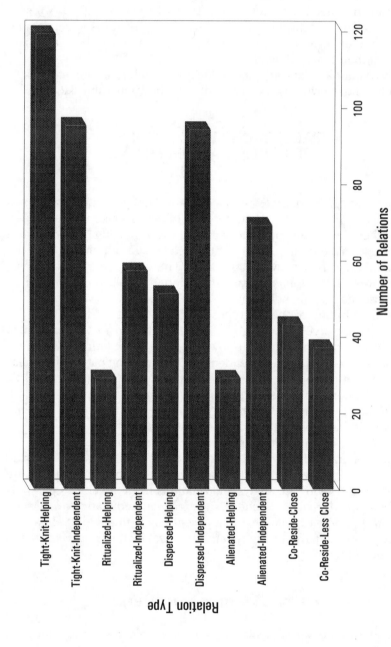

Figure 3.11 Distribution of parent–child relation types from parent's perspective.
N = 623.

of intergenerational linkages between parents and adult children. In Figure 3.12, the distribution of parent–child relation types for mothers and fathers is shown. Mothers are much more likely (27%) than fathers (16%) to have a tight-knit-helping relation with the oldest child. Overall, fathers are more likely than mothers to be functionally independent from the adult child. These results illustrate a tendency for mothers to be linked to adult children by multiple connections and of fathers to have somewhat fewer connections, and are consistent with the results obtained when the perspective of the adult child was considered (Figure 3.2).

MARITAL STATUS OF PARENT

Earlier in this chapter we have shown that, from the point of view of the adult child, the marital status of parents, in conjunction with their gender, influences the nature of the child–parent bond. From the point of view of the parent, however, there is no influence of the parent's marital status on intergenerational relations. That is, no substantial differences are found in the nature of parent–child relations among married, divorced/separated, and widowed parents. Additionally, there is no difference between mothers and fathers in the influence of marital status, as there is from the child's perspective. Whereas children describe the quality of their intergenerational relations differently depending on the combination of marital status and gender of their parents, mothers and fathers give descriptions that are not contingent on their own marital status. Perhaps the disruption of intergenerational family relations by divorce or widowhood of a parent (particularly a father) is a phenomenon that seems more salient to children than to parents.

AGE OF PARENT

The distribution of relationship types according to the age of the parent can be found in Figure 3.13. Across age groups there are fluctuations in the representation of types, but the trend is not consistently in one direction. For example, the proportion of tight-knit-helping relations rises up to the age of 65 but falls precipitously after that. At the other end of the spectrum, the proportion of those in alienated-independent relationships is largest (24%) for the parents under 45

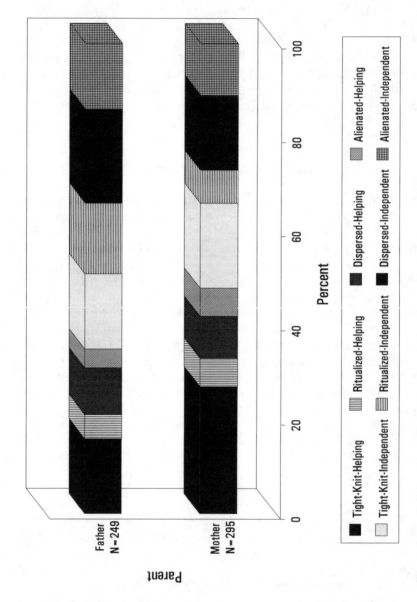

Figure 3.12 Relation types by gender of parent.

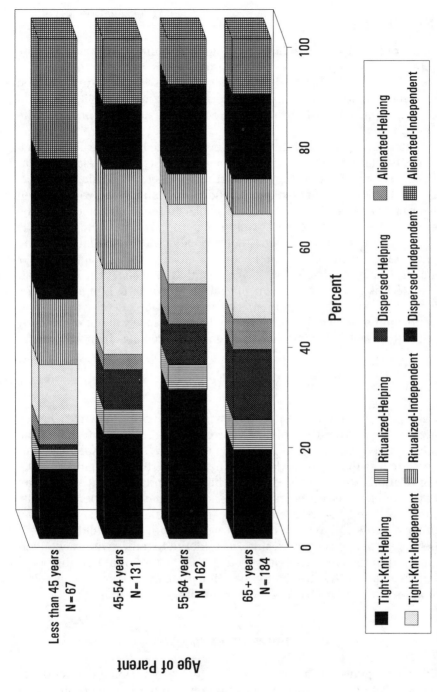

Figure 3.13 Relation types by age of parent.

69

years old, and then declines by a factor of almost one half for the three older groups. Since the aging of parents parallels the aging of their children, it is likely that older parents have older adult children who have adopted work and family roles that are more like those of their parents, thereby lessening the social disjunction between the generations.

After age 64, although there is a decline in the incidence of tight-knit-helping relations, there is an increase in two types of relations that have a strong affective component (the closeness dimension); the dispersed-helping and tight-knit-independent types increase with age and peak after age 64. These results are similar to those obtained when the child is describing the relationship (Figure 3.6). They show that the nature of the intergenerational bond is different for the family at the later stages of the life cycle, becoming more nuanced than at earlier stages. One example of a late-life change that may affect the intergenerational linkage is "retirement migration" (Litwak & Longino, 1987). Elderly parents who migrate after retirement will generally have fewer opportunities to see their children, but the distance will not necessarily affect their feelings of love and willingness to exchange help with them.

RACE OF PARENT

Race makes a difference in intergenerational relations whether they are evaluated from the point of view of the parent or from that of the adult child (Figure 3.9). As shown in Figure 3.14, African American parents are less than half as likely as other parents to have tight-knit-helping relations with the oldest adult child (8% and 23%), and more than twice as likely as other parents to have alienated-independent relations (22% and 12%). African American parents are far less likely than other parents to have the type of relations with adult children where help is exchanged. These results, considered together with race differences from the children's perspective, cast further doubt on the popular assumption that the intergenerational family functions as a social support system for African American adults.

EDUCATION OF PARENT

Education plays an important role in intergenerational connections. Parents with lower levels of education tend to have stronger links and

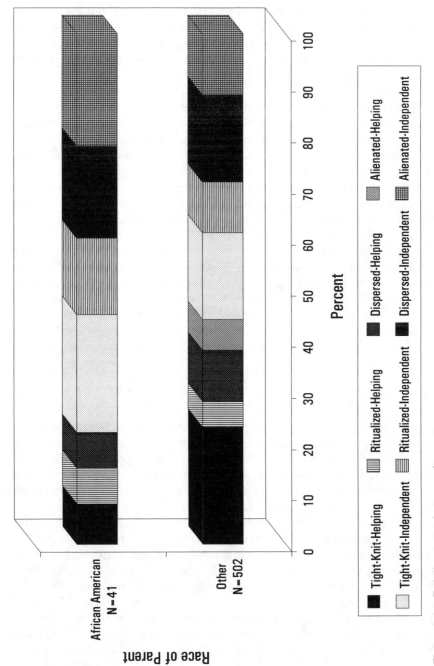

Figure 3.14 Relation types by race of parent.

parents with higher levels of education have weaker links with their children, based on all dimensions of solidarity (Figure 3.15). Only 9% of parents who have not graduated from high school characterize their relationships as alienated-independent, compared to 20% of parents who are college graduates, and more than twice as many in the lowest educational category (22%) as in the highest (11%) have tight-knit-helping relations with their adult children.

From the child's point of view (see Figure 3.10), low education is related to alienated-independent relations, but from the parent's point of view, not graduating from high school may be associated with unfulfilled parental expectation and intergenerational strain. However, the decline with parent's education in tight-knit-helping relations as reported by parents is generally similar to the association between education and family relations from the adult child's perspective. This is not surprising, in that educational achievement is associated with occupational status and with an orientation that may allow social and physical distance between the generations for the purpose of getting ahead. Consequently, more highly educated individuals tend to be less family oriented (Fischer, 1982) and to place relatively more importance on career advancement than on family relationships (Litwak, 1985).

DISCUSSION

Intergenerational family relations are complex social arrangements, consisting of multiple, often contradictory dimensions. In this chapter we have identified three of the most salient dimensions of solidarity in intergenerational linkages (opportunity for interaction, closeness, and helping behavior) and have used them to develop a 10-category typology of parent–child relations in adulthood.

The use of typologies represents a relatively new approach to the study of solidarity within families. Whereas research investigating the underlying components of solidarity has revealed important insights concerning family dynamics (Roberts & Bengtson, 1990), little attention has been paid to categorizing family relationships on the basis of these components.

Discussions about kinds of intergenerational families have largely been conceptual, with little empirical grounding. Parsons (1944) has been credited with developing the idea of the *isolated family* (defined as

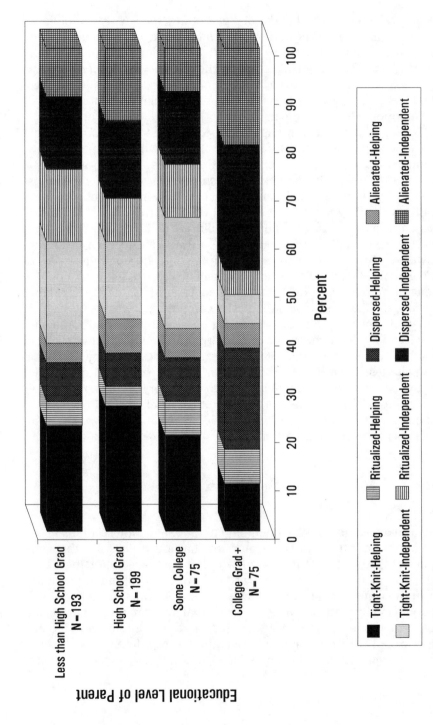

Figure 3.15 Relation types by education of parent.

one in which adult child and older parent are socially, geographically, and economically segregated from each other) as the ideal family type (i.e., as the common pattern) in America. This formulation was countered by Litwak (1985) who identified the *modified-extended family* as a type in which adult children, in spite of being economically and geographically independent of their parents, are able to maintain contact and emotional ties with them.

Ethnographic research has described families of a *traditional* type with dense patterns of interactions, often in white ethnic and low-income African American communities (Gans, 1962; Stack, 1974). Schemes for classifying family relationships have been developed most recently by Olson, Sprenkle, and Russell (1979) with respect to nuclear families; by Eggebeen and Hogan (1990) with respect to social exchange between parent and adult children; and by Gold, Woodbury, and George (1990) with respect to sibling relations in later life. However, there have been few attempts to group common types of intergenerational family relations systematically, using the full complement of *theoretically* important dimensions of solidarity, possibly because the task seems daunting in its complexity.

Typologies are intuitively appealing because they organize the multiplicity of hidden dimensions into interpretable patterns that result in rich, highly descriptive characterizations. The types of intergenerational linkages described in this chapter can be compared and contrasted with what we know of families through our everyday experience and observation. Clustering into groups and then labeling relations that are alike makes evident, *at the holistic level of the relationship,* the complexities of the intergenerational family.

SUMMARY

In our investigation of types of intergenerational family relations in the survey, we find through factor analysis that individuals use the same frame of reference regardless of whether they are reporting about someone directly up the generational ladder or someone directly down the generational ladder. Further, there is evidence that relations between family members in generations that are nonadjacent in the lineage—relations between grandparents and grandchildren—also are experienced with the same underlying frame of reference as those in adjacent generations. The three-dimensional typology thus efficiently depicts the family, capturing its most salient aspects with little loss of information.

About one in five respondents describes a cross-generational relationship as high on all three components of solidarity—opportunity for contact, closeness, and helping. This is true whether an adult child describes the relationship with the parent, or the parent describes the relationship with the oldest child. More than half of the adult children who share a residence with a parent describe the relationship as close.

Individual and family characteristics of the parent and child—gender, marital status, age, race, and education—are strongly associated with the types of relational linkages that exist between parents and adult children. Comparison between parents' and children's perspectives reveals some interesting similarities and differences in the characteristics that influence their experience of the intergenerational bond. For example, relations of children with mothers emerge as stronger than with fathers from the perspective of both children and parents. On the other hand, adult children report relations with fathers who are no longer married as weaker than relations with still-married fathers, but this difference is not reflected in the parents' descriptions of their relationships with their children.

In addition to the gender and marital status of the parent, other characteristics are related to family involvement. Race is one important factor. African Americans tend to have weaker intergenerational ties than others (especially with regard to helping exchanges), with the exception of African Americans who live with a parent. The less educated, both adult children and parents, tend to be linked by all three dimensions. Adult children who are married report stronger ties with parents, and having children of their own is also associated with stronger ties. Finally, age differences suggest a pattern whereby adult children become more functionally independent of their parents over time, and the relations of parents with children become more variegated.

Intergenerational family relations thus take on a diversity of forms that vary by differences in gender, marital status, age, race, and education. These characteristics serve as markers for differences in socialization, roles, culture, values, and access to resources; together, these differences shape behavior and sentiment toward parents and adult children.

Our findings portray intergenerational relations as less than uniform and provide a warning against sweeping generalizations about the nature of the multigenerational American family. Intergenerational families should not be summarized as *isolated* from each other, nor should they be described as *fully engaged.*

Further analysis of intergenerational ties follows in Chapter 4, where patterns of giving gifts and informal assistance in both families and communities are described.

CHAPTER 4

Volunteering, Helping, and Gift Giving in Families and Communities

Robert A. Harootyan and Robert E. Vorek

Intergenerational solidarity and cooperation, as noted in Chapters 2 and 3, are prevalent characteristics in American families. These cross-generational bonds are based on patterns of interaction, affection, similarity of opinions, and mutual assistance among family members. Still, some families lack common emotional bonds and ways of helping each other. In this chapter we move beyond the immediate family to describe how people volunteer their time and give assistance and gifts to relatives other than parents and adult children, and to others in their communities. We then ask whether their generosity outside the family is related to the solidarity within their own families.

Analysis of community involvement as measured here shows that transfers between generations take place in many ways in contemporary American society. Some of the findings are surprising. For example, assistance from younger to older persons, compared to assistance from older to younger persons, is not as prominent as might be assumed. Other patterns of helping and giving that might otherwise have remained hidden also are revealed.

Intergenerational linkages within communities include formal volunteering, informal assistance, and gift giving. We identify differences in age, gender, marital status, and opinions that are related to these types of community involvement. We also explore the relationship between the types of family relations individuals report and their community involvement.

The reasons that people choose to help are varied: a sense of social obligation, a need to maintain and solidify social bonds, and the intrinsic pleasure or satisfaction derived from helping (Schram, 1985). In the case of formal volunteerism, additional motives may be at work. Persons might volunteer to provide structure and meaning to their lives or to learn new skills that they might apply to a new career. Whatever the motivation of the helpers, their work has a common element: It benefits people in need.

We assume in this study that many people have a desire (or need) to help others and that, given the opportunity and the ability to overcome any constraints to helping, they will respond. The opportunity comes with the recognition that there is a person in need. The constraints include other commitments or obligations and a lack of resources with which to help. These constraints can prevent a person from helping or can shape the type of help that is given.

Informal assistance is the most common form of helping behavior, possibly because it has the fewest constraints. All that is required is time and the ability and willingness to help. *Volunteering* through an organization has the added constraint of scheduling—not only must persons have the time and ability to provide assistance, they may also be required to provide assistance at specific times of the day or week. *Giving large gifts* or *bequests* to others requires only that persons have the financial means to do so.

Although there have been numerous studies of relationships between generations in the family, and also studies of formal and informal assistance patterns within families and communities, the connections between these two areas have, for the most part, been unexplored. Also, previous work on helping behavior has generally focused on one aspect of community involvement, such as volunteering, or on the contributions of a particular age group, usually the young or the elderly. These studies were usually grounded in a particular analytic point of view, which limited their analysis of the complexity of society's social support components. Three points of view were common in such studies:

1. *Social Networks:* Much of the previous research on exchange networks has not focused on their *social* functions or the "relatedness needs" of volunteers (Alderfer, 1972). The exchanges described in this chapter have social as well as economic or utilitarian functions. Besides providing needed services and material goods, exchanges reinforce social bonds within families and between individuals within the community.

2. *Social Context:* Most research on helping behavior has emphasized the psychological and demographic characteristics of the
   helper or the recipient (but not both) and is often based on studies with contrived situations or laboratory settings that have little or no regard for social setting (Bar-Tal, 1984; Sinha, 1984). In
   contrast, this survey asked people about their actual behavior in
   real situations—the family and community activities that occur
   on a daily basis. In the following analysis we tie that behavior to
   psychological, attitudinal, economic, and demographic characteristics of both givers and recipients of help.

3. *Productivity:* Economists generally have concentrated on intergenerational contributions in terms of *productivity,* defined very
   specifically as paid activity, often using an implicit wage rate to
   calculate the "imputed value" of an activity (Kieffer, 1986). The
   economic value of nonmonetary contributions (e.g., time spent in
   volunteer activity and informal assistance) made by the American
   public is excluded from most studies or measures of productivity
   in society. Thus, many transfers that contribute to the well-being
   of family or community are hidden from both analytical scrutiny
   and the public's awareness, thereby limiting our picture of "productive" behavior to only a portion of the full array of productive
   activity (Morgan, 1986). This chapter describes and analyzes
   those contributions, and Chapter 5 estimates their monetary
   value as part of the total transfers that occur within and between
   generations.

Very few studies have concentrated on the full spectrum of intergenerational assistance and support; even fewer have examined *simultaneously* the contributions made by adults of all ages (Herzog, 1989). This
chapter focuses on the age differences and generational membership of
those who give and receive volunteer time, informal help, and large
gifts. We also report on characteristics other than age or generational
status that are related to these types of transfers and helping behaviors.

Intergenerational transfers at the community level are a major component of exchanges between generations. Informal transfers (such as
providing assistance and gift giving) and more formal transfers (such
as volunteering and inheritance) create a web of financial and social
connections that link generations. Yet these linkages are often hidden
from our usual perceptions of generational transfers.

Many of these intergenerational connections are explicit and
direct, while others are implicit and indirect. Assistance provided to

one generation often reduces the burden borne by other generations. For example, the person who helps an elderly neighbor or friend may also be helping that person's adult children by reducing their burden in caring for their parents. Similarly, the time, care, and expertise shared by an older person with a young child reduce the parents' burden and enable the parents to enrich the child's life in other ways. These are only two examples of the myriad connections among generations that this chapter addresses.

VOLUNTEERING

Formal volunteering, the help provided free to organizations such as charities, schools, religious organizations, and civic groups, is an important community resource. The 1990 AARP Intergenerational Linkages Survey data show that 54% of the United States population aged 18 and over volunteer at least some of their time through these types of groups (Table 4.1). These findings are similar to those from other national surveys conducted during the last decade (Independent

TABLE 4.1   Volunteer Participation Rates, by Type of Program and Age

Program type	Age group				
	18-34	35-44	45-64	65 +	Total
Total *N*	591	291	379	238	1,499
Percent who volunteer, all types	51	65	52	48	54
Of those respondents who volunteer, percent who volunteer for:					
Religious organizations	38	46	48	54	45
Education/tutoring	23	31	16	9	21
Health care	16	13	16	25	17
Community and neighborhood organizations	12	23	15	13	16
Youth programs	14	24	11	7	15
Civic and fraternal organizations	10	16	19	13	14
Disease related causes	12	12	17	14	13
Senior citizen organizations	8	8	10	21	10

Sector, 1985, 1986, 1990, 1992). But our analysis, as discussed below, also discovered some interesting age group differences in organizational patterns of volunteering.

The primary avenues for volunteer activity are religious institutions (Table 4.1). Of those who volunteer, 45% offer at least part of their volunteer time through their churches, synagogues, or other religious organizations. As Table 4.1 also shows, older volunteers are more likely to be involved through a religious institution than other age groups. Education/tutoring is the second most common type of activity among all volunteers (21%). In this group, however, volunteers among persons under age 45 are 2 to 3 times more prevalent than among those aged 45–64 or 65 and over.

Age-related differences in volunteering are noteworthy in two additional areas. Youth programs account for at least some of the time given by 15% of all volunteers, with the greatest contrast being between those aged 35–44 (24%) and those aged 65 and over (7%). Senior citizen organizations benefit from 10% of all volunteers, ranging from 8% of volunteers aged 18–34 or 35–44 to 21% of those aged 65 and over. These patterns are not surprising, because they reflect, along with other age-related factors, life cycle stages. For example, membership and participation in religious institutions are correlated with age, while likelihood of volunteer involvement in educational or recreational programs is highest for those who have school-age children—primarily parents under age 55.

The survey data also indicate that volunteers generally do not confine their activities to one organization or type of organization. On average, volunteers serve approximately two (1.8) organizations at any one time.

CHARACTERISTICS OF VOLUNTEERS

Volunteers represent every age, income, education, and ethnic group. These and other characteristics such as gender, marital status, presence of children at home, and employment status are associated with differences in rates of volunteerism. Often, however, these differences in participation rates are balanced by differences in the average number of hours that are spent volunteering (Table 4.2). In many cases a group that is high on the percentage who volunteer is low on the average number of hours per month spent in volunteer work, and vice versa. This tendency is particularly noteworthy among the groups defined by age, household income, and educational attainment. For brevity, we use the terms *prevalence* or *likelihood* when referring to the rate of participation and the terms *intensity* or *degree* when referring to the number of hours per month devoted to such participation, whether formal volunteering or informal helping.

Age.   Adults aged 35–44 are the age group most likely to report participation in some type of volunteer activity (65%), but they also report the lowest average intensity of volunteering (14 hours per month). In contrast, only 48% of those aged 65 and over volunteer, but their average monthly time is 23 hours. Among the young old (aged 65–74), 52% volunteer, with an average of 26 hours per month—by far the highest time commitment among the age groups. The oldest old (75 and older), on the other hand, have the lowest proportion of volunteers (40%) and spend an average of 14 hours per month doing volunteer work.

Household Income.   Prevalence of volunteering is highest among persons with annual household incomes in excess of $100,000 (72%) and lowest among those with annual incomes below $10,000 (35%). As with age groups, the higher the proportion within an income group who volunteer, the lower the average time spent in such activity. As seen in Table 4.2, the proportion of volunteers generally increases with higher income. Conversely, there is a sharp decline in average hours for those in the $30,000–$49,999 group.

While our analysis did not delve into factors related to this change, we suspect that it relates to the greater proportions of dual-earner families in this and the next higher household income groups. Such middle- and upper-middle-income households are more likely to have adults whose work-related time constraints reduce their opportunity and ability to spend more than a few hours per week in volunteer activity.

Educational Attainment.   As with income, volunteer rates increase sharply with years of education. Whereas 45% of persons with no more than a high school education volunteer, 72% of college graduates, including those with advanced degrees, volunteer. Once again, however, those groups with the lowest volunteerism rate spend on average the greatest amount of time in such activity.

Marital Status.   On the surface, marital status affects the likelihood and intensity of volunteering in ways that reflect other factors, such as opportunity, life cycle stage, ability, and age. For example, married persons have much higher rates of volunteering (58%) than widowed persons (39%). But widowed persons who *do* volunteer

TABLE 4.2 Volunteer Participation Rates and Average Hours of Volunteer Activity, by Individual Characteristics

Characteristic	Total N	Percent who volunteer	Average hours volunteered per month[a]
Age			
Total	1,499	54	17
18-34	591	51	16
35-44	291	65	14
45-64	379	52	18
65 +	238	48	23
65-74	163	52	26
75 +	75	40	14
Annual household income			
Less than $10,000	168	35	21
$10,000 - $19,999	239	44	21
$20,000 - $29,999	264	52	20
$30,000 - $49,999	419	61	14
$50,000 - $74,999	179	63	17
$75,000 - $99,999	56	60	16
$100,000 or more	41	72	13
Educational status			
High school	919	45	19
Some college	310	64	14
College graduate	270	72	16
Marital status			
Married	932	58	17
Separated/divorced	150	46	17
Widowed	95	39	22
Never married	317	49	15
Employment status			
Full-time	840	54	14
Part-time	175	61	18
Unemployed	267	46	22
Retired	218	54	23
Number of minor children			
None	942	52	16
One	221	52	20
Two	243	58	16
Three	70	66	18
Four or more	21	67	18
Race			
African American	137	63	21
Other	1,362	53	16

[a]Base of average hours volunteered per month equals respondents who did any volunteering.

spend considerably more time in such activity (an average of 22 hours per month) than do volunteers who are married (17 hours). The lower participation/higher intensity of volunteering among widows reflects the same findings among those in the oldest age group (i.e., those who are most likely to be widowed).

Ironically, persons who have never married had the second highest rate of volunteer involvement but the lowest average hours per month. Like those who are separated or divorced, these persons are most likely to be single earners with limited free time or inducement to volunteer. As discussed below, the presence of minor children in the household increases both the likelihood and intensity of volunteering. Because never married persons are least likely to have children, this form of inducement to volunteer is missing.

Employment Status.   The relationship between employment status and volunteering is not clear-cut. The likelihood of volunteering is highest among part-time workers (61%). Surprisingly, full-time workers and retired persons volunteer at comparable rates (54%). Not surprisingly, retired persons contribute much more time (23 hours per month), on average, than employed persons (14 hours). Unemployed persons volunteer at the lowest rate (46%), but those who do volunteer have a high degree of involvement (22 hours).

We delved more deeply into the group of respondents who are not working for pay to discern what proportion identified themselves as "homemakers." More than half (55%) of those not working for pay are homemakers. Of these, 50% say they volunteer, spending an average of 20 hours per month doing so. Interestingly, 38% of these homemakers say they are retired, probably a reflection of their age. It is also interesting that one fifth (19%) of them are men. It appears that homemakers represent a type of "middle ground" in relation to our findings regarding the relationship between volunteerism and being married or being retired. As with married persons, homemakers have a relatively high likelihood of volunteering. But like retired persons, homemakers who volunteer spend more time doing so than married persons in general. For some homemakers, available time may be the key to their degree of volunteer involvement. For others, child-centered activities and larger household size may be the key elements, as discussed later.

Children.   Rates of volunteer activity are not only higher among those with children aged 18 and younger at home, they also increase with the number of minor children, and are highest for persons with four or more children at home (67%). In comparison, 52% of respondents with no minor children or with one child volunteer. These rates indicate the likely influence of child-centered activities on the volunteer role of parents. Such activities occur through the two most common vehicles for volunteer work—religious and educational institutions. In addition, the third and fourth most prevalent types of volunteer programs—community organizations and youth programs—also increase the likelihood of youth-oriented volunteer work. Thus, factors such as being married, having children at home, and being in the middle of the life cycle are likely to complement one another as inducements to volunteerism. We investigate these multifactorial relationships in the next section.

Race. Another thought-provoking finding from the survey is the relationship of race to volunteerism. African Americans are significantly more likely to volunteer (63%) than others (53%). This finding seems contradictory to the other data indicating the positive relationship of factors such as income and education to volunteerism. Although the African American population has lower average income and educational levels than the white population, African Americans have both a higher proportion who volunteer and a higher intensity of volunteering than do white persons. Various reasons may explain this anomaly. The importance and influence of religious organizations in the African American community and their predominant role as vehicles for volunteer work are probably significant factors (Smith, 1993; Taylor & Chatters, 1986). Other possible influences are the greater likelihood of need for volunteers within the African American community and the perception of that need among African Americans (Gurin, Miller, & Gurin, 1980; Silverman, 1986).

The limited scope of the survey does not permit analysis of these potential explanations for the high levels of volunteer participation and commitment among African Americans. Additional data and multivariate analyses would shed light on the relative importance of these and other factors for volunteer activity among African Americans.

FACTORS THAT AFFECT VOLUNTEERING

The preceding discussion reviewed the relationships of sociodemographic attributes to rates of volunteering. In order to go beyond such descriptive analysis, we used multivariate techniques such as *discriminant analysis* and *multiple regression* to identify the relative contribution of several factors to the likelihood and intensity of volunteering (see Appendix D).

A discriminant analysis of 23 factors that could be expected to influence volunteer activity shows the relative influence of each factor in distinguishing between volunteers and nonvolunteers (see Table D.1, Appendix D). Three types of factors were used: demographic characteristics (e.g., age, gender, and income), attitudes and opinions (e.g., about family responsibility), and types of family relationships (as developed in Chapter 3).

Many factors emerged as significant in characterizing those who are most likely and least likely to volunteer. Factors having the most influence (either positive or negative) are as follows, in relative order of their influence:

- *Educational attainment* is the most influential factor in volunteer behavior. Only postgraduate education has a clear positive effect, while having less than a high school education has a strong negative influence on likelihood of volunteering. Even college level education has a moderately negative association with the likelihood of volunteering.

- *Middle-income and upper-middle income status* are most strongly associated with the likelihood of volunteering. Interestingly, low household income as well as very high household income also positively affect volunteerism, though less strongly.

- *Altruistic attitudes and a sense of equity or fairness* play a positive role in propensity to volunteer. The belief that "People who are wealthy should share their advantages with people who are not wealthy" is positively related to volunteerism. Clearly, those who volunteer are most likely to feel a sense of responsibility toward those who are less fortunate.

- *Positive perceptions regarding the contributions of others* are directly related to volunteer orientations. Agreement that older people and younger people "contribute a lot to their communities" has a positive effect on volunteering. Positive perceptions of those who may benefit from volunteer programs appear to induce voluntarism and, perhaps, to confirm the "worthiness" of those who benefit from it.

- *Being aged 35–44* has a very strong positive effect on the likelihood of volunteering. All else being equal, there is something unique about this age group—aside from educational attainment, marital status, existence of minor children, and other correlated factors—that induces their volunteer activity. No other age group used in this analysis exhibits this effect.

- *Having at least one family relationship characterized as high on contact (opportunity), low on closeness, and low on helping* (the ritualized-independent type, as described in Chapter 3) has a *negative* effect on propensity to volunteer. This type of perceived family relationship reflects a sense of duty (through contact) but little empathy, closeness, or actual assistance to other family members. None of the other seven family types generated in this study (see Chapter 3) showed a significant positive or negative effect on volunteerism.

- *A positive perception of one's quality of life* is directly related to volunteer activity. People who feel good about themselves are more likely to have active lifestyles and to reach out to others through volunteer work. Some researchers have suggested that the opposite process may also be operating—that volunteering may lead to high life satisfaction. But a definitive analysis of the relationship between these factors indicated that volunteerism is a consequence, not a cause, of high life satisfaction (Chambré, 1987).

- *The larger one's household,* the greater the likelihood of volunteering. Larger households are most likely to have minor children, and some large households may include elderly family members as well. Both of these circumstances may create opportunities or expectations for volunteer work related to those family members.

- *Perceptions that federal programs for youth and the elderly are too costly* reduce the likelihood of volunteer activity. This finding suggests that many nonvolunteers have negative views of public programs that benefit youth or the elderly. These individuals are also likely to have negative orientations about private responsibilities for elderly parents, as the next finding indicates.

- *Belief that adult children should not be expected to support their parents* is negatively related to volunteer work. Those who are least likely to volunteer also do not feel that adult children should have to support their parents if needed. Their lack of volunteer orientation appears to be an extension of their values in this area of intrafamily responsibilities.

- *Being married* has a small positive effect on volunteer activity. This effect, independent of household size and composition, may reflect the influence of a spouse's awareness, interests, and community involvement.

Each of these factors contributes uniquely to volunteerism in our society. Taken together, they form a complex web of sociostructural characteristics, personal values, and social perceptions that distinguish between those who are most likely and least likely to volunteer. But volunteer participation rates are only part of the picture, as revealed in the next section.

Hours Devoted to Volunteering

Volunteer activity cannot be assessed by participation rates alone; the intensity or degree of volunteer activity, expressed in hours per month, should also be considered. The latter is a surrogate measure of volunteers' available discretionary time and level of commitment to volunteer activity. When combined, participation rates and average hours spent volunteering provide a richer picture of the extent and depth of volunteerism in our society.

According to the survey, the typical volunteer works approximately 17 hours per month. Despite their lower than average rate of volunteerism, those elderly persons (65 and over) who *do* volunteer contribute the highest average time (23 hours per month) (Table 4.2). Because most older persons are not in the labor force, their discretionary time is reflected in the high number of hours they spend as volunteers. In contrast, persons aged 35–44 have the highest likelihood (65%) but the lowest intensity (14 hours) of volunteering.

We developed a Tobit regression model to identify the factors that influence a person's degree of volunteerism (Table D.2). Five factors found to *increase* the hours that volunteers devote to helping others are:

- Being a parent of a minor child
- Being African American
- The perception that the young and old make important contributions to their communities
- The belief that the wealthy should share their advantages with others
- A positive perception of one's life at present.

Three factors found to *decrease* volunteer hours are:

- Having less than a high school level of education
- Being in a two-earner household

- Having a family relationship characterized as high on contact, low on closeness, and low on helping (ritualized-independent type).

Clearly, whether looking at volunteer participation rates or number of hours volunteered per month, influential factors leading to volunteer activity are educational attainment, positive perceptions about others' lives and one's own life, and beliefs about sharing one's benefits with those who are less fortunate (ACTION, 1975; Smith, 1982). Our analysis further shows that a ritualized-independent family relationship is the only type that has a significant influence on volunteer participation and intensity; in both cases the effect is to reduce the likelihood and degree of volunteer activity.

But despite these clear effects, anomalies abound in our findings. On the one hand, lower educational attainment levels among the oldest Americans help explain their lower likelihood of volunteering. In 1990, 42% of those aged 65 and over had less than a high school education, compared to 22% of all persons aged 25 and over (U.S. Bureau of the Census, 1992a). Indeed, given such a large disparity, we wonder why the proportion of elders who volunteer is as high as 48% (52% among those aged 65–74).

On the other hand, African Americans have lower average levels of educational attainment, yet *both* their likelihood and intensity of volunteer work are higher than for others. Our regression analysis shows that, independent of other factors such as education, being African American is strongly related to high amounts of time spent in volunteer work. As discussed in the previous section, the dynamic of volunteer activity is not explained by individual or personal characteristics alone. Cultural and institutional elements—many of which are difficult to measure—appear to be important factors leading to volunteer work in the community (Jackson, 1991; Vaux, 1985).

INTERGENERATIONAL VOLUNTEERING

The previous sections have dealt with volunteer activity in general. Our findings corroborate much of what has been reported in other national surveys about age-related participation rates and the prevalence of different types of volunteer programs (Independent Sector, 1985, 1986, 1990, 1992). But we sought to explore more specifically the *intergenerational* aspects of volunteer activity in the United States.

Volunteer work that benefits individuals in other age groups is over-looked in most analyses of either helping behavior or exchanges between generations. To our knowledge, *nationally representative* data have never been reported on cross-generational aspects of for-mal volunteering.

To examine the intergenerational component of volunteer activity, survey respondents were asked to estimate the portion of their volun-teer activity that was directed toward helping specific age groups—children and teenagers, young and middle-aged adults (aged 20–59), and older persons (aged 60 and over)—or all ages in general. The mea-sure for proportion of time was "all," "most," "some," or "none." For example, a respondent could answer that most of his or her volunteer time was spent specifically helping children and teenagers and some of the time was devoted specifically to older persons.

The survey data indicate that a larger proportion of volunteers are involved in activities that particularly benefit children and teenagers than in activities benefiting elders. Two thirds (67%) of all volunteers report that at least some of their time specifically helps youth, while 56% report that at least some of it helps adults aged 60 and over (Table 4.3).

Notable differences also exist in the degree to which volunteer time is concentrated *within* a particular beneficiary group. Among volun-teers whose activity benefits youth, one half (49%) spend all or most of their time doing so. In contrast, less than one fourth (23%) of those whose time benefits older persons spend all or most of their volunteer time in this way. The limited data on this component of the survey make it impossible to explain why this difference in patterns of volun-teer time exists. One possibility is that volunteer work with older per-sons is more likely to be episodic (e.g., providing transportation assis-tance) or event-centered (e.g., a special community-based activity for seniors). For children and teenagers, volunteer work is more likely to be structured and repetitive (e.g., school tutoring programs, seasonal recreational activity such as Little League, and year-long Scouting pro-grams), often involving long-term commitments by the parents of minor children. These possible explanations warrant further investigation.

In addition to these findings, the survey indicates that 9 out of 10 volunteers (89%) spend at least some of their time helping people of all ages. We are not surprised by this result, since so many volunteer pro-grams are targeted for those who are poor, ill, or otherwise in need of assistance. Poverty and illness know no age boundaries. Hence, much of our volunteer efforts are also age neutral.

TABLE 4.3   Volunteer Participation Rates, by Age of Volunteer and Age of Benefit Group

Participation	Age group				
	18-34	35-44	45-64	65 +	Total
Total *N*	591	291	379	238	1,499
Percent who volunteer, all types	51	65	52	48	54
		Percentage distribution			
Of those respondents who volunteer, percent whose volunteer time benefits:					
Children and teens					
Any	78	74	63	35	67
All	8	8	2	0	5
Most	33	41	17	8	28
Some	37	25	44	27	34
None	22	26	37	65	33
Adults aged 60 +					
Any	57	51	61	60	56
All	0	0	1	4	1
Most	9	9	16	25	12
Some	48	42	44	31	43
None	42	49	39	40	43

Note.   Percentages may not total to 100% because of rounding.

Volunteer Service to Youth

As expected on the basis of life cycle stage and child-centered households, volunteers younger than 50 are more likely than older volunteers to devote some of their time toward children and teens (76%). Volunteers aged 65 and over, in contrast, help youth at much lower rates (35%) than do other age groups. Because the *size* of this difference—the largest difference in volunteer participation rates by age—was unexpected, we sought possible reasons to explain it.

Multivariate analyses point to several factors that influence the low participation rate of older people in youth programs. A separate regression analysis of only the data for volunteers aged 65 and older showed that higher educational attainment and disagreement with the statement that federal programs for youth are "too costly" are the two most significant determinants of volunteering for young people (Table D.3). Once again, the strong effects of education and perceived need on volunteerism emerge, showing that older Americans are no different in this regard from younger Americans.

But, as noted above, older Americans have on average fewer years of formal education than any other adult age group (U.S. Bureau of the Census, 1992a). Since a large portion of volunteer activities for youth is related to school work, older people generally are less inclined to be involved in these activities. The survey showed that while 9% of *all older volunteers* spend some time in education/tutoring, almost twice as many (16%) college-educated elderly volunteers do so.

Other evidence from the survey also points to the special importance of educational attainment in this type of volunteerism—even *within* the older population itself. Disproportionately high percentages of elders with college degrees (37%) and education beyond college (28%) volunteer in programs benefiting youth, compared to 15% of elders with some college, 22% of elders with a high school degree, and only 8% of elders with less than a high school education. Thus, whether looking only within the elderly volunteer group or at the elderly population in general, educational attainment is the primary factor in youth-targeted volunteerism. (Educational attainment is also positively related to health status, which is likely to have positive effects on participation in youth-related programs).

Elderly volunteers who do *not* feel that federal programs for young people are too costly are significantly more likely to volunteer on their behalf. These older volunteers quite possibly believe that not enough is being spent or that the costs of youth programs are a worthwhile investment. Their volunteer behavior thus mirrors these sentiments and perceptions. Three other variables significantly influence the likelihood that older volunteers will spend part of their time in programs benefiting children and teenagers. Each reflects an important attitude or perception about young people. In addition to apparently supporting federal spending on programs for younger people, youth-oriented elderly volunteers are significantly more likely to (a) agree that programs should be needs-based rather than age-based, (b) perceive that the financial status of children is better than other age groups, and (c) feel that the young do *not* receive an excess share of government benefits. Education and these four attitude and perception factors together explain most of the differences in youth-oriented volunteer activity by older persons.

The four attitude and perception factors indicate that these older volunteers strongly support federal expenditures on programs for young people and seek to help those who are most in need, regardless of their financial status. These pivotal attitudes simultaneously reflect an altruistic orientation toward the less fortunate and the need to invest in children, whether through government spending or volunteer activity.

Having explained the special characteristics that distinguish between the relatively few elderly volunteers who are youth-oriented and the majority who are not, we asked if similar processes are operating among volunteers of all ages. A regression analysis based on all adult volunteers shows that four factors significantly influence volunteering for youth (as shown in Table D.4). They are, in order of influence:

- Having more education
- Having relatively frequent contact with one's oldest adult child
- Being younger
- Supporting needs-based rather than age-based programs.

These results confirm that educational attainment is the primary determinant of volunteering in youth-related programs, regardless of the volunteer's age. Relatively frequent contact with one's oldest adult child (not living in the same household) is strongly related to this type of volunteer orientation, reflecting strong intergenerational linkages and, perhaps in some cases, a higher than average level of interest in one's grandchildren.

It is possible that as the older population reaches parity in educational attainment with younger age groups—as is projected within 15 to 20 years—the age-based disparity in rates of volunteering for youth will diminish. But the regression analysis also shows that—similar to findings about volunteering by the elderly in general (Chambré, 1987)—even when factors such as education and intergenerational contact are accounted for, older age per se still inhibits volunteering with young people. The survey did not collect information on self-reported health status and functional activity level, but another reason for the elderly's low rate of youth-oriented volunteerism may be their poorer health and rigor compared to younger volunteers (Chambré, 1987).

Volunteer Service to Older Persons

While lower in general than youth-oriented volunteering, elder-oriented volunteer activity is substantial. Half or more of all volunteers give at least some time to activities that benefit adults aged 60 and older. Volunteers aged 35–44 are least likely to devote some time to helping older adults (51%), and volunteers aged 45–64 (61%) or 65 and older (60%) are most likely to do so (Table 4.3).

Regression analysis indicates that volunteering specifically to help older persons is significantly influenced by four factors (as shown in Table D.5). They are, in order of their relative importance:

- Being older
- Feeling closer to grandparents
- Having more contact with grandparents
- Having more contact with oldest child.

In contrast to youth-oriented volunteering, older age rather than younger age is related to the likelihood of volunteering in programs that specifically benefit older persons. This is probably because awareness of need, empathy for one's age peers, and the higher likelihood of knowing an older person who benefits from formal volunteer programs are more common among elderly than nonelderly persons.

Our findings also indicate the influence on elder-oriented volunteering of emotional closeness and current interaction with one's grandparents (in contrast to responses regarding past interaction, when the respondent was a child). Volunteers would ordinarily have to be middle-aged or younger to have interaction with a grandparent. But as with older volunteers, these younger volunteers are more likely than their non-elder-oriented counterparts to be aware of the needs of older persons and to have an affinity for them.

It is less clear why contact with one's oldest adult child is significantly related to elder-oriented volunteering. By definition, such interaction occurs primarily among middle-aged and older persons, the same groups most likely to be involved in this type of volunteer activity. Interaction with adult children may be symptomatic of strong family bonds, which in turn may promote or reflect sensitivity to the needs of older members of the community in general.

GIVING AND RECEIVING HELP: INFORMAL ASSISTANCE

Intergenerational linkages are fostered in less formal ways throughout the community. Informal patterns of assistance create a rich tapestry of social interaction within and across generations—interaction that extends well beyond the extended family. But the exchange of *informal* assistance in our daily lives, while generally recognized, has not been as systematically studied as formal assistance such as volunteering. Capturing such activity was one of the goals of the research.

Informal assistance is more prevalent in the United States than volunteer behavior. An overwhelming majority of adult Americans (89%) provide informal help to others in the community (Table 4.4). But while 9 out of 10 respondents report *giving* informal assistance of one kind or another to friends, neighbors, or relatives, less than two thirds (64%) indicate that they *receive* help from them (Table 4.5). This difference in reported direction of informal help is evident in all age groups, but most notably among those aged 45–64, with a differential of 37 percentage points. These findings confirm other data suggesting that middle-aged Americans are the least likely to need informal assistance and among the most likely to provide it, whether to relatives, friends, or neighbors.

Nevertheless, a majority of Americans in *all* age groups provide help to others, but the proportion decreases with age. Whereas 93% of those aged 18–34 assist friends, neighbors, and relatives, 76% of those aged 65 and over provide such informal help (Table 4.4). Contrary to what might be expected, a similar age-based pattern occurs with the *receipt* of help: Just over half (54%) of persons aged 65 and older

TABLE 4.4 Types of Assistance Provided to Neighbors, Friends, and Relatives, by Age

Type of assistance	Age group				
	18-34	35-44	45-64	65 +	Total
Total *N*	591	291	379	238	1,499
Percent who provide assistance, all types	93	92	89	76	89
Of those respondents who provide assistance, percent who provide:					
Transportation	16	33	32	34	26
Caregiving	47	43	41	43	44
Repair work/maintenance	34	35	28	19	30
Household chores	23	27	19	23	23
Errands	40	40	32	25	36
Gardening/lawn care	20	20	18	21	20

TABLE 4.5   Types of Assistance Received from Neighbors, Friends, and Relatives, by Age

Type of assistance	Age group				
	18-34	35-44	45-64	65 +	Total
Total *N*	591	291	379	238	1,499
Percent who receive assistance, all types	75	64	52	54	64
Of those respondents who receive assistance, percent who receive:					
Transportation	32	26	22	35	29
Caregiving	36	43	8	5	28
Repair work/maintenance	26	32	35	24	29
Household chores	15	22	29	37	22
Errands	22	20	17	20	20
Gardening/lawn care	9	17	30	35	18

receive informal help, but those aged 18–34 are *most* likely (75%) to receive such assistance (Table 4.5).

The survey also asked what kind of help is received, and from whom. As noted above, people younger than 45 generally are more likely to be helped by friends, neighbors, and relatives than those 45 and older (Table 4.5). When we distinguish between *receiving help from relatives* and *receiving help from nonrelatives,* age differences become even more apparent. Three fifths (59%) of those aged 18–34 receive help from relatives and almost one half (48%) from nonrelatives. By age 65 and over, only about a third (36%) report receiving help from relatives, and about the same (35%) from nonrelatives (Table 4.6). These data demonstrate that older persons are less likely than younger adults to receive informal help from others.

GIVING AND RECEIVING HELP: TYPES OF ASSISTANCE

Caregiving—whether for infants, children, or adults—is the most common form of informal help, both within and across generations. Of those who give assistance, 44% provide such caregiving (Table 4.4). Other response categories mirror the standard set of *instrumental activities of daily living* (IADLs) such as "household chores" (e.g., clean-

TABLE 4.6   Rates of Assistance Received from Relatives and Nonrelatives, by Age and Gender

	Age group				
Gender	18-34	35-44	45-64	65 +	Total
Total *N*	591	291	379	238	1,499
	Percent receiving help from relatives				
Total	59	46	31	36	45
Male	58	44	28	34	44
Female	60	47	33	37	47
	Percent receiving help from nonrelatives (neighbors and friends)				
Total	48	47	38	35	43
Male	49	50	43	36	46
Female	46	44	35	34	41

ing, laundry, and cooking), "home repairs/maintenance," "gardening/ lawn care," "running errands," and "transportation." The survey also distinguished between assistance with those instrumental ADLs and "personal care" *activities of daily living* (ADLs) (e.g., dressing, bathing, eating, and toileting).

Providing transportation, making repairs, and doing errands are the other most common forms of assistance across all age groups. The myth of elders' general dependency is again challenged by the data showing that older persons (aged 65 and over) are as likely to *provide* informal help with transportation (34%) as to *receive* it (35%) (Tables 4.4 and 4.5). Even for home repairs/maintenance, elders are only slightly more likely to receive than to provide such assistance. But they are notably more likely to get help than to give help with gardening and household chores.

In contrast to these characteristics among elderly Americans, persons aged 18–34 are twice as likely to receive (32%) as to provide (16%) transportation assistance. But these young adults also are twice as likely to run errands for others as to receive such help (40% versus 22%, respectively). This ratio also applies to those aged 35–44 and 45–64. For reasons that are unclear, respondents in general are far more likely to report providing than receiving assistance with errands. Even those aged 65 and older are more likely to say they give rather than get informal help with errands. We suspect that some degree of response bias toward providing rather than receiving help exists among most of the survey's respondents (as discussed in Chapter 5).

The largest discrepancy between giving and receiving informal assistance is with caregiving (babysitting and/or adult caregiving). More than two fifths (43%) of older persons report providing this type of help, while only 5% report receiving it. Among those aged 45–64, the respective proportions are 41% and 8%. These stand in contrast to the figures for respondents aged 35–44 (43% in each direction) and those aged 18–34 (47% and 36%, respectively). The large differences within the two older age groups probably are explained by their low likelihood of *needing* babysitting help (e.g., only 1 in 10 respondents aged 45–64 has a child under 18 at home; none aged 65 and older do) or adult caregiving (in contrast to instrumental help with chores, gardening, etc.). But the two older groups are highly likely to *be needed for* babysitting and/or adult caregiving.

Furthermore, sampling bias in respondent characteristics may have had an effect on these data. Frail, disabled, or highly dependent older persons who receive caregiving are less likely than others to answer the phone or be available to an interviewer in a telephone survey. These potential respondents might be underrepresented in the sample compared to their healthier age peers. They are also far more likely to be recipients of formal long-term care services through community agencies (Soldo & Manton, 1985).

These general differences in giving and receiving help are corroborated by the findings on personal care assistance. Between one fifth and two fifths of persons aged 65 and older receive instrumental types of assistance with chores, gardening, transportation, and errands. But only 5% to 8% of these noninstitutionalized elderly respondents receive *unpaid* help from someone *not in their household* for personal tasks such as bathing, toileting, and dressing. According to a study by Hing (1987), those who do receive assistance with personal care are more likely to get it (a) from someone in their household (especially a spouse), (b) from formal service providers, or (c) as residents of nursing homes or other types of group quarters (Hing, 1987). Because the survey focused on intergenerational linkages outside the household and informal help in the community, these three sources of assistance are not included in our data (see Chapter 1 and Appendixes A and G).

As discussed in the next section, informal caregiving from spouses and others in the *same* household is an important contributor to the well-being of many elderly persons. Such informal care for dependent elders is also bolstered by care received through formal services. Studies have shown that *formal* services tend to complement rather than duplicate informal assistance from friends and relatives (Litwak, 1985). Elderly persons in the community are more likely than young or middle-aged adults to receive such formal help, usually through community-based service agencies that target the older clientele (Doty, 1986). Area Agencies on Aging, which coordinate and promote services for older persons, exemplify how formal services are targeted toward elders—especially those with the "greatest economic need and . . . social need, with particular attention to low-income minority individuals" (U.S. House of Representatives, 1993).

These programs focus on providing older persons with assistance in ADLs, as well as IADLs. National data indicate that 20% of all persons aged 65 and older *without* an ADL limitation (5.2 million elders in 1990) and an additional 30% of those *with* at least one ADL limitation (1.5 million persons in 1990) use some type of community service annually (U. S. Senate, Special Committee on Aging, 1991). Programs for the elderly, and those that provide family services to infants and children, are the most prevalent formal assistance mechanisms in most American communities. Although our survey did not obtain information about formal services, the data noted in Chapters 1, 5, and 6 on government outlays for youth and for the elderly also point to the predominance of public services and benefits specifically targeted to those at both ends of the age spectrum.

But our findings are consistent with other national data indicating that older persons are not as likely to receive assistance—whether formal or informal—as is generally assumed. The 1987 National Medical Expenditure Survey showed that only 25% of all noninstitutionalized persons aged 65 and over had functional limitations in one or more ADLs or IADLs. Of these impaired elderly, only 36% received any type of formal service in the community (Short & Leon, 1990). Thus, only 9% of *all* older persons living in the community receive some type of formal assistance. These national data help explain how formal care services form part of the larger picture regarding the types of assistance received by older Americans. We are impressed by the relatively low proportion of elderly persons who receive either formal or informal care from persons who are not members of their household.

Age-related patterns of informal help within the community reflect life cycle differences in family structure, living arrangements, functional capabilities, receipt of formal services, and other factors. Differences in assistance patterns also relate to whether relatives or nonrelatives are likely to be involved. The next sections explore this issue.

ASSISTANCE TO RELATIVES

When respondents were asked whether they provided assistance or help of some kind to others in the community, 57% reported that they provide help specifically to relatives who do not live with them. Those in the oldest age group are the least likely (41%) to assist relatives outside the household, and those aged 18–34 are the most likely (65%) to do so (Table 4.7). In contrast, those older persons who *do* provide help to relatives report the highest average hours of help—approximately 23 hours per month—compared to only 14 hours among those aged 18–34. The monthly average among all those who help relatives is 15 hours. As with the pattern in volunteering, helping relatives outside one's household is far more intensive among older persons than among younger persons.

Rates of assistance to such relatives are, overall, slightly higher for women (60%) than for men (54%). This gender difference is most obvious among middle-aged respondents (14 percentage points), but is

TABLE 4.7   Rates and Average Hours of Assistance Provided to Relatives, by Age and Gender

	Age group				
Gender	18-34	35-44	45-64	65 +	Total
Total *N*	591	291	379	238	1,499
	Percent providing help				
All	65	55	57	41	57
Male	65	48	50	39	54
Female	65	62	64	43	60
	Average hours of help given per month[a]				
All	14	10	17	23	15
Male	13	6	9	28	12
Female	14	13	23	19	17

[a]Base of average hours of help given per month equals respondents who provided any assistance.

observed across all age groups except 18–34, in which no difference exists. We assume that the gender difference would be even greater if the survey included assistance to relatives who live *with* the respondent, especially for the elderly. National data indicate that almost three fourths (74%) of caregivers for elderly persons live with the recipient (Stone, Cafferata, & Sangl, 1987). The high proportion (72%) of females among caregivers for elderly persons includes a large group of wives (23%) who provide care for husbands who are frail. A smaller proportion (13%) are husbands (older, on average, than wives) who care for their spouses.

Regardless of the gender differential, the predominance of within-household caregiving among the elderly makes our survey results noteworthy for the extent and intensity of assistance given to relatives outside the household. It appears that caregiving demands within the household reduce the opportunity or ability of many elders to provide help to relatives outside their household. Except for those aged 65 and over, more than three fifths of females and one half to two thirds of males provide some type of assistance to relatives outside the household (Table 4.7). Middle-aged women (45–64) provide the greatest amount of such assistance—64% do so, devoting an average of 23 hours per month (well above the average of 17 hours among all women). But also notable in this regard are the two fifths (39%) of men aged 65 and older who assist relatives, giving more than twice the average hours per month among all male helpers (28 versus 12 hours, respectively).

As we discovered in patterns of volunteering, informal assistance to relatives outside one's household is more prevalent among middle-aged Americans, but the intensity of assistance (measured in hours per month) is notably higher among helpers aged 65 and older. This age-related distinction between likelihood of providing informal help to others in the community—whether relatives or nonrelatives—and the amount or intensity of help given is a recurring aspect of our findings.

ASSISTANCE IN THE COMMUNITY

Help is provided to friends, neighbors, and other (nonrelated) members of their communities by 70% of adults. The likelihood of providing informal assistance to nonrelatives decreases somewhat with age, with 75% of persons aged 18–44 (combined age groups) and 59% of those 65 and older doing so (Table 4.8).

TABLE 4.8   Rates and Average Hours of Assistance Provided to Nonrelatives, by Age and Employment Status

Characteristic	Total *N*	Percent who help	Average hours of help given per month[a]
Age			
18-34	591	74	9
35-44	291	77	8
45-64	379	68	10
65 +	238	59	12
Employment status			
Full-time	840	72	8
Part-time	175	81	9
Unemployed	267	63	11
Retired	218	63	15

[a]Base of average hours of help given per month equals respondents who provided any assistance.

As with volunteering, employed persons are more likely to help others than are those who are not employed. Part-time workers are most likely to help nonrelatives (81%), compared to full-time workers (72%), unemployed persons (63%), and those who are retired (63%) (Table 4.8). Once again, however, the group having the lowest prevalence—retired persons—is the most intensely involved, averaging 15 hours per month.

It appears that persons who are highly engaged in the social and economic fabric of the community (e.g., those who are employed, have school-age children, or participate in religious organizations) are most likely to provide informal help to nonrelatives. The higher the level of community involvement the greater the awareness of needs and, perhaps, the likelihood of being asked to provide help (Independent Sector, 1990). For example, parents with school-age children are more likely than others to be involved in a mutual network of informal helping through their children's needs (e.g., car pools and recreational activities). Also, employed persons are most likely to have co-workers, who add to the pool of nonrelatives who may need help of some kind.

Thus, opportunity to provide help depends partly upon exposure to and awareness of need. On average, unemployed or retired persons are less engaged in their communities and thereby less likely to be involved in the web of helping behaviors, both formal and informal

(Committee on an Aging Society, 1986). For these persons, community involvement—and the informal helping patterns that evolve from it—require more concerted and deliberate individual initiative. Those unemployed and retired persons who make the extra effort to remain fully engaged in the community may be the most likely to provide informal help. Their initiative and commitment may help explain why, despite the lower rate of helping for their age group as a whole, those who do help give the highest average hours of the four age groups studied.

HOURS OF HELP GIVEN IN THE COMMUNITY

Those who provide informal assistance to nonrelatives in their communities typically help approximately 10 hours per month. As noted above, retired persons who provide such help do so for significantly more hours than average (50% more). Using a Tobit regression model, we identified five factors that most influence the number of hours (i.e., intensity) that people spend helping nonrelatives (as shown in Table D.6):

- Being retired
- Having at least one family relationship characterized as low on contact, high on closeness, and low on helping (dispersed-independent type)
- Household size
- Believing that adult children should be expected to support their parents
- Agreeing that wealthy people should share their advantages with those who are not wealthy.

Many of these factors mirror those that most influence the likelihood of providing informal help. We discussed in the previous section the possible reasons that, among all helpers, retirees provided so many more hours per month. Clearly, the level of commitment and opportunity for intense involvement are high for those retirees who do become involved in helping nonrelatives.

Another form of commitment may exist among those whose intergenerational family relationship is dispersed-independent, the second most influential factor on intensity. The explanation does not appear to depend on a process of psychosocial compensation, because there is no substantial evidence that persons compensate for role loss (e.g., from widowhood, divorce, or retirement) by volunteering or becoming more involved in community-based activity. Similarly, studies generally have not found an inverse relationship between likelihood of volunteering and level of family involvement (Chambré, 1987). But our data show an inverse relationship here.

Our regression results, therefore, are intriguing. The difference seems to be the sensitivity of our measures of family involvement. Most other studies measure only *behavior* within families, such as frequency of contact or interaction. The ten family types we developed, based on three composite factors (see Chapter 3), include measures of both behavior and emotional closeness. By including the latter in this study, our typology of family relations captures the level of emotional involvement along with the behavioral components.

In the dispersed-independent family type, individuals have little opportunity for contact and little helping behavior. But emotional closeness—or commitment—to family members is high. Thus, our regression analysis supports other studies showing that family *role* loss (i.e., at the behavioral level) is not a strong factor in intensity of community-based helping, since the other family types with low interaction do not also emerge in the regression. But hours of informal help to nonrelatives are significantly higher among persons whose family type is characterized by *both* low family interaction and high emotional closeness. For them, helping within the family probably would be high if opportunity constraints such as geographic distance did not limit such interaction.

These persons thus may gravitate toward community-based helping in lieu of family helping. Some of the research on motivations of volunteers may also help explain this pattern of informal assistance. Many volunteers are motivated by a combination of their own needs— especially social interaction needs—and altruistic orientations (the desire to help those in need) (Moore, 1985). Because persons in dispersed-independent families have strong family bonds but limited interaction, their social and altruistic orientations could be expressed in other ways, such as helping nonrelatives. Our analysis reveals a link between certain types of psychosocial bonds of family solidarity and the intensity of help to nonrelatives, whether through formal volunteering or day-to-day informal assistance.

Household size is also a significant factor in degree of help to nonrelatives, possibly reflecting the role played by exposure to a large number of persons and needs. The larger the household, the more likely the community-related network of interactions. Again, awareness of need and opportunity to provide help are increased in larger households. The regression also found that attitudes about intergenerational family responsibilities are influential. Persons who disagree with the statement that children should not be expected to support their elderly parents are significantly more likely to provide help to nonrelatives. These data mirror our findings about the influence of strong family bonds and feelings of intergenerational responsibility on the intensity of community-oriented helping patterns. Finally, norms of equity and altruism also are significantly related to degree of informal help to nonrelatives. The belief that wealthy people should share their resources with the less fortunate is another part of the value system of these highly committed helpers.

Thus, intensity of community-based helping is greatest not only among retirees but also among those whose relatively strong intergenerational family bonds are frustrated by a low level of intergenerational family interaction, especially when combined with a generalized sense of altruism and fairness. As with volunteering, community-based helping behaviors are the result of complex aspects of social structure and cultural values, factors that are difficult to measure. Clearly, family-related attitudes reach domains beyond the boundaries of the family (Kingson, Hirshorn, & Cornman, 1986). Our findings thus support the concerns of those who emphasize the importance of the family and intergenerational linkages in promoting a strong sense of community and concern for others in general.

GIVING GIFTS AND MAKING BEQUESTS

Along with volunteering and giving informal assistance to others, gifts and bequests make up the third kind of intergenerational linkage explored by the survey. The results reveal a predominant pattern of giving from parents to adult children. Also, most people plan to leave bequests to family members (defined in this question as persons other than a spouse).

GIFT GIVING

Respondents were asked if they had ever given large gifts or major financial assistance to their adult children. They were also asked if they had given such gifts or assistance to persons other than their children in the past three years. Among respondents who have adult children, 48% report having given them large gifts at some time.

Intergenerational family bonds predominate in this type of giving. Of those who had given major gifts to adult children, only 23% also gave such gifts during the previous three years to persons other than their adult children. The predominance of family ties in gift giving also is evident among *all* respondents: Only 27% report having given large gifts to nonrelatives and to relatives other than their adult children.

As estimated by the parents, the average value of gifts to adult children is approximately $5,000; the average value of gifts to others is approximately $800. Among all parent–child transfers, gifts to adult children have the highest value ($8,400) when the parents are aged 65 and over. Although the survey provides little data to discern the reasons for this large difference, we postulate that the oldest parents have both greater discretionary income and greater motivation to disperse their assets than do parents under age 65. With increasing age, a growing awareness of limited remaining lifetime, and a moderate to high degree of economic security, many elderly parents are likely to have lower self-perceptions of need. In contrast, they are likely to perceive greater economic need of their young-adult or middle-aged children, who may be struggling from the lack of growth in real income and the inflationary trend in housing and other costs during recent years (Mishel & Frankel, 1993).

Discriminant analysis shows that socioeconomic characteristics and family relationships are the key determinants of who gives gifts to adult children. The most significant factors, in order of influence, are (as shown in Table D.7):

- Being at least a high school graduate
- Reporting an annual household income between $30,000 and $50,000
- Being in a white-collar occupation
- Having a family relationship that is high on contact, closeness, and helping (tight-knit-helping type)
- Believing that adult children should be expected to support their parents.

These results expand on the descriptive data discussed above. Parents who have the resources to provide large gifts are most likely to give them; namely, those with a college degree or better, a white-collar occupation, and middle-income status. Interestingly, middle-income parents are twice as likely as those with household incomes of $75,000-$100,000 to give large gifts to their adult children. This difference may reflect different levels of need between the children from these two family-income groups; children from upper-middle-class households may be more economically secure than those from middle-income backgrounds.

Parents who give large gifts are also highly likely to describe their relationship with adult children as tight-knit-helping—the strongest of the ten family types. Indeed, large gifts are not a surprising component of families with high levels of interaction, closeness, and helping behaviors. We are struck, however, by the fact that members of alienated families—whether alienated-independent or alienated-helping—also are more likely than the other family types to give large gifts to adult children. In these families, emotional ties are weak, and helping behavior may arise out of a sense of obligation. Perhaps material gifts serve as surrogates for emotional bonds or are given because of the same sense of obligation. But regardless of family type, some sense of *mutual* dependence and reciprocity is also evident in this type of intergenerational linkage. Parents who give large gifts are more likely than other parents to feel that adult children should, in turn, be expected to support elderly parents.

In general, then, large gifts to adult children represent another hidden connection between generations, providing resources primarily from older to younger family members. For many American parents whose resources permit such transfers, giving large gifts is one part of a greater web of family solidarity, reciprocity, and mutual assistance.

RECEIVING GIFTS

The survey results regarding who receives large gifts corroborate the data on gift giving. Overall, 25% of the sample report receiving large gifts from family or friends within the previous three years. As expected, the most frequent direction of gifts is from an older to a younger generation. Parents are the most common source of gifts, with 22% of all respondents under age 65 reporting they received gifts from their parents, and 6% of those aged 18–49 reporting gifts from their grandparents. We would expect this latter proportion to be considerably higher if the survey included respondents under age 18.

Only 9% of those 65 and over reported receiving major gifts. Of these elderly recipients, one half reported receiving their gifts from adult children. The gifts included cash (52%), furniture or a major appliance (29%), clothing or jewelry (21%), vacation trip or travel expenses (23%), and real estate (13%). In contrast, respondents under age 50 were far more likely to receive cash (58%) than any other type of large gift. Despite popular impressions, financial assistance with a down payment for a house is rare; only 1% of respondents aged 18–49 report receiving such help. Similarly, only 4% received a no-interest loan, 3% received a direct transfer of real estate, and 4% vacation travel. However, large appliances are quite common (26%), as are automobiles (18%). Because the survey did not include college expenses given to or received by children who are still part of the household, we are not surprised that only 4% report receiving a gift of educational expenses (see Chapter 5 for further discussion of this form of intergenerational transfer).

Some gender differences in the source of gifts are noteworthy, depending on the characteristics of the recipient, the perspective from which the respondent answers (i.e., giving or receiving), and the time frame used in the question.

Fathers are more likely than mothers to have *ever given* gifts to adult children (52% and 44%, respectively), but this gender difference disappears (27% and 28%, respectively) for those who report giving gifts to anyone else during the previous three years. In contrast, the gender difference among gift givers reverses when reported by the *recipient.* Female relatives are more often reported as the source of large gifts during the previous three years than are males. Mothers are more frequently reported as the source than fathers (60% and 50% respectively), grandmothers more than grandfathers (14% and 10%), and mothers-in-law more than fathers-in-law (12% and 8%).

Such findings suggest that gifts across the generations are a strong but not major component of intergenerational transfers. To the extent that they exist, they are concentrated within families and predominantly flow from older to younger family members.

BEQUESTS AND INHERITANCE

Another form of giving explored in the survey is bequests. Respondents were asked if they plan to leave specific bequests to persons *other than* their spouses; 60% indicated that they plan to leave bequests to family,

friends, or organizations. Remarkably, there is no age-related difference in such planning. Just over 61% of persons under 50 have plans to
leave an inheritance, compared with 57% of those aged 50–64 and 56%
of those aged 65 and over. But marital status does make a difference.
Only 50% of married people have made bequests (to others than their
spouses), compared with 81% of those who have never been married
and 78% of those who are divorced or separated.

Turning to just those who have made specific plans for leaving
bequests, bequests to family are most common—nearly all (98%)
include family as beneficiaries. Notably, the discriminant analysis
shows that the nature of family relationships has no substantive influence on bequest planning (Table D.8). But the analysis does indicate
that family experience and a sense of reciprocity, along with concern
for children's well-being make a difference. Bequest plans are most
likely among those who have received financial help from their parents
and those who believe that parents should help their adult children.

Limitations in the survey data do not permit distinctions among
intended family beneficiaries (e.g., children versus other relatives).
Nor are we able to discern the relative amount that would be
bequeathed to different family members. Regarding nonfamily beneficiaries, one fifth (21%) of respondents plan to leave an inheritance to
friends and one third (32%) include charitable organizations in their
bequest plans. Never married (41%), childless (34%) and younger
(under 35) persons (33%) are notably more likely to include friends in
their bequest plans than those who are married (11%), widowed (12%),
or separated/divorced (17%), who have children (12%), or who are
above age 50 (9%).

SUMMARY

The results from the survey indicate that intergenerational bonds are
still strong, despite increased dispersion of family members and
decreased prevalence of "traditional" family units. Our data show that
behavioral characteristics as well as emotional components of family
solidarity must be measured and understood as significant hidden
connections between age groups. Although family interaction and
helping patterns may be lower than in previous decades, we cannot
assume that family members care less about one another or feel less
close. By recognizing and measuring these emotional aspects of family

intergenerational linkages (as in Chapters 2 and 3), we are able also to explore—more deeply than most studies to date—the connections between family solidarity and community-based behavior.

Our analyses of volunteer activity, informal helping patterns, and giving among adult Americans confirm that intergenerational connections are strong and enduring. Furthermore, these behaviors can be highly related to a complex set of factors rooted in an individual's attitudes, values, socioeconomic status, life cycle stage, household size, and primary type of family relationship. We are struck by the overriding influence of higher educational attainment, positive perceptions of other age groups, and family closeness on the propensity to volunteer, provide informal help, and give other types of assistance. The significance of these factors emerges in linkages that occur both within and across generations.

Thus, our study reiterates the fundamental importance of key institutions in society—education and family. The stronger each of these, the greater the concern, involvement, and commitment in the community. In an era of increased attention to social disorganization, family stress, and community problems, the maintenance of closeness among family members, educational opportunities, altruistic values, and norms of equity appear to be important for community involvement.

These are the hidden intergenerational connections that are unveiled by the survey, which has shown that volunteerism is more prevalent than commonly perceived and that the *intensity* of volunteer activity is an important component to measure and understand. Thus, although younger middle-aged persons are more likely to volunteer than other age groups, they spend the fewest average number of hours doing so. Conversely, although a lower proportion of elderly persons volunteer, those who do so devote significantly more time per month than their younger counterparts.

Intergenerational volunteering follows certain age-related patterns. Children and youth benefit greatly from volunteer activity, primarily from persons who are in their parents' age groups and far less so from those who are elderly. Yet our analysis indicates the overriding influence of structural factors such as educational attainment and household size or composition on these cross-generational volunteers.

Attitudes about children and their well-being do not differ significantly across the age groups. The prospects are bright that such age-related differences in rates of volunteering and in cross-generational orientations will diminish as the educational differences between older persons and the rest of the adult population are all but eliminated during the next two decades. Similar age-related contrasts are discerned in patterns of informal assistance among friends, neighbors, and relatives. But some of these patterns are counterintuitive. Lower proportions of older persons than young adults report receiving informal help from persons other than their spouses. The survey results corroborate other national data showing that older persons are not as likely to receive informal help from outside their household as is generally perceived. It is also striking that young adult and older persons are more likely to be providers of informal assistance to neighbors, friends, and relatives than to be recipients of such help.

The survey data on patterns of house sharing and gift giving indicate a general flow of such transfers from older to younger generations, especially from middle-aged and young-old groups to young-adult groups. Family connections between parents and older children are by far the predominant route for such transfers. Indeed, strong family emotional bonds continually surface along with education, altruistic values, and positive attitudes about other age groups of the population as key factors in community involvement.

Many of these factors and the behaviors they influence are generally hidden from our perceptions of everyday life. But the wide array of hidden connections discerned through our analysis of community-based behavior attests to the persistence of intergenerational ties in American society. Such linkages are a vital part of family and community life. Indeed, if such assistance was not provided freely, how would it be provided and by whom? If provided through government agencies or in the marketplace, what would they cost? The next chapter assesses the monetary value of these types of exchanges within and across generations in American families and society as a whole. The outcome of that analysis reflects the depth and importance of all these intergenerational connections—whether readily observable or generally hidden from our perception.

CHAPTER 5

Intergenerational Transfers

Karl Kronebusch and Mark Schlesinger

One important and often hidden aspect of intergenerational relations involves the flow of resources from one age group to another, flows that we refer to as *transfers* among age groups. Chapters 2, 3, and 4 have identified several forms of private transfers—personal assistance, shared housing, and financial gifts for family members; and volunteering and personal assistance for other members of the community. Those chapters described different types of exchange, the proportion of adults in the United States who are involved, and the factors that encourage or discourage intergenerational exchange.

This chapter focuses on the total economic value of these transfers. It addresses two sets of research questions. First, what is the magnitude of private transfers? What is the pattern of these transfers across the age spectrum? Second, how does the pattern of private transfers compare to the pattern of government benefits? How does the addition of private transfers change the depiction of the relative generosity of people of different generations? We present here a set of intergenerational accounts that detail the magnitude and direction of intergenerational exchange, using information provided by the 1990 AARP Intergenerational Linkages Survey and other sources. These accounts depict transfers that have been hidden from the view of policymakers because they are not regularly measured or reported in government statistics. In fact, as will be shown below, these flows are large—more than double the total of all government transfer payments—and thus are comparable in magnitude to other economic statistics that are regularly the subjects of policymakers' attention.

The private redistribution of economic resources shapes our understanding of intergenerational linkages in two distinct ways. First, private transfers may *reflect* the intensity of intergenerational relations. Those who care about other generations will, it is thought, provide them with resources, particularly if they are in need. The magnitude of the resource flows can be seen as one measure of how much each generation values the others. Second, resource flows can *affect* the nature of intergenerational ties. Transfers from one age group to another may create a sense of obligation in the recipients, a desire to reciprocate the aid that they have received. Conversely, if some age groups appear to "give" much less than they "receive," they may be seen as inadequately contributing to the well-being of their family or community. Those who give nothing at all may be thought of as not caring at all, a perception that may lead to alienation and tensions between age groups. The social importance of resource flows is thus closely linked to the magnitude of the transfers and their balance between age groups.

For most government spending, estimating the flows to and from people of different ages is reasonably straightforward. People receive government benefits and pay taxes, both of which can be assessed in dollar terms. The net flows between age groups reflect the difference between taxes and benefits. Moreover, the distribution of spending of public funds across age groups seems clear: Nonelderly adults are net payers, while the elderly appear to be the major recipients of cash transfers and youth are the beneficiaries of monies spent on public education. But this standard accounting neglects the role of private transfers, whether in the form of personal assistance, shared housing, or financial aid. Ignoring this private redistribution of resources creates a misleading picture of intergenerational resource flows.

To correct this, one must place a value on the various private transfers and combine them together into a sort of social balance sheet. This is no small task. It is also one for which there are no clear standards—the accounting principles that are accepted for private finance or government budgeting cannot be readily extended to generational accounts. People mean a variety of things when they describe something as *intergenerational,* and each definition suggests a different standard for maintaining accounts (see Chapter 1). Estimation requires that the magnitude of the flows be ascertained and dollar values assigned. Shared resources within households must be somehow allocated between those who give and those who receive.

In order to develop this accounting of intergenerational transfers, we have devised a set of principles for measuring and adding up resource flows. The details of these procedures are often complex, but they are important because the determination of the relative contribution made by each age group in American society depends on the ways in which transfers are measured. In constructing these measures, we have tried to adhere to principles that we believe reflect the ways in which most Americans think about generational exchanges.

This chapter is divided into four sections. (1) In the first, we provide some background on previous research concerning the aggregate value of private intergenerational transfers. (2) This is followed by a brief description of the methods used for constructing the accounts presented here. (3) The third section presents these accounts: the total value of giving and receiving by age group and the magnitude of net transfers by age group. In this section we identify which groups are giving to other ages and which are net recipients. The third section ends with a discussion of potential biases from the use of self-reported data on transfers. (4) In the final section of the chapter we provide estimates of the level of aggregate flows of all private transfers between different age groups and examine the effect that alternative definitions have on the picture of the relative generosity of different age groups. We then return to the broader social contexts in which transfers take place, by discussing the relative importance of public and private transfers.

These estimates provide a more accurate depiction of contribution and dependency across the age spectrum than has been available to date. The results show that private transfers in the United States are large in absolute terms, as well as relative to government transfer programs and other important economic statistics. The pattern of these transfers differs by age: Each age group and each family-defined generation has a characteristic pattern of contribution and receipt. Young, middle-aged, and elderly Americans provide different total levels of transfers, and they differ in the kinds of transfers they give and receive.

THE SIGNIFICANCE OF PRIVATE INTERGENERATIONAL TRANSFERS

Individuals tend to have the greatest needs at either end of the life cycle. Children and adolescents require a sheltering environment and

time and resources for education, and have the most intense developmental needs. Elders—particularly the oldest old—have relatively high
medical care needs, are more likely to require aid and assistance in
activities of daily living, and may require adaptive housing arrangements to be able to live better with disabilities.

But these needs exist for children and elders when their own
resources are the most limited. Most elders and youth have limited
opportunities to enter the labor market, and when they do it is often in
marginalized jobs. Children are usually raised at a time when parents
are at early stages in their work histories, earning far less than they
will in later years. In the absence of transfers of one sort or another,
many of the old and young would have substantial unmet needs.

Much of the ongoing debate over intergenerational equity is based
on the concern that too many federal dollars go to the elderly and too
few to children and their families. Federal government transfer programs, providing either cash payments or in-kind transfers, typically
attract the most public and academic attention (Howe, 1990; Johnson,
Conrad, & Thomson, 1989; Longman, 1987; Preston, 1984.)

Government spending does lead to substantial intergenerational
transfers. The Congressional Budget Office and the minority staff of
the Budget Committee of the House of Representatives have produced
estimates of total federal spending for the elderly and for children
under 18, using data on program budgets. The Congressional Budget
Office estimates that federal spending for the elderly amounted to $356
billion in 1990. Direct federal spending for children amounted to $85
billion, and the earned income tax credit, which benefits low-income
families with children, added another $9 billion to the total level of
support for children. The Budget Committee staff estimated that federal spending targeted on children totaled $55 billion in fiscal year 1987,
whereas spending targeted on the elderly totaled $259 billion (U.S.
House of Representatives, 1991, pp. 1342-1352).

These federal government programs play an important role in
addressing age-related needs. In the absence of federal programs (primarily non-means-tested social insurance), poverty rates would be
68% higher among the elderly. In the absence of public programs (primarily means-tested), poverty rates of families with children would be
17% higher (Smeeding, Torrey, & Rein, 1988, p. 113).

Older Americans thus draw a larger share of federal benefits than
do children. The federal dollars that elders receive far exceed what
they currently pay in taxes. Some observers conclude that this situation is inequitable because it inadequately protects the interests of

children, who lack the political voice to speak for themselves. Moreover, they argue that elders are becoming too great a burden, taking from others much more than they contribute (Howe, 1990; Longman, 1987).

There is, however, surprisingly little published research examining the net flow of government taxes and benefits by age, other than that which crudely classifies group benefits to "elders" or "children" (Howe, 1990). Moreover, the reported totals on government spending for "elders" and "children," like those mentioned above, are limited in several respects. They reflect only federal spending, excluding state and local government spending on education, Aid to Families with Dependent Children (AFDC), Medicaid, and other services. Nonfederal age-related government expenditures are at least 10 times higher for children and youth as for elders, due primarily to the predominance of public education costs. In 1990, 30% of state and local government general expenditures was for educational services, including higher education (Gist & Aleksa, 1993; also, see Chapter 8). These estimates also ignore the tax side of the balance sheet. Finally, they do not consider any of the ages between 18 and 65, and do not examine differences within the range of ages that constitute the "elderly." In the last section of this chapter, we improve upon these published statistics.

An equally serious omission is that government-based transfers are assessed out of context, without regard to private redistribution that occurs among age groups. Private transfers represent a social contribution in addition to paying taxes, and these must be assessed to provide a complete depiction of the social contributions of different age groups. If private transfers are high among groups that pay relatively little in taxes, this will change the picture of resource exchanges between age groups.

Private transfers may also provide a private "safety net" for individuals whose needs are not met by their own efforts or public assistance (Eggebeen & Hogan, 1990). Some even suggest that these private transfers might resolve the apparent inequities in the distribution of public resources. Groups that are the largest beneficiaries of federal dollars may share, at least to some extent, these benefits with other age groups. For example, elders are often part of extended families, and they care about their younger relatives. This personal connection, it is argued, ensures that if elders receive "too many" benefits from the public sector, they will share these with their children and grandchildren (Kingson, Hirshorn, & Cornman, 1986). In this sense, private transfers become a "safety valve" against the unequal distribution of public transfers.

The extent and role of private transfers, however, rarely plays an important part in discussions of intergenerational equity. This is in large part because private transfers are less visible. Each year, as the federal government struggles to cut its budget deficit, there are stories about how the expenses of Social Security and Medicare restrict the ability of the government to simultaneously fund other programs and achieve a balanced budget. Each year, as people complain about their annual property tax assessments, they are told by local officials how expensive it has become to operate schools. But there is no natural public forum for discussing the extent of private transfers. No government agency publishes regular statistics on them. They are often seen as personal matters, perhaps not even discussed with friends.

Past research has done relatively little to offset this imbalance in public perceptions. There has been, in recent years, substantial and important research on the provision of personal assistance and financial help between parents and grown children (Eggebeen & Hogan, 1990; Rossi & Rossi, 1990). This recent research builds on earlier studies that demonstrated a high level of help in extended families. But virtually none of this research has attempted to measure the magnitude of these exchanges. These studies differ in the precise components of exchange analyzed but are alike in using dichotomous variables that measure only the presence or absence of exchange, either within families (Bengtson, Mangen, & Landry, 1984; Eggebeen & Hogan, 1990; Rossi & Rossi, 1990; Shanas, 1978; Sindelar, 1989) or within social networks (Wellman & Hall, 1986). Even when the studies refer to the *total volume of giving* between generations (Eggebeen & Hogan, 1990, p. 217), they mean by this the number of different types of giving, not the total time or dollar value of that transfer. Thus, when these studies refer to concepts of "generational symmetry" (Rossi & Rossi, 1990, p. 395), they compare only the proportion of each generation that give various types of aid, and not the relative amounts of aid each generation provides the others.

An important exception to this pattern involves research by a small group of economists. These researchers have estimated the costs of child rearing (Espenshade, 1984); the unpaid contributions made to households by family members of different ages (Morgan, 1986); the dollar value of within-household transfers, including the value of housework (Morgan, 1978); the extent of emergency provision of time or money (Morgan, 1983); and the dollar value of interfamily financial transfers (Cox & Raines, 1985). These estimates make clear the importance of private transfers, both within and among households.

Morgan estimated that economic redistribution within the family totaled $511 to $552 billion in 1976 (Morgan, 1978) and $709 billion in 1979 (Morgan, 1983), or about a third of the gross national product. Transfers of this scale dwarf all government transfer programs and private pension programs, showing that the "family is still the main source of support for dependent persons in our society" (Morgan, 1978, p. 355).

For between-household transfers, about 11% of families report money transfers, which totaled about $25 billion in 1979 (Morgan, 1984). Cox and Raines (1985) found these transfers to be more prevalent, estimating that about 16% of families give some kind of financial transfer, 18% receive transfers, and 4% both give and receive. The transfers given average about $2,100 (in 1979 dollars) per giving family, whereas transfers received average about $2,800 per receiving family (Cox & Raines, 1985, pp. 396-397). Other researchers have estimated that time spent helping friends, neighbors, and relatives had a value of $42 billion and that time spent volunteering (in the early 1980s) had a value of $43 billion (Lillydahl & Singell, 1982; Morgan, 1984).

Although an important first step in developing accounts of intergenerational transfers, these estimates remain incomplete. They were based on data collected in the 1970s and are potentially out of date. These individual studies have usually focused on only a few types of transfers, typically financial, and virtually all studies of intergenerational exchanges have focused solely on transfers within the family. Although studies have placed a value on the aggregate helping of friends and volunteering, there have been no assessments of the extent to which these nonfamily transfers cross the generations. This chapter is designed to fill these gaps and to update this accounting.

METHODS

We followed three basic steps in creating the estimates presented in this chapter: We identified the boundaries defining transfers as *intergenerational,* allocated the transfers to particular generations and age groups, and created monetary equivalents for transfers such as personal assistance, which are not usually reported in dollar terms. The basic approach to these issues is summarized below, with a more detailed discussion of our assumptions and procedures provided in Appendix E.

Defining *Generation*

Researchers have defined generations in a variety of ways, as discussed in Chapter 1. In this chapter, we have constructed two sets of accounts, which separately convey two meaningful pictures of private intergenerational transfers. The first is divided in terms of *family generations;* the second uses socially defined age categories, which we refer to here as *policy age groups.* The two approaches provide somewhat different notions of intergenerational transfer. The former is limited to people defined in terms of family relationships. The latter is based on age rather than relationship and includes family and nonfamily categories, such as friends, neighbors, and co-workers.

Because the majority of private transfers occur within the family, it makes sense to think about intergenerational redistribution in terms of family generations—parents and children, grandparents and grandchildren. Our definitions of family generations are based on a person's relationship with the survey respondent. A respondent may engage in intergenerational exchanges within the family with his or her grandchildren, children, siblings (own generation), parents, or grandparents.

But as Chapter 4 documents, a substantial share of private intergenerational transfers takes place outside the family. Volunteer activity, charitable contributions, and personal assistance to friends and neighbors are the most common forms of these transfers. Even more resources are transferred through public programs. Thus, it also makes sense to think about intergenerational redistribution in terms of the societal age-group labels of *youth, adults,* and *elders.* Our estimates of transfers based on policy age groups attempt to capture this second interpretation of generation.

We use three policy age groups, which broadly represent policy-relevant distinctions among age cohorts: children and teens under the age of 20, adults aged 20–59, and elders aged 60 and above. We chose these divisions to distinguish age groups viewed largely as "dependent" from those viewed as "self-sufficient."

The process of becoming a self-sufficient adult takes place over a period of time; as will be shown in our estimates below, those aged 18–25 are still receiving substantial amounts of assistance from their parents. Nevertheless, age 20 is a convenient, although somewhat arbitrary, dividing line between youth who are "dependents" and adults who are "self-sufficient."

Most policy discussions follow the definition used by Social Security and Medicare that "old age" begins at 65. However, with the increase of early retirement, the early 60s are now the age when many Americans make the transition between work and retirement. In addition, the Older Americans Act uses age 60 to define eligibility for services. Depending on the context, we use either age 60 or age 65 to define elders. Redefining the boundary as 60 or 65 would not substantially change the results presented below.

The two definitions—one in family terms, the other in policy terms—can lead to different classifications of the same transfer. The average age difference between parents and children in our sample is just under 26 years. Transfers from a 50-year-old parent to a 24-year-old child are intergenerational in the family sense, but not in the policy age group sense. Similarly, assistance given by a 65-year-old to her ailing parent of 88 is intergenerational in the family sense only, because both are elders in the sense of policy age groups.

The aggregate measure of transfers between generations captures several flows of resources. Using the policy age group definition of generation, these involve transfers from adults to youth, youth to adults, elders to youth, youth to elders, adults to elders, and elders to adults (Figure 5.1). For the family generations, the flows are from parents to their children, children to their parents, grandparents to grandchildren, and grandchildren to grandparents (Figure 5.2).

The intergenerational survey collected information on a variety of transfers and on the relationship between the respondent and the recipients or providers of transfers. But because the survey did not determine the exact ages of recipients and providers of transfers, the allocation of these transfers to particular age groups requires several assumptions, which are described in Appendix E.

Another issue in defining transfers concerns living arrangements that affect the nature of shared resources. The survey provides information on the extent of personal assistance and financial transfers among family members who do *not* live together, and on whether adult family members are sharing housing. So, for example, the survey did not assess the time and money devoted to rearing young children, but does provide information on financial assistance provided by parents for their adult children who no longer live with them.

To fill some of these gaps, we obtained additional information from other studies, as noted in Appendix E. In particular, we acquired data on average parental expenditures for rearing children and paying for their college education, and combined these additional data with information from the survey to create estimates for these transfers, as described below.

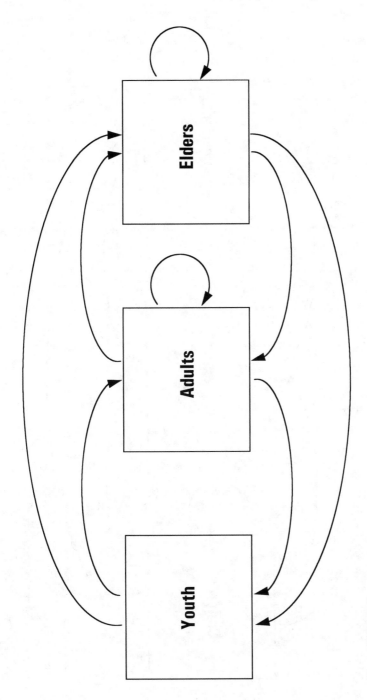

Figure 5.1 Policy age groups.

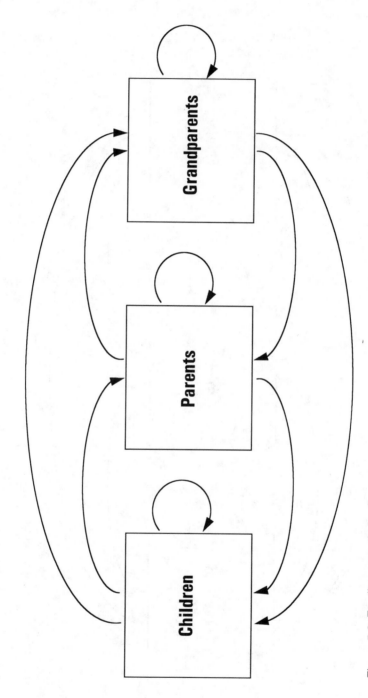

Figure 5.2 Family generations.

MEASURING TRANSFERS

Intergenerational transfers fall into three broad categories: time, money, and housing. Time may be devoted to personal assistance or formal volunteering. Financial transfers consist of gifts, charitable contributions, and inheritances. Housing given and received occurs with shared living arrangements.

From the survey we can evaluate some, but not all, of these components. Personal assistance given and received were both ascertained. Both the giving and receiving of gifts are available from the survey, although not to the same level of detail. The survey provides information on whether a respondent currently lives with his or her parent(s) or with an adult child. For inheritances, the amount of inheritance *received* was determined by the survey. The value of inheritances that were *bequeathed,* however, obviously could not be ascertained from this sample of living respondents. To correct this, we obtained supplemental information on the aggregate size of estates.

CREATING MONETARY EQUIVALENTS

To construct an aggregate index of intergenerational transfers, there needs to be a common unit to measure various forms of giving and receiving. Although limited in important ways, the most common method for constructing such an aggregate is to express each component in dollar terms. The survey itself provides the monetary value of inheritances and gifts. For housing, volunteering, and helping, monetary equivalents are estimated using the prices of substitute goods and services that would be purchased if the transfers were not available. The method of measuring and creating monetary equivalents for transfers is described in Appendix E.

PRIVATE TRANSFERS BETWEEN GENERATIONS

In this section we present information about private transfers between generations, based on the methods described above, in two ways. First, we describe the total level of transfers given and received across the age spectrum, and how the different types of transfers vary by age. Second, we combine giving and receiving to create measures of net exchange, and describe how net exchange varies across the age spectrum.

MAGNITUDE OF PRIVATE TRANSFERS

Giving. The average level of giving (of all private transfers) for all ages is the equivalent of about $9,100 per adult per year (Figure 5.3). The level of giving changes with age, forming an inverted U-shaped pattern. For young adults up through early middle age, giving rises rapidly with age, reaching a peak at about $14,000 per year for those aged 35–44. Above that age, giving declines with age.

Each of the different transfers follows its own characteristic age pattern. The costs of raising children are highest for those between ages 25 and 44. Not surprisingly, transfers to adult children are at their peak for somewhat older age groups. As shown in Figure 5.3, the costs of higher education and shared housing provided to adult children are highest among those aged 45–54, but substantial amounts of these types of assistance are provided by those aged 35–44 and those aged 55–64. The peak for major gifts and financial assistance is found among those aged 55–64.

The value of personal assistance or help given to others is relatively constant across age groups. The value of volunteering is also relatively stable across the age spectrum, with some increase above the average for those between ages 65 and 74. Charitable contributions are highest for people who are in the latter half of their working careers.

Receiving. The average adult reports receiving the equivalent of about $2,700 in private transfers, far less than the average value of reported giving (Figure 5.4). Although it may be "more blessed to give than to receive," the combined giving of all age groups should equal the combined receiving of all age groups. There are several factors that contribute to the discrepancy reported here. The first is that giving to children is included, but receiving by children under 18 is not. Second, as discussed below, there appears to be some reporting bias, due to recall and sample selection, which tends to make reported giving larger than reported receiving.

As with giving, the dollar value of receiving varies across the age spectrum. Young children are major beneficiaries from their parents' expenditures on child rearing. Young adults (aged 18–24) are significant recipients, as well. Although they are legally adults, they are in a sense still dependents, receiving about $6,200 per year. Over the mid-

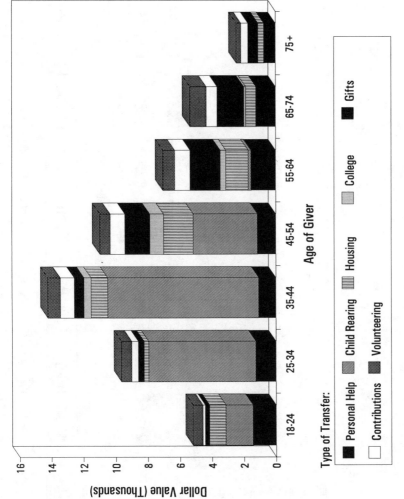

Figure 5.3 Private transfers given, by age of giver and transfer type.

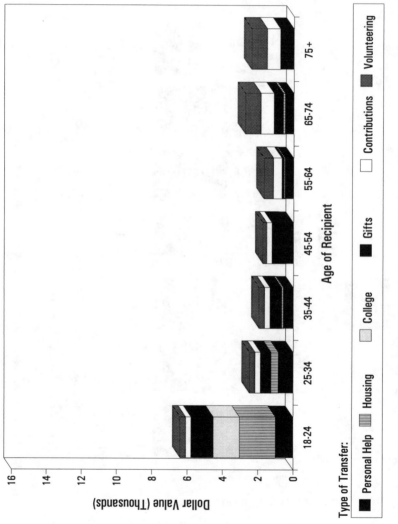

Figure 5.4 Private transfers received, by age of recipient and transfer type.

dle part of the age spectrum, from ages 25 to 54, receiving is at a level lower than for any other age group. For this age group, the emphasis is on giving of various sorts. In the older age groups, receiving of private transfers increases somewhat, due to increases in the receipt of personal assistance and the benefits of volunteering and charitable contributions.

Who Benefits from Private Transfers? Transfers given and received may stay within a generation or may be intergenerational. Figures 5.5–5.8 present these transfers using the two definitions of generation—family generations and policy age groups. Figures 5.5 and 5.6 show giving to and receiving from family. Figures 5.7 and 5.8 show giving to and receiving from family and community and include personal assistance given to nonfamily (friends, neighbors, co-workers, etc.), as well as formal volunteering and charitable contributions. The average value of giving to family alone is about $7,100 per year, and the total of family and nonfamily transfers average about $9,100. Thus nonfamily transfers average nearly $2,000 per year, about one fifth of total giving.

As can be observed in Figure 5.5, private transfers within the family primarily flow downward, from parents to their children. Young and middle-aged parents give to their young children by supporting them through childhood; middle-aged and elderly parents provide housing, pay for college education, and give gifts to their adult children. Giving to children peaks between the ages of 35 and 44, then declines. Transfers from adult children to parents are much smaller. They represent a large share of total transfers only for young adults. There are some two-generation exchanges—that is, giving and receiving between grandchildren and grandparents—but these transfers represent a relatively small share of the total, even for the oldest old and the youngest adults.

The results shown in Figures 5.7 and 5.8 provide an important addition to the literature on transfers and exchanges because they include the value of transfers to people outside the family. Failing to include these types of giving by focusing only on within-family transfers or public sector transfers provides an incomplete picture of private transfers.

NET TRANSFER FLOWS

Reported giving and receiving can be combined to determine the net flow of transfers, which we define as the amount given minus the amount received. The averages across the age spectrum are presented

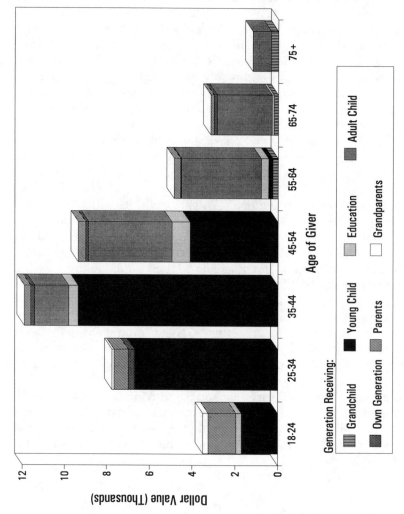

Figure 5.5 Giving to family, by age of giver and generation receiving. (Education is shown separately because it largely reflects parents' help to children, but also some grandparents' contributions toward education. Young child and adult child categories do not include education.)

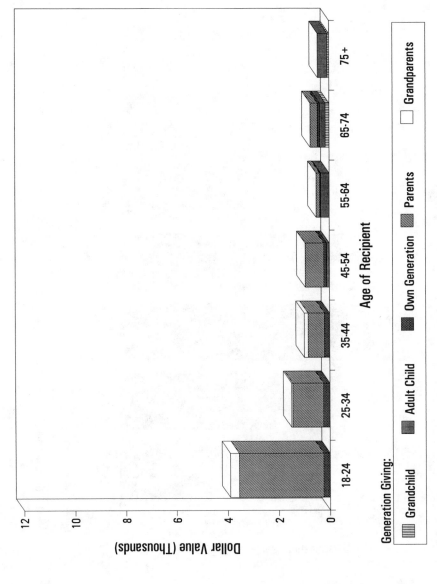

Figure 5.6 Receiving from family, by age of recipient and generation giving.

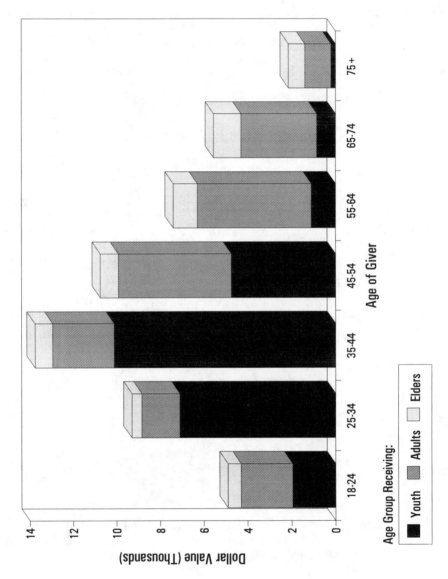

Figure 5.7 Giving to policy age groups, by age of giver and age group receiving. (Includes personal assistance given to nonfamily, formal volunteering, and charitable contributions.)

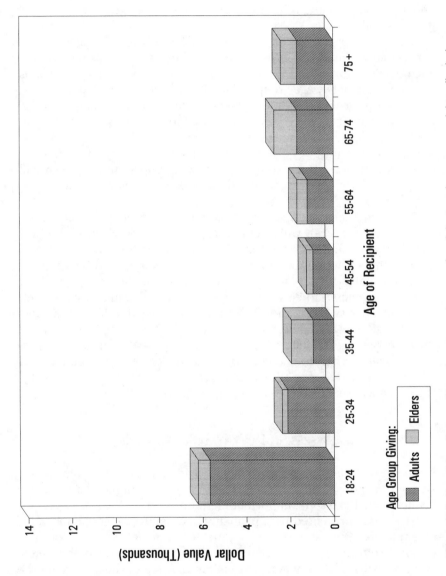

Figure 5.8 Receiving from policy age groups, by age of recipient and age group giving. (Includes personal assistance given to nonfamily, formal volunteering, and charitable contributions.)

by family generation and by policy age group in Figures 5.9 and 5.10. As these figures show, it is possible to be a net giver with respect to one generation and a net receiver with respect to another. A summary line in Figures 5.9 and 5.10 indicates the net for all generations or age groups combined.

The net transfer index varies substantially with age. Young adults are net recipients; adults over the age of 24 are net givers. This positive balance declines for older adults, but remains positive for all age groups, except for the policy age groups allocation for those 75 and older.

Most age groups are net receivers with respect to their own parents: The flow from parents is substantial for those 18–24 and the net flow with respect to parents remains negative up through age 44, after which the amount received from parents is very close to zero. Moreover, all age groups are net givers with respect to their own children, except for those aged 75 and above, who have a balance very near zero.

It is sometimes assumed that private transfers follow a life course or life cycle model in which elders receive aid from their children in exchange for the assistance that they gave as parents. For some individuals this is undoubtedly true, but in the aggregate this is not the dominant pattern. Instead, the middle-aged and the youngest of the elderly are giving to their own children, and young adults are receiving from their parents. The oldest old give and receive relatively smaller amounts than other age groups; their net position is not one in which they receive large transfers from *family,* but instead their net receipt is close to zero. When the benefits of volunteering and charitable contributions are added, the oldest old become net recipients, although their balance is still close to zero (Figure 5.10).

Assessing Potential Limitations

Although we believe these estimates provide a reasonably comprehensive and accurate depiction of private intergenerational transfers, the estimates do have some important limitations.

The totals presented here probably understate the economic value of family ties. Our estimates do not include financial expenses for caregiving provided to adults, such as disabled parents or spouses. Moreover, it is not only actual transfers that have value, but also the availability of family members who might potentially provide transfers if the need arises. (Economists refer to this as the *value of insurance* or

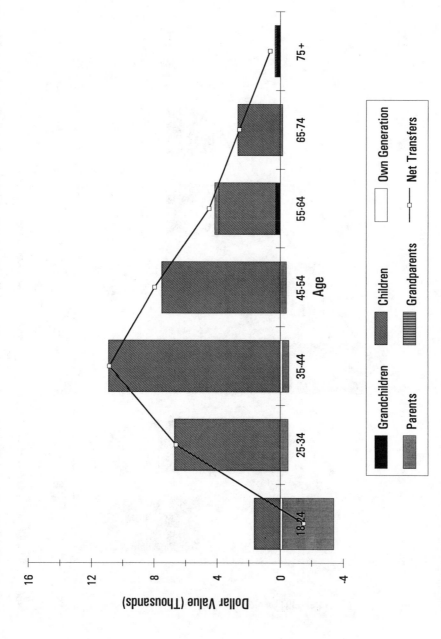

Figure 5.9 Net giving minus receiving, family generations, by age and generation.

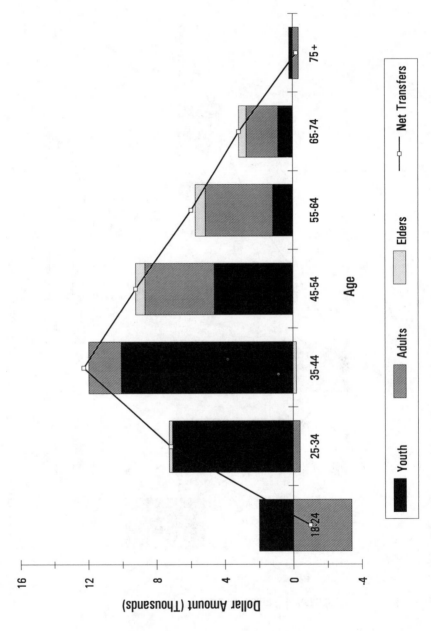

Figure 5.10 Net giving minus receiving, policy age groups, by age and generation.

as an *option value*.) For example, to the extent that individuals believe that they could share housing with their parents or adult children if they needed to, potential shared housing may be valued even by those who do not actually receive shared housing.

Reported Giving and Receiving.   The most important potential limitation is that these estimates largely rely on self-reported information. The estimates presented above primarily use the survey responses of givers about their giving, which we believe will be subject to fewer biases than the responses of the recipients of transfers.

If all transfers are accurately and completely measured, then the sum of giving over all ages should equal the sum of receiving over all ages, but for several reasons we do not obtain a perfect match with these data. First, because the survey included only adults, the totals presented above include adults' reports of giving to children, but not children's reports of receiving. This leads to an apparent imbalance of giving and receiving.

For transfers between adults or between elders and adults, the survey should, on average, include equivalent responses from the givers and the recipients. Discrepancies between these responses can arise for two different reasons: errors and biases in reporting, and sample selection.

First, the accuracy of recall may differ systematically between givers and recipients. Givers and receivers may simply have different impressions of the amount of time or the value of a particular transfer. There also may be social stigma in admitting to the need for help and social status to be gained by portraying oneself as a giver.

A second source of discrepancies is sampling bias, which is more subtle; it is similar to the problem raised by transfers to children. Some of the transfers from adults to elders, especially informal helping and shared housing, will occur when the elder becomes disabled. Bias may occur since the givers (*adults* in this case) are more likely still to be alive and living in the community than the recipients (*elders* in this case). Thus, the givers are more likely to be included in the survey sample, which was limited to noninstitutionalized adults, than are the recipients. An estimate of the total amount of help given by adults to elders will then spuriously appear to be larger than the amount of help that elders received from adults, simply because relatively healthy givers are more likely to be included in the survey, while the relatively more disabled recipients are less likely to be included.

If information had been collected simultaneously from both the givers and receivers in a family, it would be possible to assess the magnitude of the reporting or recall bias. For example, to assess the recall biases of parents and their adult children, information on transfers would be collected from both the parents and the children. The survey does not contain the information necessary for this direct comparison. But to approximate this comparison, we have examined two subsets of the respondents from the survey—parents with one or more adult children and adult children with one or more living parents. On average, if there were no biases in recall, the parents' reports of giving to their children should be matched by the children's reports of receiving from the parents.

The actual data reveal a complex picture in which both types of reporting bias appear. On average, the children report larger flows *in both directions* than do the parents for help and housing. The disparity is especially striking among young adults, who report substantial help given to parents that is not reflected in the parents' reports. For gifts, however, the reports of children and parents on the value of gifts from parents to children are similar in magnitude.

It is often argued that, because parents have a greater stake in generational relations, they report higher levels of closeness and consensus with younger family members (Bengtson & Kuypers, 1971). But these data show that the "generational stake" hypothesis can work in both directions. For many young adults, generational relations may be more important than they are for their parents because they provide needed support when their personal resources are limited. When measured in terms of *economic transfers,* young adults perceive these relations in more active, reciprocal terms than do their parents. But it is also noteworthy that this pattern does not extend to older adults. Older parents are more likely to report that their children are assisting them, but much *less* likely to report that they are helping their children. They see, or at least report, greater asymmetry in their patterns of informal assistance.

Unfortunately, it is impossible to completely resolve the uncertainties about reporting and sampling biases. The issue is nevertheless important not just because it affects the accuracy of our estimates, but also because perceptions about the magnitude of giving and receiving may affect perceptions about the relative contributions of different generations, which could influence the emergence of intergenerational tensions, as discussed in Chapters 6 and 7.

To summarize, Americans give transfers valued at an average of $9,100 per adult per year. Of this, about $7,100 represents giving within the family. The flow of resources is predominantly down the age spectrum—from parents to their children.

The average value of all transfers given (per person annually) varies substantially with age, starting from about $5,000 for those aged 18–24, rising with age to nearly $14,000 for those aged 35–44, and then falling at higher ages.

Each type of transfer shows its own characteristic age pattern. The value of personal assistance given is relatively constant across the age spectrum, although there are some variations. In contrast, shared housing provided to adult family members, gifts, major financial assistance, child rearing costs, educational costs, inheritances, volunteering, and charitable contributions all show substantial age-related variations. Housing, gifts, educational costs, and charitable contributions peak in middle age, while child-rearing costs are highest for somewhat younger age groups, those aged 35–54. The value of volunteering peaks among those aged 65–74.

ASSESSING INTERGENERATIONAL RESOURCE FLOWS

In the results presented above we report transfers at the individual level, expressed as the dollar value per person. In this section we present several alternative measures to assess transfers across the age spectrum. We also compare, across the age spectrum, the level of private transfers to household income and to public, government-provided transfers.

AGGREGATE MAGNITUDE OF PRIVATE TRANSFERS

In 1990, aggregate private transfers amounted to about $1.6 trillion. This giving is largely between, rather than within, age groups: Intergenerational transfers between policy age groups amount to $1.1 trillion, or about 70% of the total (Figure 5.11).

These totals can be compared to more familiar economic statistics. In 1990, government transfer payments (Social Security and unemployment, veterans', and welfare benefits) amounted to just under $700 billion, less than half the total of private transfers. Private transfers of $1.6 trillion amount to just over 40% of total consumer expenditures on all goods and services, and are comparable to total consumer spending for food, clothing, motor vehicles, gasoline, and health care combined (U.S. Department of Commerce, 1991).

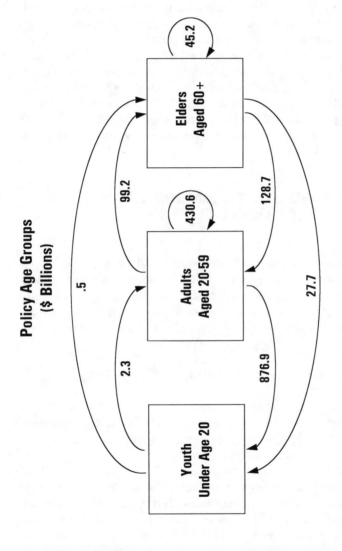

**Policy Age Groups
($ Billions)**

**Total Value of All Private Transfers = $1.611 Trillion
Total Value of All Intergenerational Private Transfers = $1.135 Trillion**

Figure 5.11 Private transfers: Intergenerational flows between policy age groups. (Excludes bequests and inheritances.)

Intergenerational private transfers consist of flows of resources from one policy age group to another, with downward flows from adults to youth dominating this picture. Over $1 trillion flows from adults and elders to youth, while upward flows from youth are only about $2.8 billion. The downward flow from elders to adults ($129 billion) is also larger than the corresponding upward flow from adults ($99 billion), although elders and adults are, in aggregate, more nearly reciprocal in their transfers.

Overall, about 56% of private giving goes to youth, 35% to adults, and 9% to elders. For both adults and elders, almost two thirds of giving goes to the next younger age group (for adults this is youth, and for elders, adults). Adults provide the bulk of giving—$1.4 trillion, or about 87% of the total. They are both the largest population group and, on average, the largest givers.

Although most giving is intergenerational, some giving stays within age groups. Adults' giving to other adults consists largely of transfers from nonelderly parents to their adult children. This giving is intergenerational in the family sense, although it is within the same policy age group. Elders tend to give relatively more to their age group than adults do, largely because elders' volunteering and charitable contributions tend to benefit elders disproportionately. Still, 78% of elders' giving goes to either adults or youth.

In transfers between family generations, the magnitude of the flows depends on the ages chosen. We present one possible depiction of these flows, choosing the ages where grandparents, parents, and adult children are most likely to be alive. In Figure 5.12 the middle generation, labeled *parents,* are the cohort aged 45–49. With an average age gap between generations of about 26 years, this places their adult children in the cohort aged 18–24, and their parents (labeled *grandparents*) in the cohort aged 70–75.

As with flows among the policy age groups, most transfers within families are to adjacent generations and the dominant flow is downwards. Unlike transfers among the policy age groups, with substantial giving within a particular age group, in the family context nearly all transfers are intergenerational. The survey reveals only a very small amount of giving among those of the same family generation, that is, among siblings. (Shared housing among siblings, however, was not ascertained in the survey.) Although two-generation transfers (from grandparents to grandchildren) do occur, they represent a modest portion of intergenerational transfers.

From the perspective of the aggregate total of private transfers

Family Generations
($ Billions)

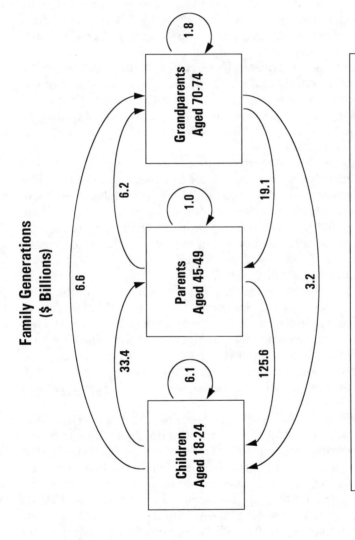

Total Value of All Private Transfers = $247.3 Billion
Total Value of All Intergenerational Private Transfers = $238.3 Billion

Figure 5.12 Private transfers: Intergenerational flows between family generations (hypothetical example of cohorts). (Excludes bequests and inheritances.)

among both policy age groups and family generations, elders aged 60 and older are not a dependent group. Measured as a policy age group, elders give to other generations 50% more than they receive. As a family generation, grandparents aged 70–75 give 75% more than they receive. (This picture changes somewhat with the incorporation of public transfers, as discussed below.)

PRIVATE TRANSFERS RELATIVE TO INCOME

Private intergenerational transfers are larger for some age groups than for others; some age groups are net givers and others are net receivers. These inequalities in giving and receiving might be interpreted as indications of inequity. But for most Americans, how much the members of a given age group should receive is determined in part by their needs. How much they should give is determined in part by their resources, both financial and nonfinancial. Transfers will be considered inequitable only if people give too little or receive too much by these standards.

To provide at least a crude adjustment for differences in financial resources across age groups, we compare the level of intergenerational transfers to individuals' reports of their current household income. This comparison reveals that the private transfers evaluated here are large relative to household income (Figure 5.13).

The inverted-U shape of the age distribution of net transfers (as shown above in Figures 5.9 and 5.10) persists, even after adjusting for family income (Figure 5.13). Giving as a fraction of income rises somewhat for those in the early child-rearing years (25–44), and is roughly constant at about one third of income for all other age groups, including the elderly. Receiving as a fraction of income is substantially higher for both young adults and elders than for the middle-aged. For young adults, the transfers they receive are largely from their parents. For elders, the rise in receiving is largely due to the receipt of charitable contributions and the benefits of volunteering. In addition, for those aged 75 and older, there is a rise in the receipt of personal assistance.

Thus the apparent "relative dependency" of young adults and the elderly is not due to a difference in their *giving*, as expressed as a fraction of their income. Instead, "dependency" relative to income depends on the *receipt* of transfers. Moreover, because elders' volunteering and charity disproportionately aid the elderly, the relative dependency of the elderly does not necessarily reflect dependency on

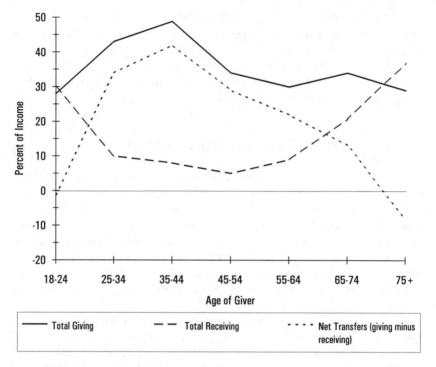

Figure 5.13 Private transfers relative to income, by age of giver.

other age groups, as is generally assumed when dependency ratios are used in debates over intergenerational equity.

Relative dependency among the elderly, calculated in this way, arises only for those 75 and older. Elders aged 60 to 74 are net contributors with respect to private transfers. The generosity of these elders is larger than the dependency of the oldest old, and thus the aggregate total for the elderly age 60 and over is one of net contribution (as in Figure 5.11 and discussion above).

ALTERNATIVE DEFINITIONS OF TRANSFERS

The age-related patterns described above are sensitive to the choice of transfers included in the total. In Figure 5.14 we present the net of giving minus receiving using three alternative definitions, focusing on family transfers. (The results for the transfers with policy age groups are qualitatively similar.) The net flow depicted above (Figures 5.9 and

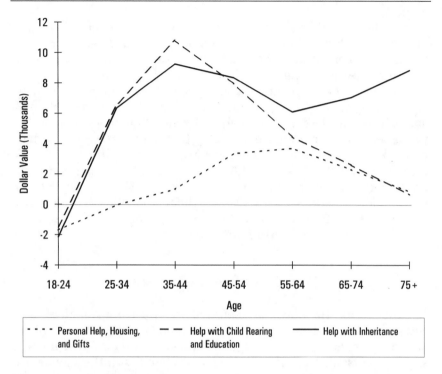

Figure 5.14 Alternative transfer definitions, family transfers. Alternatives are (1) excluding college and child-rearing costs, (2) including these costs, and (3) including bequests and inheritances.

5.10) was based on the value of personal assistance, housing, gifts, volunteering, charitable contributions, college education costs, and costs for rearing young children. Figure 5.14 presents the patterns of net transfers (1) excluding college and child-rearing costs, (2) including these costs, and (3) including bequests and inheritances. Excluding college costs and child-rearing expenses restricts the transfers to those assessed directly in the survey (i.e., informal assistance, shared housing, and financial gifts). Incorporating bequests and inheritances measures transfers most inclusively, but includes transfers that occur after the death of the giver.

The exclusion of the costs of college and child rearing reduces the magnitude of transfers and shifts the peak to older age groups. The addition of bequests and inheritances leads to a large change in net position of those aged 55 and older, especially among the very oldest. Using the definition that excludes bequests, those aged 65 and above give on net less than the average for all adults, but the inclusion of inheritances shifts them to a position above the average for younger adults. For family generations that shift is so large that those aged 75 and above nearly become the most generous age group.

These results demonstrate a potential role for bequests in thinking about intergenerational equity. But, compared to other types of public and private transfers, bequests are different in a number of important ways. Bequests occur after death; only their anticipated effects shape relations among the living. Bequests are infrequent, their magnitude uncertain, and their value highly concentrated in a small number of households. The effect of bequests on perceptions of the relative contribution of the elderly is thus likely to differ from other types of transfers. How this difference should be assessed in aggregate measures of transfers is a matter for further research.

PUBLIC AND PRIVATE TRANSFERS

The discussion thus far has been limited to private transfers, both within families and with the larger community of friends, neighbors, and co-workers. Now we add public transfers, which cover the substantial redistribution of resources associated with the payment of taxes and receipt of government benefits (such as transfer payments, educational services, and medical services), as well as the flow of tax payments that support the general operations of government.

To compare private with public transfers and to provide a net measure of intergenerational exchange, we present estimates of the benefits received from public programs and taxes paid by each age group. These estimates are based on data from surveys of individual participation in government programs and consumer expenditures, as well as aggregate data on government spending, as explained in Appendix E. (Our estimates are for a single point in time, neglecting cohort differences that are important over time. See Kotlikoff, 1992, for one approach to analysis of cohort differences.)

The level of net public transfers for each age group is the difference between average government revenue attributed to that age group and average government benefits received by that age group. Unfortunately, information on the various taxes and transfers is most conveniently reported by age of household head. Thus, in the following discussion, any transfers to children are included under the age of the head of the household in which they live.

Public Transfers. In Figure 5.15 we present the average level of benefits received by households from four different types of government spending (non-means-tested, means-tested, retirement, and general government). For those aged 25–54, the benefits of public education for their children represent the largest portion of the non-means-tested benefits they receive. For the elderly, the non-means-tested benefits are largely Social Security and Medicare. Welfare programs for poor families with children tend to dominate political debate about means-tested programs. But, in fact, the value of means-tested programs is, on average, highest for those aged 75 and older, largely because of the value of Medicaid benefits.

The *general government* category includes all the other federal, state, and local government programs that do not represent cash or in-kind transfers to individual beneficiaries. These programs range from national defense to local fire and police protection. (As discussed in Appendix E, some of these are allocated by person and some by household.) The age pattern for the benefits of general government depicted in Figure 5.15 reflects the size of households for each age group. Age groups with relatively large households, such as those raising young children, benefit more from general government because their households have more people. The elderly, in contrast, benefit less because their households are smaller. These general benefits of government constitute the majority of the public benefits received by all nonelderly age groups. For the youngest adults, the benefits of general government represent nearly all of the public benefits they receive.

Figure 5.16 reproduces the total of benefits received, and adds the age pattern of government revenue. Revenue, largely taxes paid to government, rises and falls with age-related changes in labor force participation and earnings. The *net* public benefits curve in Figure 5.17 represents the difference between revenue and benefit. Those aged 25–64 are net contributors, while young adults and the elderly are net recipients. Young adults are net recipients largely because they contribute relatively little in taxes paid. The elderly are net recipients because their current contributions are modest and their receipt of government benefits is high. In addition, while those aged 55 to 64 are net contributors on average, their net contribution is surprisingly close to zero, indicating that a substantial portion of this age group are net recipients of government benefits. Compared to the next younger age group (aged 45–54), their contribution in taxes paid is lower (possibly due to early retirement), while the receipt of retirement benefits (particularly military retirement benefits) is higher.

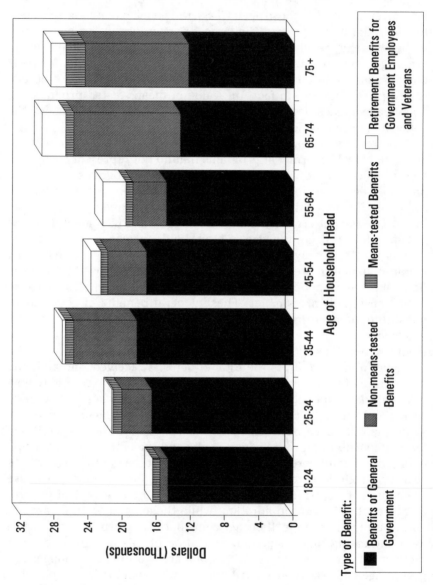

Figure 5.15 Government benefits, 1990 dollars, per household, by age of household head and type of benefit.

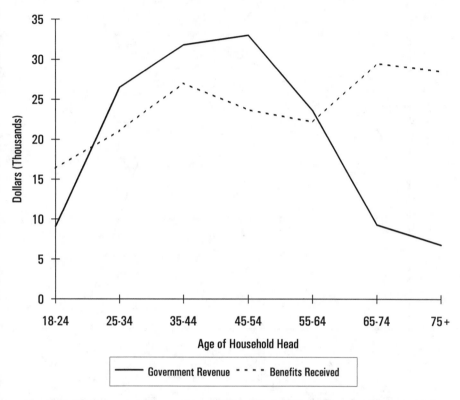

Figure 5.16 Government revenue and benefits, 1990 dollars, per household, by age of household head.

Net Public and Private Transfers.   The public sphere is represented by the net of government revenue and benefits depicted in Figure 5.17. We incorporate private transfers in two different ways: first including only transfers between households (Figure 5.18) and second, including all private transfers, within households as well as between households (Figure 5.19). The addition of private transfers to public transfers shifts the net exchange curve upwards somewhat, reflecting the net social contribution beyond the payment of taxes (Figure 5.18). This effect is largest among those aged 35–64. As before, the addition of bequests has a noticeable effect on the relative position of the oldest age group.

The main difference that occurs after adding the intrahousehold transfers is an increase in the level of net transfers for households raising children, primarily those aged 25–54 (Figure 5.19).

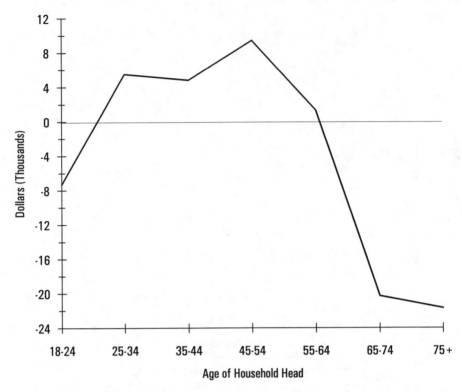

Figure 5.17 Net government revenue minus benefits, 1990 dollars, per household, by age of household head.

CONCLUSION

In summary, we estimate that total private transfers amount to about $1.6 trillion in the United States, while intergenerational private transfers account for $1.1 trillion of that total. These transfers are large—more than double the magnitude of government cash transfer programs.

The bulk of private transfers flows down the age spectrum—from parents to their children. Most Americans are net recipients with respect to their parents, and all, except the oldest old, are net givers to their children. Thus, in contrast to the literature that emphasizes reciprocal exchanges among family members, we find that the value of

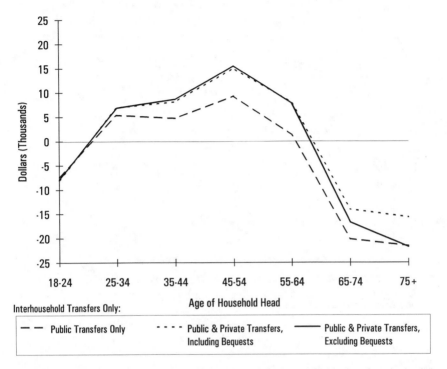

Figure 5.18 Net public and private transfers, interhousehold transfers only, by age of household head.

transfers flowing down to younger generations is substantially larger than the value of transfers flowing up to older generations.

Elders as a group give more than they receive in the sphere of private transfers. They are net dependents only in the public sphere of government transfers and benefits. Adults are substantial net contributors, while children are net recipients.

Transfers have specific age patterns. The value of personal assistance given is relatively constant across the age spectrum. The costs of raising young children are borne largely by those aged 25–44. The costs of college education and shared housing provided to adult children peak for those aged 45–54, while gifts and major financial assistance peak for those aged 55–64. Volunteering is found among all age groups, with those aged 65–74 providing the highest value for this type of transfer. Charitable contributions are substantial for those aged 35 to 64.

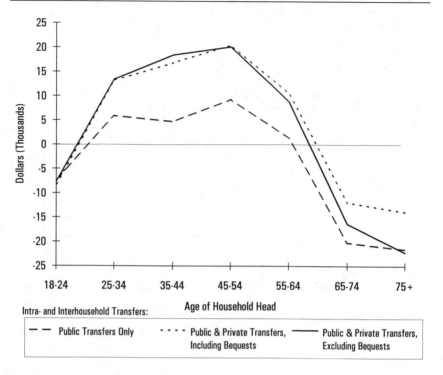

Figure 5.19 Net public and private transfers, all intra- and interhousehold transfers, by age of household head.

Evaluations of the relative generosity of the generations are dependent on how broadly transfers are defined. Limiting the definition to personal assistance, housing, and gifts, and excluding bequests, those aged 55 to 64 appear to be the most generous. With a broader definition that includes child-rearing and educational expenses, those aged 35 to 44 represent the peak givers. Still more broadly, by including the value of bequests given and inheritances received, the apparent position of the elderly changes from a modest level of contribution to a substantial level of contribution.

The distribution of benefits, public and private, and the extent to which different age groups are net givers or net recipients may become important to policy discussions on the appropriate allocation of government benefits by age. For example, it is common for policy analysts to talk about "dependency ratios," measured as the relative size of the "productive" and "unproductive" segments of the population. In these discussions, dependents are assumed to be those under 18 and those 65 and over. But the findings reported in this chapter suggest that if dependency is measured by actual practices, it lasts longer in youth and, with respect to public programs, it begins earlier in late middle age for many individuals.

It should also be remembered that when today's elderly were middle-aged, they too may have been generous givers. Moreover, the middle-aged may be able to be generous precisely because of the existence of Social Security and Medicare. These federal programs reduce the likelihood that middle-aged children will need to provide financial support to their elderly parents. At the same time, these programs provide some assurance about the financial standard of living that they will have in retirement, and provide insurance against many medical expenses. Expecting these benefits, the middle-aged are able to give extensive financial and nonfinancial support to their adult children.

Views about equity across the generations will be based in part on the magnitude of perceived contributions and perceived needs, along with views about the appropriate bases for judging the distribution of resources. The inclusion of parents' contributions in time and money toward rearing young children changes the apparent balance of resource flows for those in the peak child-rearing years. The combining of private transfers with the flow of public transfers reduces, but does not eliminate, the apparent dependency of the elderly on other age groups. But there may be substantial differences across the age spectrum in recognizing these contributions. For example, parents with young children may feel that their contributions are not being adequately recognized, or that their needs for assistance in raising children are not being met. They may also fail to perceive the social contributions of the elderly, and perceive only their relatively large Social Security benefits. These perceptions may affect their attitudes and become a source of tension, as is discussed in Chapters 6 and 7.

CHAPTER 6

Intergenerational Tensions and Conflict: Attitudes and Perceptions About Social Justice and Age-Related Needs

Mark Schlesinger and Karl Kronebusch

The 1980s were a time of social and political paradox. The federal government accumulated a staggering deficit while political leaders of both parties preached doctrines of fiscal restraint. Capitalism triumphed over communism internationally, at a time when two of every three Americans reported that the "lot of the average man" in this country was getting worse. A septuagenarian President achieved unprecedented levels of political popularity, while elders as a group were increasingly portrayed as a threat to the well-being of younger Americans.

It was during the 1980s that the term *intergenerational equity* first came into common usage. This history has been reviewed in earlier chapters. But the paradoxical nature of much of the debate over intergenerational equity has often been overlooked. Elders were portrayed as needy (Kingson, Hirshorn, & Cornman, 1986) yet greedy (Howe, 1990), vulnerable (Palmer, Smeeding, & Torrey, 1988) yet politically powerful (Dychtwald & Flowers, 1989; Gibbs, 1988). The scope of intergenerational tensions was simultaneously reported to be ubiquitous (Longman, 1987), currently moderate but imminently explosive (Dychtwald & Flowers, 1989), and virtually nonexistent (Gerber, Wolff, Klores, & Brown, 1989; Kingson et al., 1986). Those warning about the potential for intergenerational conflict were often labeled provocateurs and enemies of the elderly (Kingson et al., 1986; Minkler &

Robertson, 1991; Quadagno, 1989), though many of these same concerns had been raised a decade earlier by advocates of America's elders, who warned about growing "anger toward the old" (Neugarten, 1973, p. 574) and about conflicts in which "youth demand fundamental changes, the resistance of the old is aroused, and the militancy of youth is increased" (Foner, 1974, p. 193).

Many of these apparent paradoxes and disparate assessments can be explained by the fact that the popular press and academic writers on this topic have relied on vague and inconsistent notions of what exactly is meant by intergenerational tensions. These notions range from extreme forms of "age wars" (Dychtwald & Flowers, 1987; Gerber et al., 1989) to more subtle disagreements over the just allocation of societal resources (Gibbs, 1988). Confusion over terminology has been exacerbated by the fact that most discussions of intergenerational concerns have taken too narrow a perspective on the ways in which tensions emerge around social programs. Most analyses, both contemporary studies (Gerber et al., 1989; Marshall, Cook, & Marshall, 1993; Thomson, 1993) and those dating back two decades ago (Foner, 1974; Kreps, 1977) presume that tensions are produced by competition among organized interest groups representing Americans of different ages. This perspective has led, in our assessment, to a misleading portrayal of the scope of intergenerational discord and has overlooked the most important ways in which tensions may emerge.

To provide a more complete perspective on the nature and scope of intergenerational tensions, we explore three questions in this chapter:

- What are the various ways in which intergenerational tensions might be created?
- How prevalent is each type of tension in contemporary American society?
- What does the nature of current tensions and their distribution among different groups tell us about the potential growth of future tensions?

We explore the second and third of these questions using data from the 1990 AARP Intergenerational Linkages survey. Our discussion focuses on tensions emerging from government programs and policies, though we set this within the context of generational relations within families. (We examine the connections between family and public policy concerns more fully in Chapter 7.)

INTERGENERATIONAL TENSIONS IN CONTEMPORARY SOCIETY

Past discussions of intergenerational conflict have defined this almost exclusively in terms of "age wars" between organized interest groups. From this perspective, intergenerational tensions develop only if (a) people identify themselves in terms of an age group or cohort (e.g., think of themselves as "elders" or "baby boomers"), (b) age groups are able to act with sufficient cohesion that they can pursue a consistent political or social agenda, and (c) different age groups or cohorts are unable to negotiate satisfactory working arrangements to manage their differences (Binstock, 1983; Foner, 1974; Minkler & Robertson, 1991). Unless each of these stages holds true, intergroup conflict does not occur.

This perspective makes extensive intergenerational conflict seem quite unlikely. First, few people overtly identify themselves with a particular age group or cohort, since they have a variety of other more salient affiliations (Bengtson, Cutler, Mangen, & Marshall, 1985; Foner, 1974; Heclo, 1988). Second, because people in each age group tend to have diverse ideological beliefs and group affiliations, it is difficult for an age-defined group to pursue a coherent political agenda (Binstock, 1983; Minkler, 1986). Third, because advocacy groups for the young and old often work collaboratively, there are ample opportunities for them to negotiate mutually acceptable positions on issues that might otherwise be laden with conflict (Quadagno, 1989).

But "age wars" defined in these terms are too narrow a characterization of intergenerational tensions. First, they focus exclusively on interest groups and ignore less organized tensions. Second, they focus on overt instances of conflict and ignore less obvious sources of tension.

Intergenerational discord may arise from individuals' perceptions rather than group agendas in several ways. If, for example, taxpayers are concerned about the size of the federal deficit, they may favor cutting back on Medicare spending not because they feel any antipathy toward the elderly as a group, but rather because they simply see Medicare as the fastest growing part of the federal budget. Such proposed cuts would surely generate intergenerational tensions.

A second form of individualized tension can develop because people of a given age are *seen* as a group, even if they do not *act* as a group. Witness the long history of racial tensions in this country, which involved the tendency of people to think in stereotypical terms. Public perceptions of different age groups are also shaped by stereotypes (Palmore, 1988). Consequently, intergenerational tensions may emerge, based on what the public *thinks* about different age groups, even when these perceptions are inaccurate.

These individualized tensions reflect perceptions and values that differ from one individual to the next. Indeed, this variation in itself may stimulate or exacerbate tensions. Because these forms of tension are decentralized, there is not the same opportunity for negotiation and collaboration to diffuse tensions as when conflicts exist between organized groups.

To better understand the nature of these individualized tensions, it is useful to define several related aspects of what we might mean by "tension." Past discussions of intergenerational relations have generally used the terms *tensions* and *conflicts* interchangeably. We, however, use them to mean distinctly different forms of social interaction. Both are in turn defined in terms of a third distinct concept, which we refer to as a *stressor*. Because we are all most familiar with intergenerational relations within our own families, we initially illustrate these strains in a familial context.

A *stressor* refers to any demand on individuals that impinges on their personal welfare and thus becomes a "burden." Within the family, stressors involve the needs of other family members, although not all needs are necessarily sources of stress. Many people receive great gratification in caring for or aiding others. It is only when others' needs are seen as burdensome that they become a source of stress. Stressors are intergenerational to the extent that they cross the boundaries of family generations, such as providing child care, paying for a college education for youth, aiding grown children who are not self-supporting, or caring for ailing elder parents.

We use the term *tension* to refer to any stressor, or burden, that an individual judges to be "unfair." Someone caring for an ailing parent might, for instance, feel that his or her siblings should share more of the burden. All the children might feel that their parent should take more responsibility for himself or herself.

In contrast to stressors, tensions can be intergenerational in two ways. First, if the stressor or burden is intergenerational, then the tension related to that stress is intergenerational as well. If children feel that an impaired elder parent is not doing enough to help himself or herself, there are obvious intergenerational tensions. But even if the stressor is not intergenerational, the tension may be so if the way the person tries to resolve the tension shifts costs to those of other generations. For example, a young dual-earner couple may feel overburdened by the costs of housing. If they insist that their parents should help with these costs, they may produce intergenerational tensions even though the initial stresses were within a single generation.

We use the term *friction* to refer to a tension whose cause is attributed to the conscious actions of some other person or group. In our example above, if elder parents feel unfairly burdened by their children's requests for assistance, this represents an intergenerational *tension*. If in addition they feel that they have been forced to help out because their children are shirking their own responsibilities, then this becomes a source of *friction*.

Intergenerational discord can take each of these forms, which may build on one another. *Stressors* discomfort the individuals in question. They feel burdened by various age-related needs. Given their other needs and the other demands on their time and resources, they may feel that some of these age-related needs represent an *unfair* burden, and thus *tensions* develop. The more the parties attribute their tensions to the deliberate actions or willful neglect by others, the more likely these tensions are to create *frictions*. Overt intergenerational *conflict* is most likely to emerge from this latter set of circumstances.

Not all intergenerational problems will emerge in this sort of multistage process. As we document in Chapter 7, under some circumstances tensions may be felt even if there is no sense of burden. But these interlinked forms or levels of tension provide a useful conceptual schema for categorizing intergenerational strains and for understanding the differences in their reported prevalence.

INTERGENERATIONAL TENSIONS IN A BROADER SOCIETAL CONTEXT

Intergenerational discord around social programs is connected in several ways to tensions within families. The same broad process, the progression from perceived burdens to expressed tensions to friction, is likely to shape the scope of societal tensions. In addition, there are likely to be several more direct linkages to individuals' family circumstances.

The first connection between family and societal-level tensions involves perceptions: The family serves as a lens through which people view intergenerational relations and burdens more generally. Many people lack experience with age-related needs and norms beyond their immediate family and perhaps the families of a few close friends. Consequently, if they feel burdened or not burdened in their own relationships, they may assume that this feeling is shared by others of the same age. They may thus project these feelings and experiences onto all relationships between parents and children. In contrast, those who have little or no personal experience in these relationships may be influenced by media representations—either positive or negative—of intergenerational family relationships.

A second link between family and societal-level tensions stems from the fact that family and public programs represent alternative means of meeting age-related needs. Those who feel the greatest family burden from a particular need are likely to be the most receptive to government programs that could reduce the burden of their family obligations. Conversely, those who have not experienced this family burden—because they have had no family members in need, they have felt no burden in responding to the needs of family members, or they have felt no responsibility to meet those needs—are likely to feel the most burdened by government programs that address these needs.

Although tensions felt within families and society are thus interconnected, the nature of intergenerational conflict at the societal level differs from that within families in several important ways. Perhaps the most fundamental difference between intergenerational tensions within families and those in society involves exposure. As documented in earlier chapters, most individuals in families have considerable contact with each other that crosses generational boundaries. Family members are likely to share a common understanding of their mutual circumstances (though they may often disagree on the causes). With societal interactions, there is more distance. Most Americans simply do not know very much about the well-being or needs of the average older person or the average child. One would thus expect that differences in perceptions across different ages might play a far more important role in intergenerational relations in society than they do within the family.

Another important difference between family and societal tensions involves the norms of equity by which relations are judged, by which people decide whether particular age-related burdens are fair or unfair. Within the family, Americans generally favor norms of equality, with some consideration of need (Hochschild, 1981). Most bequests, for example, are divided equally among children (Hurd, 1989). As one goes beyond the family, however, the norms of contribution and equal opportunity play a larger role, as discussed in the next section.

Intergenerational Tensions and Norms of Societal Equity

Norms of intergenerational equity are part of the broader set of norms by which Americans judge the fairness of social institutions. By *norms* we mean those criteria that most people agree are legitimate standards against which actual practices or policies may be compared. Three norms prove most influential.

Under *norms of contribution,* people are thought to "deserve" the benefits they get because they have earned them through their effort and productivity (Alves & Rossi, 1978; Kluegel & Smith, 1986). Individuals are viewed as a sort of societal investment. Society owes to them in proportion to what they contribute. "In a society governed by a norm of investments, all people would be able to earn respect and rewards, but they must *earn* them" (Hochschild, 1981, p. 62).

A different set of norms emphasize the primacy of assuring that individual *needs* are met—that no one goes without food, clothing, or shelter. Concerns for the needs of others may stem in part from what philosophers term the *duty of beneficence,* the obligation that members of society have to aid others in distress (Baybrooke, 1987; Dougherty, 1988). Within the context of the Social Security program, this standard is sometimes referred to as the principle of *social adequacy* (Schulz, 1988).

Under a third set of norms, those invoking notions of *equality,* social arrangements are just if all members of society are treated in a like manner. But notions of equality can be mutually contradictory. Treating all people equally (procedural equality) may lead to quite unequal outcomes if their needs differ, while achieving equal outcomes requires that treatment be unequal (Rae, Yates, Hochschild, Morone, & Fessler, 1981). In general, Americans favor norms of procedural equality over equality of outcomes (Hochschild, 1981; Kluegel & Smith, 1986). They emphasize most the procedural norm of *equal opportunity*—that is, that all Americans have an equal chance to participate in important social institutions. One major exception involves government and political participation, where norms of *equal outcome* (e.g., "one man, one vote") dominate popular thinking.

Each of these norms plays an important role in defining what Americans believe to be a fair distribution of social resources and a just allocation of responsibility for meeting various individual and social needs. People balance off these three norms against one another in deciding whether particular individuals or groups have been fairly treated.

Assessments of *intergenerational* equity are made according to a comparable balance. In most writing on this subject, the norm of equality is invoked most frequently. Authors suggest that age groups differ in the degree to which they experience various good or bad outcomes, or the extent to which they can draw on societal resources (Longman, 1987; Preston, 1984; Thomson, 1993). Historically, the well-being of elders was compared most often to that of working-age adults, a comparison that legitimized a number of public policies targeted to elders, including the Medicare program (Blumenthal, Schlesinger, & Brown-Drumheller, 1988). More recently, comparisons between elders and children have become more common. Whether inequalities between age groups are inequitable, however, depends in part on how needs differ with age (Palmer et al., 1988).

The fairness of current practices and policies will also depend on the extent to which different age groups are judged to be deserving. Although both children and elders are often portrayed as dependent groups—those who rely on the support of others to assure their well-being—norms of contribution have not entirely disappeared from judgments of intergenerational equity. Binstock, for example, has argued that the growing tendency to divide elders into the *young-old* and *old-old* (typically at age 75 or 85) represents an effort to treat the younger group according to norms of contribution, holding them "capable of and obligated to earn their own living, rather than to view them as exempt from the Protestant work ethic" (1990, p. 436).

More generally, the norm of contribution remains a part of discussions of intergenerational equity, but with a change in tense. For elders, the shift is into the past. What matters in this case is what elders have contributed to others and the obligations these past contributions create. "Members of all generations may harbor the expectation that the devotion and care given by the young parent to the infant and child . . . should be reciprocated and the indebtedness repaid in kind when the parent, having grown old, becomes dependent" (Brody, 1985, p. 26). In a societal context, past contributions extend beyond the family to include work history, military service, and general citizenship. Benefits legitimized through these past contributions are often referred to as *earned benefits*.

The focus for children is more on what they will contribute in the future. Thus, public programs to benefit children are invariably described by their proponents as good "investments" for society, in the sense that a healthier and better educated cohort of children can be expected to be a more productive cohort of workers when they are grown (Minow & Weisbourd, 1993; Schlesinger & Eisenberg, 1990).

From these various norms emerge several sources of intergenerational tension, as we discuss in more detail below.

SOURCES AND CATEGORIES OF INTERGENERATIONAL TENSIONS

In our schema developed above, intergenerational tensions emerge when people judge some set of age-related burdens to be unfair, in the sense that they violate their norms of equity. There are three ways in which these tensions can develop (Figure 6.1).

Dissonance.   In the first case, there is a mismatch between how particular age-related needs are being met and how a person thinks that they should be met. This is the principle form of tension described in most writings about intergenerational equity. For example, some observers have argued that children in the United States today are neglected and receiving too little, given their needs and

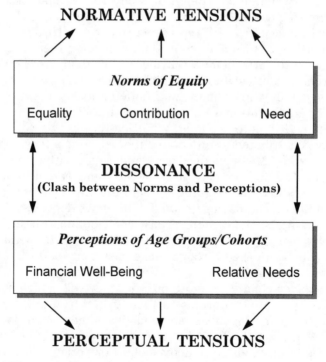

Figure 6.1 Types of intergenerational tensions.

potential future contributions (McCormick, 1991; Minow & Weisbourd, 1993; Preston, 1984).

We refer to this first form of tension as *intergenerational dissonance,* the clash between what people see and what they expect. Perceived inequities arise when family practices or government policies violate this notion of equity. This may happen more or less inadvertently, because our collective attention has been diverted to other concerns (Preston, 1984). In other instances it is attributed to the deliberate actions of groups that have more political influence and thus can appropriate a larger share of public resources (Longman, 1987). As with intrafamily tensions, the latter form of tension seems more likely to produce overt intergenerational conflict.

Normative Tensions. The second source of intergenerational discord has received little attention: People do not always share common values, and thus may differ in the relative importance that they place on particular norms of equity. For example, about 5% of all Americans can be viewed as strong egalitarians, in the sense that they favor having all people receive roughly equal incomes (Kluegel & Smith, 1986). To them, the retirement income benefits of the Social Security program may seem unfair, because monthly payments to retired workers are based in part on what one earned during one's working years and are thus higher for those who previously had higher paying jobs. But the program benefits levels are purposely designed to be progressive—monthly payment amounts represent a *higher* proportion of preretirement income for lower paid workers and a *smaller* proportion of preretirement income for these higher paid workers (Olsen, 1982). About half of our respondents, however, believe that Social Security benefits should be proportional to past earnings, reflecting the norm of earned benefits. To them, current arrangements may overcompensate low-income workers.

Differences in the norms by which people judge societal equity can thus become a source of intergenerational tensions and friction. We refer to these tensions as *normative tensions.* Again, these tensions can be intergenerational in two senses. First, people of different ages may place greater or lesser importance on particular norms. The "generation gap" that drew so much attention in the late 1960s and early 1970s was largely a result of differing norms between young adults and their middle-aged parents (Kriegel, 1978). Second, those who favor particular norms may inadvertently discredit claims by particular age groups to a share of societal resources. For example, a person who places little importance on earned benefits may implicitly discount the norm that legitimizes elders' claims to entitlements such as Social Security. Thus, even though opinions for or against the norm of earned benefits do not vary by age, their implications can be unintentionally intergenerational.

Perceptual Tensions.   A third source of tensions involves differences in perceptions. Even if people agree on how particular age groups should be treated or what particular age cohorts should be able to expect from life, they may differ in their perceptions of how they are actually treated or what opportunities they actually have. These we refer to as *perceptual tensions.* When perceptions differ systematically by age or among different cohorts, or where perceptions differ about particular age-related needs, these tensions can have important ramifications for intergenerational relations.

PUBLIC ATTITUDES AND INTERGENERATIONAL TENSIONS

Using data from the intergenerational survey, we can begin to explore how each of these three forms of tension emerges, as well as assess its current prevalence. We begin with comparisons between perceived practices and norms of equity, then explore different concepts of what is equitable and different perceptions of the well-being or treatment of various age groups.

PUBLIC ATTITUDES AND INTERGENERATIONAL DISSONANCE

The focus of most discussions of intergenerational equity has been on the unequal distribution of government spending on elders and children relative to their needs. Inarguably, the federal government has assumed more responsibility for the needs of the elderly, while families retain most responsibility for children, apart from the financing of primary and secondary education. The inequalities in federal spending are thus most noticeable. As of 1990, about 7% of all federal spending went to those under 18 and their families, compared to 29% to those 65 and older (U.S. House of Representatives, 1991, pp. 1342–1344). In contrast, the age-related pattern of total spending by state and local governments is the reverse of the federal pattern. As discussed in Chapters 1 and 5, nonfederal government expenditures for children and youth are almost four times higher than those for the elderly. But these expenditures are generally less noticeable to the public.

Dissonance and Intergenerational Burdens

Substantial federal government spending on the elderly could be expected to create perceived burdens. In the words of one national columnist, "Spending too much on the elderly will inevitably short-change other important goals, everything from improving schools to fighting crime and cleaning up the environment" (Samuelson, 1990, p. 61). Results from the survey suggest that this sentiment is shared by only a minority of Americans. Asked whether "federal programs that provide benefits to older persons" are too costly, 29% agreed that they are. (In this chapter when we report percentages who *agree* or *disagree* on 5-point scale questions, we combine "strongly agree" and "agree," and "strongly disagree" and "disagree," respectively, unless we specifically refer to separate categories of agreement and disagreement.)

Although almost a third of all respondents thus judged federal programs for elders as too costly, this number is somewhat deceptive. About two thirds of those who agreed that programs for the elderly are too expensive *also* thought that programs for children are too expensive. This suggests that these respondents were feeling burdened by federal spending generally, and not just by spending on the elderly. To the extent that intergenerational discord evolves from attributing burdens to a particular age group, these respondents seem less likely candidates for intergenerational tensions. Also, some of those who feel that elders' federal benefits are too costly are elderly persons themselves. Moreover, recognizing that government spending for elders is large, or even perceiving it as burdensome, does not suggest that it is inequitable and thus a source of intergenerational tension.

Dissonance and Intergenerational Tensions

If elders were seen as needier than children, their greater share could be justified in terms of the norm of need. There are two ways in which relative need can be assessed: by comparisons among age *groups* and by comparisons among age *cohorts*. Some have argued that both comparisons make the federal government's disproportionate spending on elders seem inequitable (Longman, 1987; Thomson, 1993).

Comparing age groups, it is children who are typically portrayed as the most economically needy. Government statistics on poverty show that 12% of elders live in poverty, compared to about 20% of children and 10.5% percent of working-age adults (Howe, 1990, p. D-18). Poverty rates for children grew throughout the 1980s, while poverty rates for the elderly declined to their lowest point before increasing slightly during the early 1990s.

Government statistics may overstate the disparities between children and elders. A substantial proportion of elders (about 8%) live just above the poverty line and poverty is measured in a way that may understate economic deprivation in smaller, elder-headed households (Lazear & Michael, 1980; Schulz, 1988). Nevertheless, most academics who have studied the distribution of economic well-being conclude that children are the age group that is comparatively worse-off (Bane & Ellwood, 1989; Hurd, 1989).

Americans' perceptions of the well-being of different age groups, however, are somewhat different from the portrayal in either the academic literature or in government statistics. The survey asked whether particular age groups were among the "best-off" or "worst-off" financially, on a 5-point scale. In response, 14% thought that children were the worst-off, and another 19% felt that they were worse-off than average (Figure 6.2). Similarly, 11% thought that elders were the worst-off, and 22% that they were worse than average. In short, exactly the same proportion believed that elders were doing less well than average as believed that children were.

Given these perceptions, the federal government's current focus on the needs of elders may not be judged inequitable by the population as a whole. Despite their greater benefits, elders are seen as no better-off than are children. In the absence of government support, they would clearly be worse-off. To the extent that children and elders are expected to have equal outcomes, the current balance of federal spending by this measure would seem to be about right, so long as reported perceptions accurately reflect Americans' judgment about the well-being of different age groups.

A second comparison of age groups involves the burdens that their needs impose on others. Survey respondents were asked whether the costs of child care or the burdens of caring for disabled elders are too great for many families. Sixty-two percent felt that child care is too costly, and 45% felt that elder care is unduly burdensome. The disparity in these assessments suggests that child care is seen by the public as a more pressing need. Greater spending on the elderly, or the enactment of new programs paying for long-term care, could exacerbate tensions unless similar increases in programs that support child care are implemented.

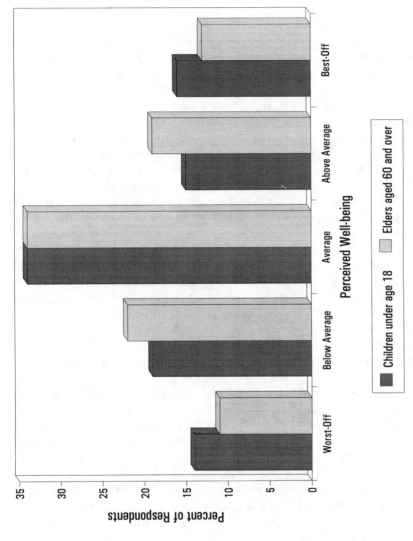

Figure 6.2 Perceived financial well-being of children and elders. (Based on 5-point scale.) N = 1492.

Intergenerational comparisons can be made in terms of cohorts as well as age groups. Some have argued that inequities exist because this current cohort of elders is receiving more than its fair share of government benefits. One claim is that those now elderly are receiving in public benefits more than they have earned (Longman, 1987). We turn to this issue in the next section of the chapter. The second claim is that current elders had a relatively easy time during their working years, working in an era when the American economy was growing and opportunities for advancement were more readily available than now exist for their grown children (Thomson, 1993).

To what extent do Americans see those who are now working as experiencing a more difficult time than the cohort that is now elderly did at a comparable age? Respondents in the survey were asked to make comparisons between the status of their own cohort and those of cohorts past and future. The results suggest that the economic hardships that began in the mid-1970s have only slightly tarnished the American dream of each generation doing better than its parents (Daniels, 1989; Kluegel & Smith, 1986). A third of all respondents under the age of 50 agreed that their parents' generation "had a better standard of living than my generation has," but 47% disagreed. When asked if young people today still have opportunities "to achieve a better life than their parents," more than three quarters of the respondents agreed. About a third of those who felt that their own generation had done less well than their parents were still optimistic about opportunities in the future.

Contemporary Tensions and Intergenerational Dissonance

Most Americans do not seem to believe that unequal spending on children and elders is necessarily inequitable, since, despite that spending, respondents judged elders as frequently as they judged children to be badly off. But it is clear that *some* Americans do see children's needs as greater than elders'. About one in five respondents saw children, but not elders, as worse-off financially than average. Almost two thirds see the costs of child care as unduly burdensome for many families. To the extent that these attitudes coincide with a perception of burden from federal programs for the elderly, intergenerational tensions are likely to arise.

We can explore these potential tensions in two ways. The first involves the overlap of perceived needs and burdens. Those who feel that children are substantially worse-off than average, but feel that elders are not, *and* that federal programs for the elderly are too costly are likely to be focal points of intergenerational tensions. The same is true of Americans who feel that child care burdens families *and* that federal programs for older persons are too costly. These combinations of attitudes are presented in Figures 6.3 and 6.4. We estimate from these interactions that about 10–20% of the American public experience implicit or explicit intergenerational dissonance around federal spending for the elderly.

A second way to measure these tensions is to ask the question more directly. Asked whether they believed that elders had gotten "more than their fair share" of government programs and tax benefits, 18% believed that they had. This falls in the range of our estimates based on the overlap of perceived need and the burdens of federal benefits (Figures 6.3 and 6.4).

Intergenerational tensions of this type are thus modest in scope. They may, however, increase in the future. Given current federal commitments, the proportion of federal spending on the elderly will grow significantly over the next half century, as the Baby Boomers come of age for federal entitlement programs (Howe, 1990). Those who feel that elders and children are currently equally well-off may

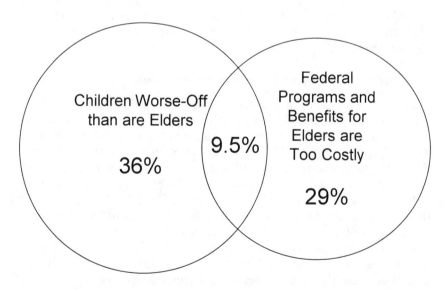

Figure 6.3 Intergenerational tensions: Percent agreeing that children are worse-off *and* elders' benefits are too costly.

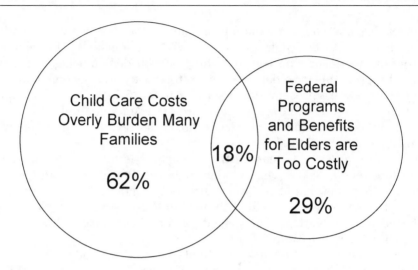

Figure 6.4 Intergenerational tensions: Percent agreeing that child care is burdensome *and* elders' benefits are too costly.

consider this growing federal emphasis on elder benefits inappropriate. Those who feel that families are unduly burdened by the needs of children are likely to be even more sensitive to these shifts in federal funding unless state and local government spending for children also increases.

Dissonance and Intergenerational Frictions

We have suggested that age-related tensions develop into frictions primarily when perceived inequities are attributed to the deliberate actions of the beneficiary group. Frictions about the distribution of federal government benefits to elders may emerge from perceptions that this group exerts undue influence over the political process. The American public was until recently relatively sanguine about elders' political influence. In a Harris poll conducted in 1981, for example, two thirds of the public reported that elders had *too little* influence on American society; only 3% felt that they had too much (Harris, 1981). Since that time, however, the popular media have increasingly portrayed elders as having considerable political influence, certainly more than that available to advocates for children (Gibbs, 1990).

When respondents in the survey were asked whether "advocates for older Americans have been more successful than those for children and youth," 37% agreed; 17% disagreed. (A large group in the middle were apparently undecided.) Most of those who have a firm opinion on this issue thus believe that elders have become relatively powerful in a political sense.

This perceived political imbalance threatens the interests of other groups only if elders act out of narrow self-interest. In fact, evidence suggests that the opposite is true. Individually, elders tend to be the *least* supportive of any age group of government benefits targeted to the old. For example, when asked if federal programs for the elderly had become too costly, 35% of respondents 65 and older agreed, compared to 26% of those under the age of 50.

But individual attitudes by elders are not necessarily reflected in the actions of their advocates. And the key issue precipitating inter-generational conflict is how Americans *perceive* that elders use their political influence. We cannot address this directly, but we can make some informed estimates. Of the respondents who felt that elders received more than their fair share of government spending, 59% also believed that elders and their advocates had a more effective political voice than did advocates for children (Figure 6.5). This subgroup of respondents thus represents 11% of the sample. Of the respondents

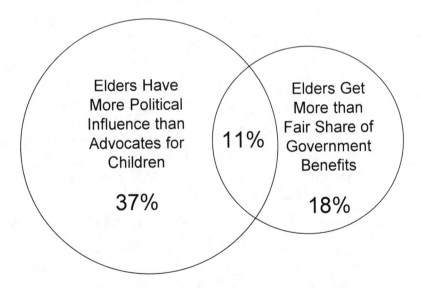

Figure 6.5 Intergenerational friction: Percent agreeing that elders have a large political voice *and* elders get too many benefits.

who felt that child care was too costly for many American families, 42% also believed that elders had more political influence than children (Figure 6.6). These respondents comprise 26% of the sample.

It is the intersection of these beliefs that creates the potential for intergenerational tension or friction. Not all those with a *potential* for feeling intergenerational conflict will actually do so. Although these respondents see both unequal political influence and excess burdens, they do not necessarily attribute the burdens to the political influence. To the extent that they do not, this combination of perceptions should not lead to intergenerational tension or friction.

Returning to our three-stage model, we can create a more accurate estimate of the intensity of existing frictions. Of the 62% who feel that child care costs are excessive, 29% also feel that elder programs are too costly. Almost two fifths of these people feel that elders have more political influence than children (Figure 6.7). Thus 7% simultaneously perceive burdens for families with children, see some unfairness in federal benefits to elders, and also perceive elders as having disproportionate political influence. This is a prime group for intergenerational conflict. Similarly, of the 29% who see elders' programs as too expensive, less than two fifths think elders get an unfair share of government benefits. And only about half of this group see elders as having

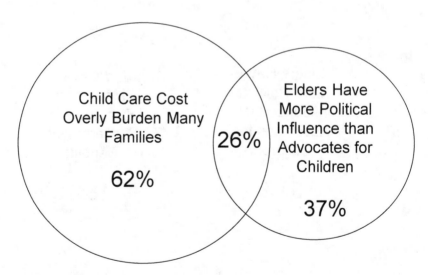

Figure 6.6 Intergenerational friction: Percent agreeing that elders have a large political voice *and* child care is burdensome.

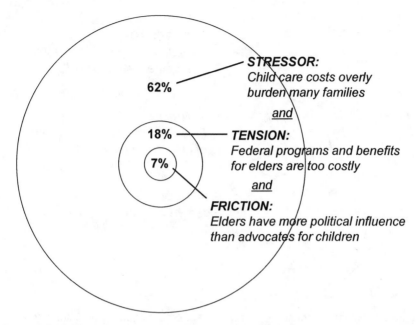

Figure 6.7 Stressors, tensions, and frictions: Percent agreeing on 3 items (child care burdens, cost of elder programs, and elders' political influence).

disproportionate political influence. The prime group for conflict around elders' benefits is thus 5% of the total population (Figure 6.8).

These percentages are very small. While it is useful to consider the potential for and sources of intergenerational conflict, it is equally important to recognize that most Americans do *not* associate elders' greater political influence with unfair benefits.

PUBLIC ATTITUDES AND NORMATIVE TENSIONS

The history of federal policy toward the elderly reflects a balancing act between the different norms of societal equity. The criteria for judging Social Security and Medicare have changed over time as the relative importance of contribution, need, and equality have shifted in importance (Blumenthal et al., 1988; Meyers & Wolff, 1992). Because different people hold somewhat different views about the relative importance of each norm, tensions may develop among these standards for assessing equity.

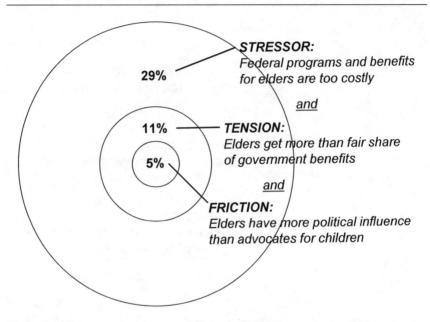

Figure 6.8 Stressors, tensions, and frictions: Percent agreeing on 3 items (cost of elder programs, elders' share of benefits, and elders' political influence).

These normative tensions are most closely linked to the concept of *earned benefits,* a version of the norm of contribution. Medicare and Social Security are both broadly considered earned benefits—82% of the survey respondents considered these programs an "earned right." A similar principle is often extended to less formal benefits for the elderly. For example, 78% agreed that "senior citizen discounts are fair because elders deserve special treatment." This is not because elders were seen as unusually needy, since the vast majority of those who favored "special treatment" felt that elders were as well-off or better-off financially in comparison to other age groups.

But even those who believe that elders have earned special status and benefits may question whether this norm legitimizes benefits as extensive as elders currently receive. The benefits that elders receive from Medicare and Social Security income programs are only partially earned in an actuarial sense. The payroll taxes from those who are now retired cover, on average, only about 15% of their expected benefits from Medicare and 40% of their expected cash payments under old age and survivor's insurance (Longman, 1987, p. 76; Vogel, 1988; Wolff, 1987). It is likely that Americans think of these benefits as earned in a less literal sense—that people paid in the payroll taxes that were asked of them and thus have a right to expect the benefits that were promised to them. When the norm of earned benefits conflicts with other norms, however, the rather vague link between what people have contributed in the past and what they receive in the present can generate considerable tensions.

The primary challenge to the norm of earned benefits comes from standards linked to need. Programs like Medicare are based on the presumption that elders have all earned roughly comparable benefits, even when this presumption obviously conflicts with differences among elders' financial needs and resources (Schlesinger & Brown-Drumheller, 1988). But although Americans generally favor the norm of contribution over need when distributing earnings for working-age adults, they appear to strongly favor the norm of need over the concept of earned benefits in distributing public resources. When asked if government benefits should be allocated "on the basis of need instead of age," 76% in the survey favored need. This included three fourths of those who had stated that Medicare and Social Security were "earned rights."

As noted earlier, under current Old Age, Survivors and Disability Insurance (OASDI) provisions, those who have paid in more in payroll taxes generally receive more back, in dollars per month, in their Social Security checks. Although lower paid workers have a higher *proportion* of their preretirement income replaced by OASDI benefits, this may not assure sufficient protection to the most needy elders. Forty-nine percent of the survey respondents were in favor of making Social Security benefits "highest for those who are poor."

The norm of need appears in a different form in proposals to tax Medicare and Social Security benefits as forms of income. Because low-income elders face lower marginal tax rates, taxing benefits indirectly places a greater emphasis on need in the distribution of public benefits. At the time of the survey, only half the amount of Social Security benefits of recipients with incomes above certain levels was taxed as income. But 23% of respondents in the survey agree that the total amount should be subject to federal income tax. A third of all respondents favored taxing the dollar value of Medicare benefits as a form of income.

There is, therefore, considerable normative tension associated with the distribution of benefits to elders. Between a quarter and a half of our survey respondents favor increasing the role of need in the distribution of benefits, depending on the particular way in which this might be done. These tensions are much more prevalent than is the intergenerational dissonance that is the focus of much of the debate over intergenerational equity.

Proposals to tax federal benefits for elders more heavily would certainly exacerbate intergenerational tensions. But it is too simplistic to assume that such a debate would put younger Americans in one camp against a united group of elders on the other side. Although a significant number of elders would oppose changes of this sort, a substantial minority of the elderly would in fact favor these changes (Table 6.1). A considerable proportion of elders are strongly supportive of changes that run counter to group self-interest. Elders, for example, are the age group most likely to disagree with the notion of special discounts for seniors. Also, a larger proportion of elders than any other age group strongly support changing the distribution of Medicare and Social Security benefits.

Compared to other age groups, elders have more strongly held beliefs—both for and against change—about government programs and policies that provide them with benefits. This greater salience is not surprising, since this is the group with the greatest personal experience with these benefits and the group with the most at stake if bene-

TABLE 6.1 Support for Changes in Elder Benefits, by Age of Respondent

Respondent's age	N	Percent who				
		Strongly disagree	Disagree	Neutral	Agree	Strongly agree
		Medicare benefits should be treated as taxable income				
18-49	980	17	10	35	18	17
50-64	279	32	9	26	11	19
65 +	240	35	11	12	7	24
		Social Security benefits should be highest for those who are poor				
18-49	980	16	14	22	16	32
50-64	279	20	12	18	12	38
65 +	240	18	10	14	11	44
		Senior discounts are fair because older people deserve special treatment				
18-49	980	5	3	9	18	65
50-64	279	7	6	14	16	56
65 +	240	8	5	18	14	52

fits are changed. The greater extremes of support and opposition suggest that the most intense normative conflicts may occur *among*
elders, or between coalitions in which different groups of elders are on
either side of the issue. Thus, *intragenerational* tension may prove to
be one of the most important sources of ongoing discord around age-
targeted benefits.

PUBLIC ATTITUDES AND PERCEPTUAL TENSIONS

A third source of societal tension has been largely ignored in past discussions of intergenerational equity. This involves differences in the
way people perceive age-related need and treatment. All else equal,
those who see elders as well-off can be expected to favor redistribut-
ing government benefits to children, and those who see them as
worse-off than others can be expected to oppose this change. Those
who believe that dependent elders demand more time and attention
from their caregivers than do children will favor government programs
that support the needs of the older group.

To the extent that people differ in these perceptions, they will differ
in their assessment of just distributions of societal resources and the
appropriate role for government. To explore this source of intergenerational tension, we focus on Americans' varying perceptions of the relative well-being of different age groups and cohorts.

Perceived Well-Being of Different Age Groups

As noted earlier, about a third of all Americans see elders as worse-off
financially than other age groups (Figure 6.2, above). An almost identical proportion reported that children were worse-off than other age
groups. This in itself does not imply a conflict in perceptions, since
both young and old might be seen as worse-off than working-age
adults. However, 23% see children as worse-off than average, but
elders as not. A different 22% see elders as worse-off than average and
children as not. Because most Americans favor allocating government
benefits according to need, these different perceptions will lead to
conflicting conclusions about which age groups should have the highest priority for public benefits.

But this is only a part of a complicated story. While many see old
and young Americans as facing the greatest financial difficulties, many
others see them living a life of relative financial security. Fourteen percent of survey respondents reported that children were the age group

worst-off financially, but 16% saw them as the best-off. Eleven percent saw elders as the worst-off, 13% as the best-off (Figure 6.2).

Because so many Americans have such widely disparate views about the well-being of different age groups, these perceptions represent perhaps the most significant source of tension affecting intergenerational public policy. There are two plausible explanations for these divergent perceptions: differences in self-interest and differences in knowledge.

The self-interest hypothesis argues that people generally see themselves as facing the biggest hardships and discount hardships of others. If this were true, one would expect to see elders labeling themselves as least well-off, and see other "competing" age groups as relatively better-off. In fact, exactly the *opposite* is true. Elders are significantly less likely than others to report that older Americans face the biggest financial hardships. Compared to adults aged 18 to 49, for example, elders are about half as likely to report their own age group as least well-off, and more than two times as likely to label themselves as the group financially best-off (Table 6.2).

Elders' perceptions of children's well-being is more complicated. Elders are more likely than others to see children as the *best-off* group. This could stimulate intergenerational tensions or friction if the perception led elders to argue that children and their parents are thus less deserving of benefits. But a substantial number of elders see children as the *worst-off* group (Table 6.2). Potential *intragenerational* tensions again emerge from these results.

TABLE 6.2 Perceived Financial Status of Children and Elders, by Age of Respondent

| Respondent's age | N | Percent who feel | | | | |
		Worst-off	Below average	Average	Above average	Best-off
		Children under 18 years old				
18-49	980	14	19	36	15	15
50-64	279	10	26	31	16	15
65 +	240	18	12	30	13	23
		Older adults, aged 60 and older				
18-49	980	12	24	35	18	10
50-64	279	11	21	35	21	13
65 +	240	6	11	33	23	25

The survey provides some support for differences in knowledge as an explanation for differences in perceived well-being. There is a striking relationship between education and perceptions of financial well-being. Better educated Americans are much less likely to view children as the age group best-off financially. Only 6% of those who have graduated from college see children as best-off, compared to 21% of those who did not go beyond high school. This may mean that disseminating information more widely could shift public perceptions about the relative well-being of different age groups. These data also reflect the effect of education on perceptions of financial well-being in general. Adults with less than a high school education are more likely than others to be poor themselves. Their perceptions of children's *relative* well-being may be much more positive than those of college graduates, who are far more likely to be financially well-off.

Perceptions of Age-Related Needs

Americans have sharply divergent perceptions of the economic well-being of children and elders. But the "need" for age-targeted government benefits involves more than just financial well-being. The perception of need is also shaped by the burdens that various age-related conditions place on family members, and by the opportunity of individuals in an age cohort to do better than their parents. In each of these dimensions, we find significant differences in perceptions that could stimulate intergenerational tensions.

Burdens. We have seen that Americans in general believe that both child care and elder care are too much of a burden on many families. Yet 20% think that child care is not unduly costly, and 30% think that caring for elders is not unduly burdensome. These differences in perceptions could create tensions around proposals for government benefits targeted to those needs.

Respondents 65 and over are more likely than any other age group to judge care for the elderly as being burdensome on families. The perceived burden of child care, in contrast, is highest among younger adults. By combining the responses to these two questions, one can get some sense of how respondents differ in their perception of the *relative* burden of elder care and child care. Here the age differences become most pronounced. Elders are much more likely than younger adults to conclude that care for elders is burdensome but care for children is not, whereas young adults are more likely than elders to see things the other way around (Table 6.3). In neither age group, however, does the proportion who feel this way exceed one fourth. To the

TABLE 6.3   Perceived Family Burdens: Child Care Versus Elder Care, by Age of Respondent

| Respondent's age | N | Both are burdens | Percent who agree | |
			Elder care is a burden, child care is not	Child care is a burden, elder care is not
18-44	881	34	7	25
65 +	240	38	17	9

extent that perceived burdens become a rationale for government intervention, these differences suggest that some elders and young adults—a minority in each group—could become engaged in a tug of war over which of these forms of family caregiving should get the highest priority.

But the results allow for another interpretation. More than a third of all elders and young adults believe that the care of *both* elders and children is unduly burdensome. This suggests the potential for an *intergenerational coalition,* albeit one that does not yet represent a majority of public opinion.

Opportunity.   Most Americans remain optimistic about the opportunities for future cohorts, even the third that believe that their generation has not been able to do better than their parents' generation. But 10% think that opportunities are more limited for the latest cohort of young people, and another 12% are uncertain. One might expect that those who have in fact had a harder time themselves would be less optimistic about opportunities for the next generations, and that pessimism would be concentrated among economically disadvantaged groups (Heclo, 1988). Several groups appear to be prime candidates. Real income for nonaged Americans in the lower half of the income distribution (roughly speaking, annual household incomes under $30,000) has fallen over the past 15 years (Howe, 1990). African Americans have experienced the most extensive declines and see themselves as facing more limited opportunities than their white counterparts (Kluegel & Smith, 1986).

The results from the survey are somewhat surprising. Respondents in the lowest income brackets are substantially more optimistic about prospects for future cohorts than those in the highest income brackets. African Americans are more optimistic than others. This aspect of the American dream—the opportunity for young people to do better than their parents—thus appears remarkably resilient even for those with the most severe personal hardships.

The most substantial difference in cohort expectations is, interestingly, related to age. Young people are more pessimistic about future prospects than are older Americans. Sixty-six percent of those 65 and over, but only 53% of those under 25, *strongly* agree that young adults have opportunities to do better than their parents. (This difference is smaller when the "agree" and "strongly agree" categories are combined.) But the age difference is apparently less a product of personal experience than a general sense of trepidation, since those who have had more difficult personal histories (measured as change in their well-being over the past five years) are no more pessimistic than their peers. Young adults have not lost faith in the American dream, since they remain for the most part optimistic. However, they are less optimistic than are elders, and this difference could exacerbate tensions due to differences in the age-related needs reported above.

Perceptions, Frictions, and Political Influence

As noted earlier, intergenerational friction is more likely to occur among those who blame disparities across age groups or cohorts on the actions of the better-off group. A substantial number of Americans (37%) believe that elders' interests have been better represented than have the interests of children. Some of these individuals could become prime candidates for catalyzing intergenerational conflict. What distinguishes this group from other respondents?

Again, it has been hypothesized that younger economically disadvantaged groups who see themselves as politically disenfranchised will be most likely to interpret elders' disproportionate share of government benefits as the result of imbalanced political influence (Heclo, 1988; Longman, 1987). Data from the survey suggest that this portrayal is too simplistic. The perceptions of racial and ethnic minorities are sharply divergent: African Americans of working age (under age 65) are among the least likely to see elders as having greater political influence; Hispanics in the same age group are much more likely to perceive a political imbalance (Figure 6.9). Working-age respondents with incomes in the lower half of the income distribution are no more likely than other respondents to see elders as having more political influence than children. But respondents in very low income households (under $10,000 in annual incomes) are slightly more likely to feel that elders have more influence. And the elderly themselves are *most* likely

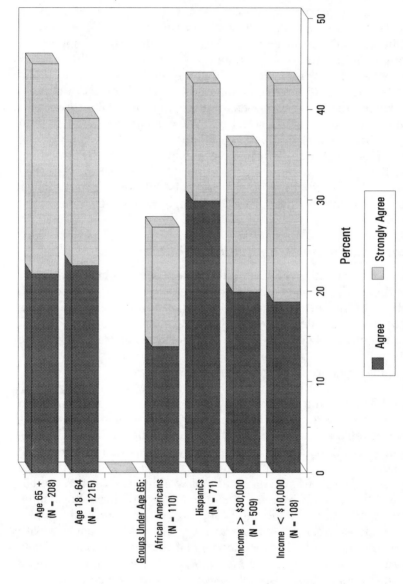

Figure 6.9 Perceptions of political influence: Percent agreeing that "Advocates for older Americans have been more successful than those for children," by age, ethnicity, and income.

to agree with this assessment. In no case, however, does the proportion who feel this way exceed 45%.

Although there has been considerable speculation suggesting that intergenerational tensions would emerge first among young, politically and economically disenfranchised groups, the survey data presented here show that these groups cannot be seen as homogeneous sources of tensions. Differences in perceptions among lower income households and between racial and ethnic minorities are striking. In Chapter 7, we explore more fully the personal characteristics, attitudes, and circumstances that are associated with higher levels of perceived burdens and reported tensions involving age-targeted government benefits.

DISCUSSION AND CONCLUSION

The findings from the intergenerational linkages survey shed considerable light on the nature and prevalence of intergenerational tensions. Given these findings, we now return to the questions with which we began this chapter.

How are Intergenerational Tensions Created? Most past discussions of intergenerational equity have focused on what we have defined here as dissonance—a disparity between how age groups are seen to be treated, and how it is believed that they should be treated. The survey data suggest, however, that this source of tensions is not the most important in contemporary American society. Differences among Americans in how they think age groups should be treated, and differences among them in how they perceive them to be treated, are the most significant sources of tension and may potentially engender more intergenerational conflict.

How Prevalent are Intergenerational Tensions? The striking differences between the survey results and past assessments of the scope of intergenerational tensions can be explained in light of the various ways in which tensions can be defined and measured. The survey data suggest that the pool of Americans with the strongest potential for intergenerational conflict is small—perhaps 5–10% of the public. However, a much larger group, perhaps 15–20% of the public, feel some intergenerational tensions, as reflected in their beliefs that certain age groups are getting more than their fair share of government benefits. A larger group perceives burdens either for themselves or others from age-related needs—almost 30% concerning age-targeted federal government programs, 45–65% for familial obligations in general.

How are Tensions Distributed Among the American Public? Contrary to most predictions, intergenerational tensions do not appear to be concentrated among politically or economically disenfranchised groups. Younger Americans as a whole do appear to be less optimistic about their future opportunities, and more likely to feel burdened by familial obligations such as child care, than are elder Americans. If these differences grow or become embodied in political debates, they may become significant sources of intergenerational tension. But perhaps the most striking differences in norms and perceptions occur *among* the elderly, suggesting that *intragenerational* tension may become an important aspect of the politics of age-targeted government benefits.

It is important to set these specific findings in a broader conceptual context. We have suggested that it is misleading to portray generational conflict in the form of competition among organized interest groups, analogous to the tensions associated with competitive lobbying between business and organized labor. We see the most important sources of tensions resting in individual norms and perceptions, more analogous to the sources of racial tension and conflict that have long polarized American society. If intergenerational conflict involves interest groups, then disagreements about how to define equity within each group make it less likely that conflict will occur, because no group can establish a firm position conflicting with another (Kingson et al., 1986). If tensions are individualized, however, differences in norms may become an important source of tension, and potentially exacerbate intergenerational discord.

What do these findings suggest for generational relations in this country in the long term? As befits an era of political paradox, many of these implications are likely to play themselves out in seemingly paradoxical ways:

- *The Paradox of Displaced Compassion.* Elders are particularly sensitive to the burdens that their care creates for their extended families. Past studies suggest this reflects a strong empathetic bond with their children (Doty, 1986). But this very concern for others may create a situation in which elders are perceived politically as self-oriented. In emphasizing the family burdens of elder care, older Americans may be seen as protecting their own interests. Although motivated out of a concern for their children, they

may be accused of neglecting the well-being of younger generations by placing a higher priority on government benefits for
elder care than on government programs financing child care.

- *The Paradox of Age-Related Salience.* Reforms involving programs
  for the elderly naturally draw the greatest attention and concern
  from elders, and may be largely ignored by younger adults. This
  creates a situation in which elders become the most fervent
  advocates *and* the most committed opponents of a given reform.
  This can lead to important *intra*-generational tensions. In addition, because the general public (and many politicians) continue
  to assume that elders are a relatively homogeneous group,
  whichever side has the louder political voice may be assumed to
  represent the collective position of all elders. The divisions
  among elders will hamper the efforts of interest groups representing the elderly to speak with a coherent collective voice.
  This will in turn limit their ability to negotiate with other interest
  groups to promote intergenerational coalitions and diffuse intergenerational tensions.

- *The Paradox of an Ill-defined Social Contract.* Policymakers have
  never been explicit about the benefits that elders have "earned"
  under the auspices of Social Security. For example, should Social
  Security guarantee an adequate minimum retirement income?
  Should Medicare provide financial security against health care
  costs? This ambiguity allows many people to endorse the idea of
  a program, without much concern for its specific details. But it
  also creates the potential for considerable intergenerational tension. As the relative needs and well-being of different age groups
  and cohorts change over time, the norm of need suggests that
  program benefits should change as well. But because there was
  never a clear agreement on what those benefits were, much less
  what they should be, any particular change may be viewed as
  inequitable even by those who endorse this norm.

To date, intergenerational tensions and friction appear relatively
modest. The potential for conflict appears limited to less than 10% of
the population. Tensions are more widespread, but most who feel intergenerational tensions are unlikely to act upon them, since some tensions will be diffused by ties of empathy that cross generational boundaries. Nonetheless, as American society ages, the scope and intensity of
intergenerational stressors could increase, depending on the direction
of changes in major government spending and the perceptions of the

American public about the fairness of these changes. Without appropriate attention, each of these stressors could become a trouble spot in future political debates.

CHAPTER 7

The Sources of Intergenerational Burdens and Tensions

Mark Schlesinger and Karl Kronebusch

In Chapter 6 we described several different forms of intergenerational tensions, each of which was linked to a combination of public perceptions and attitudes. Identifying these different forms of tension reveals some of the various ways in which tensions can be generated. But this does not fully describe the *process* through which tensions emerge and are either exacerbated or diffused over time. The goal of this chapter is to develop a better understanding of this process. In so doing, we hope to more fully explain the nature of contemporary tensions and their future scope.

Public attitudes about societal equity have complicated origins (Hochschild, 1981; Kluegel & Smith, 1986). The particular factors that most influence these attitudes differ from one individual to the next, and any single survey can measure only a portion of the factors that may affect intergenerational relations. Statistical analyses that link these factors to reported tensions convey only the average associations reported by the survey respondents and say nothing about variations among the respondents.

To simplify our analysis, we focus in this chapter on the form of tension that we labeled *intergenerational dissonance* in Chapter 6, the perception that a particular age group is being treated in a manner that is unfair or inequitable. Although we have demonstrated that this is not necessarily the most prevalent form of intergenerational tension, it is the one most extensively discussed in past writings about intergenerational equity. These prior discussions provide us with implicit and explicit hypotheses about the factors that shape intergenerational tensions, hypotheses that can be at least partially tested using data from the 1990 AARP Intergenerational Linkages Survey. We provide these tests by estimating a set of regression models that link respondents' beliefs about the burdens and fairness of age-targeted public programs to their characteristics, attitudes, and perceptions. Findings from these analyses can be used to address several questions:

- To what extent do the assumptions made in most discussions about intergenerational equity accurately portray the attitudes and perceptions that shape reports of intergenerational tensions?
- Do reports of intergenerational tensions follow the multistage model of perceived burdens leading to reported tensions, as hypothesized in Chapter 6?
- What are the various norms of equity that are applied to determine whether a particular age group is getting its fair share of public resources?
- To what extent do the standards applied to children as recipients of public dollars differ from those applied to the elderly?

FRAMING THE ISSUES

The factors that influence assessments of intergenerational equity depend on Americans' assessments of burdens or fairness. Previous writing on this topic suggests that these judgments will be driven largely by concerns of self-interest, either directly or indirectly. Following from our discussion in Chapter 6, however, we believe that a broader array of perceptions and norms of equity are likely to play an important role.

COMMON ASSUMPTIONS IN THE INTERGENERATIONAL EQUITY DEBATE

A number of assumptions undergird most past writing about intergenerational equity. The first can be referred to as the *self-interest* hypothesis. It is generally assumed that people will judge the fairness of public programs largely in terms of the costs and benefits that these programs have for them, either directly or indirectly (Kreps, 1977;

Longman, 1987). This leads to a set of predictions about the groups that should report the greatest tensions involving age-targeted government benefits.

We would expect direct benefits and costs to differ by the age and economic well-being of the respondent. Therefore, with respect to benefits, a self-interested older respondent should report above average tensions for programs targeted to children, and below average tensions for programs benefiting the elderly. For younger respondents, these attitudes should be reversed. The costs of programs for the elderly fall most heavily on working-age adults with moderate incomes, since the payroll taxes that support Social Security and Medicare were until recently applied only to incomes below a specified ceiling (in 1993, about $55,000 a year). Conversely, programs for children are financed by a combination of general revenues and property taxes (for public education), which are borne to a somewhat greater extent by higher income recipients. Programs for children are more often means-tested, so that their benefits are limited to Americans with modest incomes. This combination of costs and benefits has led to predictions that tensions around programs for elders would be greatest among moderate-income, younger adults, with tensions around programs for children greatest among high-income older adults (Heclo, 1988; Longman, 1987; Richman & Stagner, 1986).

Individuals may also indirectly benefit from age-targeted public programs, if those programs assist family members they care about or feel some obligation to help. Programs for elders are thought to be embraced by working-age adults who care about the well-being of their parents, and programs for children are thought to be supported by elders who feel close to their grandchildren (Kingson, Hirshorn, & Cornman, 1986). For somewhat similar reasons, familial obligations create a class of people who benefit from public programs that relieve them of that obligation. For example, it is often argued that Social Security payments to elders also help their grown children, by reducing the need to financially assist their parents (Binstock, 1989). These indirect benefits may be greatest for women, who often have the closest intergenerational bonds and are the most likely to provide care for older and younger family members (Doty, 1986).

Such familial connections create what we will term the *family safety valve* hypothesis, which suggests that intergenerational tensions from age-targeted programs are reduced by the indirect benefits experienced by family members of other generations. This reduction in tensions will hold, of course, only for those who have family members of the relevant ages. Property taxes for public education benefit only those with children (or grandchildren), and payroll taxes indirectly benefit only those with living older parents. For example, among survey respondents aged 55 to 59, only 40% have at least one parent alive. It is only this group who will feel emotionally tied to elder beneficiaries, or potentially relieved of an obligation for caring for those beneficiaries.

Another common, though sometimes debated, assumption involves the extent to which the public perceives social issues in terms of age groups or cohorts. Much of the discussion of intergenerational equity presumes that people implicitly or explicitly compare the well-being of different age groups or generations (Longman, 1987; Thomson, 1993). This assumption has been questioned on the grounds that most Americans simply do not see themselves as part of an age group and do not define equity in these terms (Binstock, 1989; Kingson et al., 1986). Moreover, it is suggested that most people assess their well-being in terms of a life cycle, anticipating that they will benefit from certain programs when they are young and other programs when they are older (Bengtson & Murray, 1993; Foner, 1974; Kingson et al., 1986). Inherent in this competing hypothesis is the assumption that young people expect to have children at a certain age, to benefit from public education, and to receive the benefits of Medicare and Social Security when they reach retirement age.

RECASTING THE TERMS FOR MEASURING INTERGENERATIONAL TENSIONS

In most past discussions of intergenerational equity, notions of burden and tension are intertwined and are often treated as identical (Binney & Estes, 1988). In Chapter 6 we proposed a somewhat different way of framing the study of intergenerational discord. Several different levels of discontent were identified, ranging from burdens to tensions to friction among age groups. Although these different forms of discord are to some extent interconnected, we suggested that they are distinguishable from one another and exacerbated by somewhat different factors.

Perceptions of either burdens or tensions will depend on a basic comparison. A sense of burden results from a comparison of the perceived costs of age-targeted programs with the ability of the individual or society to shoulder those costs. Tensions follow from the comparison of the treatment of a particular age group (e.g., the burden that age-targeted benefits entail) against norms for how that group should be treated.

Within this common framework, different considerations shape each comparison. Burdens are affected primarily by perceptions, tensions by attitudes about societal equity. Consequently, not all burdens will lead to intergenerational tensions. Programs that meet age-related needs that are viewed as legitimate by all concerned will be supported, even if they are seen as burdensome. Conversely, tensions may arise in the absence of perceived burdens, if the programs designed to meet age-related needs are judged to have emerged from an inequitable political process.

One can thus view the process generating intergenerational tensions as beginning with burdens, which are translated into tensions in a manner that is mediated by other attitudes and perceptions. Some of these mediating factors diffuse or *buffer* tensions, others exacerbate or *catalyze* them.

The assumptions and hypotheses that underpin past discussions of intergenerational equity fit within this framework. Direct self-interest can shape both perceived burdens and tensions. The balance of costs and benefits from age-targeted programs depends on personal circumstances—the age and financial well-being of the respondent. Similarly, expectations of an improved personal financial situation in the future may prevent current burdens from being perceived as future tensions, while limited future opportunities may increase those tensions. Indirect benefits associated with familial bonds may reduce perceptions of burden from public programs, if these programs reduce familial obligations that might otherwise prove burdensome. Family connections may also diffuse tensions, by creating the possibility that the government benefits received by one generation will be shared with other generations within the family. Public perceptions that are cast in terms of age groups may affect perceived burdens, by juxtaposing the needs of some age groups with those of others. Cohort comparisons may diffuse or exacerbate tensions, depending on whether individuals believe that their cohort is experiencing greater or lesser opportunity than was available to previous cohorts.

Past discussions of intergenerational equity thus implicitly contain a set of assumptions or hypotheses about the ways in which people assess burden and judge equity. These generate a set of questions which can be explored using data from the intergenerational survey. Can one predict the extent of burdens associated with age-related programs based on perceptions of the aggregate costs of those programs, the probability that an individual will directly benefit from the program, the family connections to those who will directly benefit, or the relative needs of different age groups? To what extent are tensions associated with those programs linked to these perceived burdens? How are tensions associated with different standards of equity, or with either direct or indirect self-interest?

In this empirical analysis, *burdens* are measured using responses to the survey questions asking whether federal programs that provide benefits to older persons or to children are "too costly." Overall, 29% of the respondents felt that programs for elders were too costly and 22% felt this about programs for children. *Tensions* are measured by respondents' perceptions that either children or elders receive more than their fair share of government benefits. Eighteen percent agreed with this statement for children; an identical percentage agreed for elders.

In the analyses that follow, we relate these measures to two sets of regression models. The first set of models identifies *who* reports intergenerational discord. The measures of burden and tension are the dependent variables in regressions with sociodemographic characteristics of respondents as independent variables. We explore with these models the simple hypotheses of self-interest that predict that the greatest discontent with programs for elders will be found among disadvantaged working-age respondents, with the greatest tensions about programs for children found among the elderly. We then estimate a second set of regressions focusing on *why* respondents report intergenerational burdens and tensions. In these regressions, the independent variables are the attitudes and perceptions reported in the survey. These latter models provide some preliminary answers to the questions about the origins of intergenerational tension in contemporary American society. Complete results from the regressions are provided in Tables F.1 through F.4 in Appendix F.

WHO FEELS INTERGENERATIONAL BURDENS OR TENSIONS?

Past writings on issues of intergenerational equity presume a primary role for direct self-interest, predicting that the greatest tensions around programs for elders would be found among young adults in economically and politically disadvantaged groups (Hayes-Batista,

Schink, & Chapa, 1988; Longman, 1987). Tensions and burdens associated with programs for children are argued to be highest among those who have no children in their households, primarily older adults (Richman & Stagner, 1986).

To test these predictions, the explanatory variables in each regression model include measures (age, race, ethnicity, and socioeconomic status) that are generally thought to identify the economically and politically disadvantaged (Kluegel & Smith, 1986; Palmer, Smeeding, & Torrey, 1988). The results of these regressions (Tables F.1 and F.2) suggest that direct self-interest offers at best an incomplete explanation for observed patterns of intergenerational burdens and tensions.

Race/Ethnicity. Racial and ethnic minorities are no more likely to report intergenerational burdens or tensions than otherwise comparable non-Hispanic whites. Controlling for socioeconomic status, African Americans are significantly less likely to report tensions around government benefits for elders.

Unemployed Status. Respondents who are unemployed are more likely than others to feel burdened by the costs of programs for either children or elders. But the unemployed were no more likely than other respondents to feel that elders or children received an excessive share of benefits. For this group, being disadvantaged seems to foster a sense of burden, but does not lead to greater intergenerational tensions.

Income. The relationship between income and burdens or tensions is complicated. Burdens and tensions are most often reported by two income groups. The first includes those whose incomes are modest, but too large to be eligible for most means-tested government benefits. Respondents who feel more burdened by their limited financial means may also feel unfairly excluded from government assistance (Coughlin, 1980).

A second, more surprising, finding is that both burdens and tensions are reported relatively often among those who are financially best-off. This is *not* because this group is more burdened by federal taxes; taken in aggregate, federal taxes in 1990 represented about the same fraction of income for the well-to-do as for the middle class (U.S. Department of Commerce, 1991).

In assessing benefits to the elderly, respondents with household incomes between $75,000 and $100,000 are by far the most likely to report intergenerational tensions, yet they are relatively unlikely to report perceived burdens. Here then is an example that runs in exactly the opposite direction as unemployment; tensions exist even where there is no evidence of perceived burden. This anomaly is perhaps explained by the generally positive relationship between higher income and conservative political philosophies. Wealthier Americans are more likely than the less wealthy to resent and oppose government benefits that are funded by income-based taxes—no matter whom they benefit.

Education. Limited education is quite strongly linked to both burdens and tensions. Because education and income are correlated, past studies confused the influence of one with the influence of the other. Comparing two otherwise similar respondents, the one with postgraduate training is 20–25% less likely to perceive burdens than the respondent with a grade school education. Better educated respondents are also less likely to report tensions involving government benefits for children, but not for elders.

There are a variety of possible explanations for the relationship between education and reported burdens or tensions. Some, however, appear to be more compatible with our other findings. Because these regressions control for the age of the respondent, the correlations with education are not simply the result of higher education in the younger cohorts, who might also have children at home and thus support benefits for children out of self-interest. (We show later in the chapter that having children living at home is not in any case related to tensions or burdens involving government programs for children.) A more plausible explanation involves the relationship between education and perceptions documented in Chapter 6: More educated respondents believe that children are worse-off than other age groups. We demonstrate later in this chapter that perceptions of relative well-being are important predictors of reported tensions for age-related government programs.

Age. Reported intergenerational burdens and tensions also have a complicated relationship with the age of the respondent. Overall, the age pattern for the perceived intergenerational burdens of federal programs is not very pronounced. Perception of *burden* from government benefits for elders follows a generally U-shaped relationship—reports of stress are highest in the very young (aged 18–24) and those 65 and over, although they dip back down for those 75 and over. Reported burdens in the younger group are consistent with the self-interest hypothesis; reported burdens by the older group fly in its face.

Age differences associated with *tensions* about government benefits are more striking. Tensions around benefits for *elders* follow roughly the same U-shaped pattern as burdens; reports of tensions over elder benefits are highest in the old and the young. In contrast to feelings of burden, however, the pattern for tensions is more pronounced and there is no decline among those aged 75 and over. Here again is a group that is more likely to feel tensions without reporting comparably higher burdens. It is not surprising that the oldest respondents are not burdened by programs such as Medicare or Social Security, which are financed through payroll taxes. It is interesting that these oldest respondents do feel tensions about these benefits, perhaps reflecting their concern that the programs might have become too costly for society to continue to support.

Burdens from programs for *children* follow a similar age pattern as for elder programs, but tensions follow a different pattern. Tensions are less likely in young adults, but more likely for those above age 45. Both the middle-aged and the elderly report more tensions than burdens. Elders report burdens about as often as do young adults, but report tensions much more often.

Consequently, only attitudes towards benefits for children fit a simple model of age-based self-interest—young adults are the least likely to report tensions, older adults the most likely. More often, the findings run *counter* to stereotypes from the debate around intergenerational equity. Reports of tensions and burdens involving elder programs are highest among elders themselves. The most disadvantaged are not those feeling the greatest discord, although the unemployed do feel burdened by federal benefits. Tensions are reported most often from those with the greatest incomes. And we have documented that tensions and burdens are inconsistently related to one another. We have identified groups that are more likely to report burdens, but no more likely to report tensions, as well as other groups for whom tensions exist without a sense of burden. Next, we examine some of the attitudes and perceptions that might account for these patterns.

WHY MIGHT SOME PEOPLE FEEL INTERGENERATIONAL BURDENS OR TENSIONS MORE THAN OTHERS?

Past discussions of intergenerational equity suggest that various attitudes and perceptions, along with a respondent's age and family situation, will shape reports of intergenerational burdens and tensions. To assess the importance of each of these factors, we estimated four regression models. In the first two regressions, the dependent variables were the measures of burdens from age-related federal programs, analyzed separately for programs for children and elders (Table F.3). The second two regressions use measures of tensions as the dependent variables (Table F.4). The reported measure of burden is included in the second two regressions as an explanatory variable, to determine if in fact perceived burdens are associated with greater reported tensions. The complete results are presented in Appendix F and are summarized below.

SOURCES OF INTERGENERATIONAL BURDENS FROM FEDERAL PROGRAMS

We hypothesized that perceptions of burdens of age-targeted federal benefits are shaped by respondents' assessments of the value of using societal resources in various ways. Burdens thus depend on the costs of the age-targeted benefit, measured against other competing needs and a person's financial ability to pay for those needs. More specifically, this involves five considerations: (a) the perceived size of the age group that is receiving benefits, and thus the aggregate cost of the program; (b) the perceived importance of other needs that compete for societal resources; (c) the emotional reward that people experience when government benefits help those whom they care about; (d) the extent to which government benefits relieve individuals of the burdens of personal responsibility to help family members; and (e) respondents' perceived ability to pay for those government programs. These factors may either exacerbate or reduce perceived burdens.

Factors that Exacerbate Burdens

The two factors that are likely to exacerbate perceived burdens from age-targeted programs involve the anticipated costs of the program benefits and a sense that there are societal needs that deserve more priority for federal spending. These factors are in turn affected by public perceptions of the size of the age groups receiving benefits and the intensity of needs of Americans of various ages.

Costs of Programs

All else equal, the more that government programs for the old or the young are expected to cost, the more they will be seen as burdensome. Costs are a product of the generosity of the benefits and the number of beneficiaries. The first open political discussions about intergenerational tensions around the Social Security program began almost immediately after benefits were substantially expanded in 1972 (Kreps, 1977). Scholars began to write about intergenerational tensions during this same period.

It is unlikely that most Americans have an accurate impression of the number of needy children or elders in the country as a whole (Kluegel & Smith, 1986). Their perceptions are more likely to be shaped by their experience in their own communities. At this level, they can make some firsthand assessments of how many people are likely to benefit. Therefore, people in communities with large numbers of low-income elders or children should be most likely to claim that benefits for these groups are burdensome.

Measures. The survey did not ask respondents about how many people they thought would use government programs for children or elders. As an indirect measure of this exposure, we use data on the low-income population in the county in which the respondent lived. In each community, the greater the proportion of poor who are children, the more respondents should expect national programs for children to cost. The greater the proportion of poor who are elders, the more programs for the elderly should cost.

Findings. The size of the age group that would be receiving benefits was among the factors consistently related to reported burdens. Respondents who live in communities in which many of the poor are children more often report burdens from federal programs for children. Similarly, respondents who live in communities in which many of the poor are elders more often report burdens from federal benefits for elders. It thus seems quite likely that public perceptions of burden are shaped in significant ways by the demographics of local communities, which serve as a lens that colors an individual's perception of the country as a whole.

Competing Needs

Regardless of expense, the extent to which benefits to children or elders are seen as a burden will depend on perceptions of competing needs. The larger these other needs are, the more likely that particular age-targeted benefits are seen as excessive. A crucial issue in the formation of intergenerational tensions is whether the public sees the needs of one age group as competing with those of another.

Measures. To assess burdens from federal programs for *elders,* we measure competing needs by whether respondents feel that (a) the costs of child care are too big a burden for many families, (b) most communities cannot afford a "quality public education," and (c) most employers are unable to pay for the health care costs of their employees and families. Each of these beliefs represents an important social problem that could be better addressed by diverting resources away from programs for elders. The proportion of respondents agreeing that each of these was a substantial problem was 62%, 30%, and 48%, respectively.

In measuring the burden of federal programs for *children,* the question on child care was replaced by a comparable question about families caring for frail elder parents. Forty-five percent of the respondents felt that elder care was too big a burden for most families.

Findings. The greater are competing needs, the more evident are burdens from age-targeted programs. This is true for all three measures of competing need: unmet family needs, educational needs, and health care needs. These findings also provide evidence that the competing needs of different age groups add to perceptions of burden to a significant extent. The unmet need that most exacerbates perceived burdens from federal benefits to elders was the concern that communities could not pay for an adequate education. Concerns about the burden of federal benefits to children were heightened by the belief that families were being overburdened by the need to care for frail elders. Interestingly, however, perceived burdens from federal programs for children were also highly sensitive to the perception that communities could not pay for an adequate education. In this case, it appears that locally financed needs, such as education, were seen to be competing with federally supported programs for children.

Factors that Reduce Burdens

Three factors have been predicted to reduce perceived burdens: emotional ties that cross generations; an intergenerational sense of family obligation; and resources of time and money.

Emotional Bonds

The extent to which those who are paying for federal programs feel emotionally connected to those who are the recipients of benefits is expected to reduce the perceived burden of those programs. Those who care about other generations are thought to see this commitment as a positive expression of generational solidarity, rather than a burden (Kingson et al., 1986).

Measures. We measure intergenerational emotional bonds using the measures of emotional closeness that were developed in Chapter

3. In assessing the burden of benefits for elders, we also include a measure of whether respondents agreed with the statement: "I've always known that I could count on my parents for emotional support when I needed it." Seventy-three percent of the sample agreed with the statement.

   Findings.   Whatever the effect of emotional bonds on intergenerational relationships within the family, they appear to have little impact on perceived burdens from age-targeted programs. Respondents who currently have close emotional bonds with their parents are no less likely to report that federal benefits for elders cost too much. Those who could count on emotional support from their parents in the past did report burdens less often, although this relationship was only marginally significant statistically.

Family Obligations

The second set of buffering factors involves a sense of obligation or commitment to help meet the needs of other age groups. These are predicted to create an indirect self-interest among caregivers in supporting the benefit programs, reducing the sense of burden.

   Measures.   We measure feelings of personal responsibility using data from the survey identifying (a) whether respondents have adult children or living parents and (b) whether they feel an obligation to assist them. Respondents were asked to agree or disagree with the statement that "grown children should not be expected to support their parents." Thirty-five percent of all respondents agreed. Respondents were also asked about parents' obligations to their grown children, in terms of (a) assistance in child care, (b) helping to meet the costs of housing and health care, and (c) leaving an inheritance. Support for these intergenerational obligations ranged between 34 and 44%. Because those who supported one obligation tended to support the others, these three questions were combined into a single variable measuring parental obligations to grown children.

   Findings.   Perceived familial obligations were not significantly related to reports of tensions or burdens. Nor was there even consistency in the directions of these relationships; the coefficients on the family obligations variables were as often positive as negative in sign.

Personal Circumstances and Resources

A fifth factor shaping perceived burdens is the relative well-being of those paying for federal programs. Two aspects of well-being are potentially important: time and financial resources. Those whose living arrangements allow them less free time are likely to feel more burdened by family obligations, and thus to be more accepting of public programs that would partially relieve them of these obligations (Doty, 1986). Conversely, those with limited financial resources are likely to feel more burdened by the taxes required to pay for federal benefits (Heclo, 1988; Longman, 1987).

Measures.   We measure time availability by whether the respondent is married, since couples have significantly more time for caregiving than single adults (Doty, 1986). For respondents who are married, we also assessed whether both husband and wife worked, since this should significantly reduce time available for caregiving (Hagestad, 1986). In addition we include a variable measuring whether the respondent is female, since women bear a disproportionate share of caregiving.

The availability of financial and other resources is measured through three variables: (a) whether respondents are employed or unemployed, (b) whether respondents' well-being has increased or decreased over the past five years, and (c) whether respondents see their own age group as relatively well-off financially, compared to other age groups.

Findings.   Personal circumstances have little influence on perceived burdens. Those who might have less time to meet family obligations (unmarried or two-earner households) were no less likely to see age-targeted benefits as burdensome than others. Women were as likely to see these programs as burdensome as were men, even though women might be expected to be the caregivers who would most benefit. Employment status or assessments of personal well-being have little relationship to perceived burden.

The one measure in this category that was consistently important involved respondents' perceptions of the financial well-being of their own age group. Those who see their own *age group* as relatively well-off were less likely to report that age-targeted benefits represented an undue burden. This effect was slightly larger for benefits targeted to elders, but was substantial for children's programs as well.

SOURCES OF INTERGENERATIONAL TENSIONS FROM GOVERNMENT PROGRAMS

All else equal, the greater the perceived burdens from federal benefits for elders and children, the greater the intergenerational tensions associated with those benefits. The statistical analyses presented here

(Table F.4) support the hypothesis that greater burdens are associated with greater tensions. For tensions around programs for children, perceived burden is the largest single influence on reported tensions. Consider two respondents, who have identical attitudes and perceptions, except that the first sees programs for children as not too costly, and the second feels they definitely cost too much. The second respondent is 22% more likely to report intergenerational tensions around these programs. The relationship of burdens to tensions around programs for the elderly is slightly less pronounced, but is still statistically significant and large in magnitude.

But we observed that people report intergenerational burdens without reporting intergenerational tensions and vice versa. We thus must look beyond perceived burdens to identify the factors that mediate the translation of burdens into tensions. These can be placed into two broad categories: considerations of fairness *(norms)*, and various types of personal expectations.

Norms of Equity

Controlling for differences in perceived burden, notions of fairness or equity are likely to shape intergenerational tensions in several ways. Most past discussions of intergenerational equity have focused on comparisons between age groups or cohorts (Longman, 1987; Preston, 1984; Thomson, 1993). But we believe that norms of fairness are also applied in broader ways, both to the programs that provide benefits and to societal institutions.

The "Deservingness" of Particular Age Groups

Given prevailing American values, two norms are most likely to legitimize special treatment for particular groups. The first involves *needs:* Groups that are seen as particularly needy merit greater assistance, even if the costs are burdensome (Hochschild, 1981; Kluegel & Smith, 1986). The rationalization of age-targeted programs on the basis of need might include the *needs of caregivers.* Almost two thirds of all Americans believe that child care has become too burdensome for most families. Almost half see the care of ailing elders as too burdensome. For these people, tensions around age-targeted programs would be reduced if the programs were seen as assisting caregivers.

A second potentially important norm involves *contribution*—those who contribute more to society are thought to deserve more in return (Hochschild, 1981). Those who think that elders or young people are making important contributions to society should thus be more willing to bear the cost of benefits directed to these groups.

Current contributions are only one aspect of this norm. Elders may be viewed as particularly deserving because they have contributed in the past, by having "earned" current benefits. As we observed in Chapter 6, more than 80% of the American public think about programs such as Social Security and Medicare as earned benefits. This measure of deservingness may also reduce intergenerational tension.

Measures.   *Need* was measured by the question asking respondents to rank the relative financial well-being of different age groups in the United States. (See Appendix F for details of this measure.) As discussed in Chapter 6, Americans are split in their perceptions of the relative financial status of children and elders, with the number of respondents seeing them as better-off than average equal to the number reporting them to be worse-off than average. One would anticipate that those in the first group (children and elders better-off) will feel the greatest intergenerational tensions, those in the second group (children and elders worse-off) the least.

Measures of family burden and the *needs of caregivers* were based on the questions about whether child care or elder care are too large a burden for most American families.

Measures of *contribution* were questions about whether "older people" and "younger people" were seen as making important contributions to their community. In response to this question, 73% saw elders as making important contributions; 43% thought that young people were making important contributions.

Because elders may also be seen to have earned special treatment as a result of their past efforts, we included responses to a question about whether senior discounts are fair because "older people deserve special treatment." Seventy-eight percent felt that they were. Because this belief was unrelated to people's perceptions of whether elders are needy, we believe that the "special treatment" is legitimized by elders' past contributions and seniority. The group agreeing that older people deserve special treatment should report fewer tensions around government benefits for elders.

Findings.   Perceptions of the relative financial well-being of different age groups appear to be strong predictors of intergenerational tensions. They are equally influential for tensions around programs for children and elders (with one important exception, discussed below). Those who feel that children or elders are better-off financially more often report tensions around age-targeted benefits. This effect is particularly striking involving benefits for elders; it is two-and-a-half times as large as for children. It is the most influential predictor of intergenerational tensions for government benefits for older Americans. Again comparing two respondents with otherwise identical perceptions and attitudes, the respondent who thinks that elders are among the best-off financially is 79% more likely to report tensions around benefits for elders than a respondent who sees elders as among the financially worst-off.

The primary difference between tensions around programs for children and programs for elders appears in the link to caregivers. As hypothesized, if families are seen as unduly burdened by child care, tensions around government benefits for children are reduced. But the same is *not* true for elders. Tensions around government benefits to this group are entirely unrelated to perceptions that families are over-burdened when taking care of frail elders. This suggests that the public does not believe that existing government programs for elders are reducing caregivers' burdens.

Needs are not the only influential norm. Tensions around benefits for both children and elders are reduced by the perception that they are contributing to their community. This effect is somewhat larger for elders, suggesting that they are held more accountable to a norm of contribution. Respondents who think that elders deserve special treatment such as senior discounts are also less likely to report tensions about benefits targeted to elders.

Assessments of Programs Providing Age-Targeted Benefits

Perceptions of equity may also shape intergenerational tensions through judgments about the fairness of the programs that address age-related needs. Programs that are seen to operate unfairly are more likely to be sources of tension even if beneficiaries are seen as deserving assistance. One aspect of fairness involves the allocation of benefits among recipients. In the context of age-targeted programs, this becomes a concern for the *intra*-generational equity of the program. If the program is seen to benefit "undeserving" recipients in an age group, it will become a source of intergenerational tensions.

Similar considerations apply to the political process through which these programs are enacted. Americans strongly value norms of equal representation in the political sphere (Kluegel & Smith, 1986). Even burdensome programs will be more readily accepted if they are seen to have emerged from a just political process. If the political process is seen as biased toward a particular group, then even modest benefits for that group may lead to substantial tensions.

Measures.   To measure perceptions of fairness involving the allocation of age-targeted benefits, respondents were asked whether Social Security benefits and college assistance should be limited to those with annual family incomes of under $30,000. Twenty-three percent favor means-testing Social Security, 24% favor means-testing college assistance. Both groups should report greater tensions over existing government benefits, which are not strictly means-tested.

Fairness of the political process in terms of equal representation was measured by the belief that elders' advocates have been more successful than advocates for children. Almost 40% expressed this belief, which might heighten tensions around benefits for elders and diffuse tensions around benefits for children.

Findings.   Although typically overlooked in past discussions of intergenerational equity, perceptions of fairness in programs also appear to be important influences on tensions that may have intergenerational ramifications. Whether programs are targeted to children or elders, issues of *intra*-generational equity are associated with intergenerational discord. Respondents who think that these programs should be means-tested are more likely to report tensions. The effects are about equal in magnitude for benefits targeted to both the old and the young.

Perceptions of inequality in the political process affect tensions as well, but only in one direction. Respondents who believe that advocates for elders have more influence than advocates for children are more likely to report tensions around benefits for the elderly, but not around benefits for children. The magnitude of the effect on tensions for elder programs is substantial. Comparing two otherwise equivalent respondents, the one who feels that elders' advocates have clearly been more politically effective is 30% more likely to report tensions than the respondent who does not perceive that there is unequal political influence.

Assessments of Societal Institutions

A third context in which perceptions of fairness may affect intergenerational tensions involves perceptions about how just society is overall. The more people feel that social institutions are inequitable, the more they are likely to turn to "scapegoats" who somehow embody these inequities (American Association of Retired Persons, 1987). If a member of a particular group feels unfairly treated, all other groups getting public benefits may be seen to get more than their "fair share" (Hayes-Batista et al., 1988; Heclo, 1988). Similarly, if an individual thinks that government programs (or taxes) have simply become too large, then he or she may conclude that the beneficiaries of any and every government program are getting more than they deserve. For example, those who feel overburdened by taxes may express tensions about programs such as Medicare or Aid to Families with Dependent Children (AFDC) not because they are, respectively, government programs for elders and children, but simply because they require more tax dollars.

Measures. We measure two aspects of these broader concerns. The first involves the realization of what has often been characterized as the "American dream"—that each generation has a reasonable expectation of doing better than did its parents. When this expectation is violated, tensions may result. About a third of all respondents under the age of 50 reported that their parents' generation had a better standard of living than their own. This group may be more likely to judge existing programs to be unfair, particularly those that benefit elders, who were the more advantaged cohort (Thomson, 1993).

To measure discontent with the general role of government in American society, respondents were asked whether, if they were in need, they would prefer help from government or from their family. About two thirds favored the family. Those with a strong preference for family may report tensions around government benefits for elders or children simply because they are seen to inappropriately substitute for family support.

Findings. As anticipated, perceptions that one's parents' generation fared better than one's own were linked to tensions around age-targeted benefits. Contrary to expectations, this effect was larger for benefits targeted to children. (There was no significant increase in tensions around benefits targeted to elders.) Those who feel they have somehow lost ground in achieving the American dream thus appear antagonistic to all government benefits, but are significantly more hostile to government efforts that benefit children.

In contrast, the regressions provide no support for the hypothesis that preference for family aid would be associated with tensions around government benefits. Rather, respondents who were more family oriented were slightly less likely to report tensions about benefits for elders (although this was only marginally significant statistically).

Personal Expectations

A second set of factors predicted to affect intergenerational tensions involves the hypothesis of self-interest, measured by individuals' expected benefits from government programs and their expectations of their own well-being in the future.

Direct Benefits

From a simple model of self-interest, tensions associated with age-targeted benefits should be least prevalent among those who currently benefit directly from such programs. For programs such as Medicare and Social Security, current beneficiaries would include all elders and, for Medicare, disabled persons. Federal programs for children have a less clearly defined target group—some benefits are strictly mean-tested, and others, such as aid for education, are more widely available. Nevertheless, families with children are certainly more likely to benefit from these programs than are families without children.

A second group for whom tensions may be lower are those who can expect to benefit from the programs in the future. For example, it has been argued that tensions around programs for elders are diffused by the fact that most young people expect or aspire to live long enough to be a beneficiary one day (Foner, 1974). But for more than a decade, the majority of young Americans have been convinced that Social Security and Medicare would not remain solvent long enough for them to reap substantial benefits (Chen, 1989). Consequently, only middle-aged respondents may be sufficiently sure of future benefits that they feel less tension associated with programs for elders.

A comparable situation may exist involving government benefits for children. As families have fewer children and delay child-bearing, more households of child-bearing age actually have no children. Consequently, "child-bearing age" may have become a poorer predictor of the potential benefits that families expect from programs targeted to children (Richman & Stagner, 1986).

Changing family structure, however, may increase the perceived need for programs that serve age-related needs and thus reduce tensions. Government-supplied benefits may be particularly important for respondents who have divorced, since marital breakdown tends to disrupt networks of family support.

Measures. We measure expectations of benefits by the age of the respondents, by whether they currently have children, and by their marital status.

Findings. Models of direct self-interest suggest that elders and parents with children should be the least likely to report tensions about government programs for, respectively, the old and the young. However, self-interest (at least in this simple sense) is a poor predictor of intergenerational tensions associated with public programs. Respondents with children were no more likely than those without children to report tensions about programs for children. Elders, in contrast, were much more likely to report tensions involving programs of which they were the beneficiaries.

People who are divorced are less likely to report tensions involving government benefits for elders. This is consistent with the hypothesis that they feel that their family support network has been frayed by divorce. These respondents may see government assistance to elders as a welcome alternative resource. Curiously, this same effect does not extend to benefits for children, perhaps because government programs are not seen as substitutes for the nuclear family.

Indirect Benefits Through Intrafamily Transfers

Tensions around age-targeted programs may be reduced if people expect that any generation that gets benefits will share its windfall with family members who are younger or older. It has been argued that tensions created by programs such as Social Security are diffused by the expectation among young adults that benefits will eventually be shared with them, through gifts or inheritance (Kingson et al., 1986). This is another version of the family "safety valve" hypothesis.

For this to operate, individuals must have family members of the appropriate age, and must believe that older adults will help younger family members. Many young to middle-aged adults have living parents, but findings from our survey suggest that fewer than half of all young adult respondents believe that parents have any obligation to assist their adult children. One might expect that adult children who do think that their parents are obligated to assist them would be least concerned about government programs that make elders better-off, since the programs assist their parents who in turn are obligated to assist them.

Measures.   To measure these effects, we include variables measuring whether (a) the respondent has a family member in the appropriate age group; (b) the respondent believes that the other family member has an obligation to assist the respondent if the latter is needy; and (c) the respondent has actually received assistance in the past (gifts or help with tasks around the home) from the other generation, which might predict future transfers.

Findings.   The hypothesis that intergenerational tensions are reduced by actual or expected intrafamily transfers is not supported by these findings. Tensions around programs for children appear to be completely unrelated to whether the respondent has received, or expects to receive (if needed), assistance from younger generations. Tensions around programs for elders occur no less frequently among people who have received gifts or other assistance from their parents in the past. In fact, those who believe that parents are obligated to help grown children (through financial assistance or inheritance) actually are *more* likely to report tensions about benefits targeted to elders (though this relationship is only marginally significant statistically).

Personal Prospects

When future prospects are promising, current burdens may be borne without undue tension. This is particularly true for younger adults, who may expect as part of the normal life cycle to make sacrifices early in life, in return for later rewards (Foner, 1974). Conversely, those who anticipate no improvement in their well-being may feel greater tensions for any given level of burden.

Measures.   Respondents were asked to rate their current well-being (on a 10-point scale) as well as their expected well-being five years from the time of the interview. From this we calculated a variable measuring whether respondents expected their well-being to increase or decrease over the next five years. Fifty-four percent anticipated that their standard of living would improve, 13% that it would decline.

Findings.   Our analyses suggest that future personal prospects—at least as measured by expected well-being over the next five years—have no impact on perceived tensions. This provides further evidence that well-being at the individual level is a poor predictor of tensions at the societal level.

SUMMARY AND DISCUSSION

We have identified in this chapter a number of factors that appear to be related to perceived burdens and tensions associated with government benefits for children and elders. We have demonstrated that tensions emerge, at least in part, through a two-stage process. In the first stage, certain perceptions and experiences lead to the conclusion that age-targeted programs are too costly. In the second stage, all else equal, perceptions of burden foster intergenerational tensions. But other factors are at work as well, catalyzing or buffering potential tensions.

We can now return to the questions with which we began this chapter. What do our findings suggest about the assumptions common to the debate over intergenerational equity? The primacy of self-interest as a motive is assumed by virtually all writing on this topic. Those who predict substantial intergenerational tensions expect that these will occur among people who bear most of the costs but expect to personally receive few of the benefits from age-targeted programs (Longman, 1987). Those who expect tensions to be less common claim that potential tensions will be diffused by intergenerational connections within families, which lead to indirect benefits (self-interest) even for those who are not themselves program recipients (Kingson et al., 1986).

The findings reported here cast doubt on both these predictions. Personal self-interest (as measured by age, having children or elder parents, or personal financial situation) appears to have little influence on intergenerational tensions. Intergenerational family ties, whether based on emotional bonds or a sense of obligation, do little to reduce a sense of burden or diffuse tensions associated with age-targeted government programs. Personal circumstances do sometimes matter, but they do so in a complex and somewhat inconsistent manner. For example, those who are divorced, and who might need to rely on government programs to supplement a weakened system of family support, do in fact report fewer tensions around programs for elders. But divorce does not alter the tensions they report for programs benefiting children.

Self-interest thus seems a poor and inconsistent predictor of intergenerational tensions. A second assumption, much more debated in the literature on intergenerational equity, seems more robust. People do appear to think in terms of age groups and cohorts when making assessments that affect intergenerational burdens and tensions. Increased needs associated with one age group increase the burden reported for public programs benefiting other age groups. The worse-off financially one sees one's own age group, the greater the burden associated with government programs benefiting other ages. The better-off an age group is seen to be, the more tensions are reported around government programs targeted to that group. Conversely, the more that an age group is seen as contributing to society, the smaller the tensions. The more political influence that an age group has, the greater the tension around the government benefits that they receive. The more one cohort is seen to do less well than its parents, the greater the tensions around government programs for both old and young. One may argue that the allocation of public resources *should* not be judged by a comparison between age groups, but such comparisons are clearly important in the thinking of the American public today.

The second question that we raised addressed the relationship between burdens and tensions, which are often equated in the literature on intergenerational equity. Our analyses suggest that these concepts should be treated as distinct—that some people feel that age-targeted programs are burdensome, yet report no tensions about these programs, while others report tensions without a sense of burden. All else equal, a sense of burden does lead to tension, but other factors mediate this process.

The most important of these mediating factors are the norms of equity that are applied to judge whether particular age groups are being treated appropriately. Our analyses suggest that the norms of need and contribution both play a role in this assessment. And the norm of need is applied not only to the group that is the recipient of the services, but also their caregivers, at least in the case of programs targeted to children.

The results presented here also suggest that norms of fairness are applied to the programs that benefit an age group, as well as to the age group receiving benefits. Programs that are seen to unfairly distribute benefits are associated with intergenerational tension, even among those who feel that the beneficiary group deserves assistance. Those who believe that the political process is biased in favor of particular age groups report tensions more frequently around programs serving those groups, even if they are seen as needy or otherwise meriting benefits.

One important aspect of this analysis involves comparing the origins of reported burdens and tensions for programs benefiting elders and those targeted to children. For the most part, the processes which generate perceptions of burdens and tensions appear to be quite similar. Burdens are affected primarily by the anticipated size of the recipient group and the competing needs of other age groups, as well as the perceived financial well-being of the age group of the respondent. With both age groups, tensions are related to perceptions of the financial well-being of the age group, their contributions to society, the fairness with which programs distribute benefits among recipients, and the extent to which each age cohort can expect to do better than the one that preceded it. There are some notable differences: divorce affects tensions around programs for elders, but not those for children; caregiver burden affects tensions around programs for children, but not for elders. And the magnitude of the influence of certain attitudes and perceptions is different. Tensions around programs for elders, for example, appear to be more sensitive to both the group's relative financial status and their contributions to society than are tensions around programs for children.

We believe that these results provide some useful insights into the scope and nature of intergenerational tensions in contemporary American society. Do they say anything useful about the potential growth of tensions in the future? One common prediction is that future tensions will develop among groups that are economically and politically disenfranchised (Hayes-Batista et al., 1988; Heclo, 1988). Our findings cast doubt on this prediction. The groups that are most often expected to feel intergenerational tension—racial minorities and low-income populations—do not report burdens and tensions more often, and the regression analyses suggest that personal circumstances have little influence on expressions of intergenerational tension.

Our findings do suggest a second factor that may be of greater concern. Both tensions and burdens are strongly influenced by perceptions of how many "needy" members there are in each age group, of the group's financial well-being, and of their contribution to society. (In Chapter 4, similar factors were found to influence the likelihood and degree of formal and informal assistance in the community.) As suggested in Chapter 6, most people have little global sense of the status or actions of elders or children in the nation as a whole. Our analysis suggests that their impressions are shaped in part by characteristics of their local communities. But they can also be influenced by information and impressions conveyed through the media. If these perceptions are easily influenced, and are swayed in the relevant direction, then the extent of intergenerational tension could substantially increase.

As we emphasized at the beginning of this chapter, our analyses have been based on a simplified model of generational interactions. The analysis nevertheless reveals how complex these interactions can be. Far more study is required before we can adequately understand the processes that create intergenerational tensions and frictions. At this point, we are able to point to only the most obvious of these connections. But even a crude approximation gives us a better understanding of how to deal with intergenerational tensions in ways that may reduce frictions and establish stronger bonds among age groups and cohorts.

CHAPTER 8

Generational Linkages and Implications for Public Policy

Vern L. Bengtson and Robert A. Harootyan

It has been the goal of this study to examine the nature and extent of linkages between generations in American society today, as reflected in a nationally representative sample of 1,500 individuals age 18 and over who were interviewed in the 1990 AARP Intergenerational Linkages Survey. Our intent was to assess the concerns, perceptions, and exchanges that exist across age groups at three levels of social structure analysis: family, community, and nation. There were three general research questions that provided focus for the design and data analysis in this investigation:

1. What connections and conflicts are most evident across age groups and generations in America today, at the family, community, and societal levels of analysis?
2. How can these intergenerational linkages best be explained in terms of underlying theoretical dimensions—processes that may be "hidden" from current journalistic or political discussions, but made evident from concerted social science investigation?
3. What are the social and political implications of these connections, in the context of growing public concerns about intergenerational equity and age-based entitlement programs?

In reviewing the data reported in the preceding chapters, we have been struck by four general conclusions. First is the relative strength of the ties that bind generations and age groups in contemporary

American society. To cite some examples, the intergenerational bonds in today's extended families appear strong and are manifested in various sentiments and behaviors; there is considerable public support for current federal programs that benefit targeted age groups; and there is much evidence for mutual patterns of assistance and exchange between younger and older members of our society.

A second important conclusion from our survey is that heterogeneity is an important aspect of American cross-age relationships. For example, while closeness and contact within families are the most prevalent patterns within our sample, emotional distance and ritualized or obligatory patterns of helping emerged in the responses of a significant proportion of the survey respondents. While there is support from a vast majority of respondents for current federal policies supporting the aged, a significant minority feel these are too costly and should be revised. And a slightly smaller minority of respondents feel that federal programs benefiting children and youth are too costly.

Third, we have seen that the web of factors which can explain the attitudes and behaviors of Americans toward other age groups are complex and not intuitively obvious. Moreover, these intergenerational linkages exist in feelings, perceptions, and behaviors that are often unrecognized by pundits and politicians. They thus represent *hidden connections* across age groups in contemporary American society.

Fourth, these findings provide a warning to avoid overly simplistic or narrowly defined assessments concerning societal resources that are allocated across age groups. For one thing, measures of federal outlays to different age groups are only part of the picture of contemporary intergenerational exchanges; to these must be added state and local governmental expenditures, especially the large proportion that is targeted to education. For another, interactions among extended family members form a complex web of interdependent connections. And added to such family linkages are important interactions among community members, ranging from formal volunteer activities to day-to-day types of informal assistance that Americans provide to members of other age groups.

To this broad overview must be added the more specific findings of our study, which we will discuss in terms of six aspects of "hidden connections" between generations today as reflected in our data. Then we turn to a discussion of some policy implications and concerns suggested by these findings.

HIDDEN CONNECTIONS AND FAMILY
INTERGENERATIONAL SOLIDARITY

In Chapter 2 we examined generational linkages within the family, based on respondents' reports about relationships with parents, adult children, grandparents, and grandchildren. The conceptual framework involves six dimensions of intergenerational solidarity—structural, associational, affectual, consensual, normative, and functional—reflecting the complexity of contemporary intergenerational family bonds (Roberts, Richards, & Bengtson, 1991). Two general findings stand out. For one thing, most survey respondents perceive family intergenerational linkages as quite strong—surprisingly so, in the context of frequent media depictions today of family weakness. But second, these bonds differ across the six dimensions and on the basis of gender, age, parents' marital status, and socioeconomic characteristics—suggesting the heterogeneity and diversity of today's multigenerational families (see Bengtson, Rosenthal, & Burton, 1990; Maddox & Lawton, 1993).

Several specific findings support these conclusions. First, the large majority of adult children report some type of contact with their aging parents at least weekly, either by phone or in person. However, there are significant gender differences: Such contact is greater with mothers than with fathers. The gender difference is further highlighted when considering parents' marital status. Adult children report less closeness and contact with unmarried and remarried fathers, compared both to married fathers and to mothers regardless of their marital status. Second, nine out of ten adult children report feeling close to a parent: 63% feel "very close" and an additional 27% feel "somewhat close." Again there are gender differences: Higher proportions feel "very close" (73%) or "somewhat close" (an additional 24%) to their mothers than to their fathers (55% and 33%, respectively).

Third, the general sense of intergenerational closeness is even more pronounced for middle-aged and aging parents than for adult children. More than four out of five parents (84%) feel "very close" to their adult children, with an additional 15% feeling "somewhat close." This sense of closeness by parents is more evident toward children who are married than toward those who are not, perhaps reflecting greater likelihood of shared family experiences or the presence of grandchildren.

Fourth, our data suggest that the middle generation is the "pivot" in grandchild-grandparent relationships. Moreover, the greater the influence that grandparents had when one was a child, the greater is the emotional closeness felt with one's parents. Thus, one "hidden connection" at the family level is found in the bonds that transfer across multiple generations and relationships.

Fifth, our respondents report a high degree of help and assistance (functional solidarity) across family generations. And again, gender contributes to the greatest differences in these relationships. More children report exchanging assistance (either receiving or providing "hands-on" help) with mothers (about one third) than with fathers (about one fourth). Marital status and gender of both the adult child and the parent(s) influence the helping pattern, as with the other five solidarity dimensions. For example, mother–daughter assistance patterns are more prevalent than those of mothers and sons, especially if the mother is married (neither divorced nor widowed) and the daughter has children.

A sixth finding concerns normative solidarity—the sense of responsibility of adult children to parents, and of parents to adult children. Our data reflect a strong commitment by young adults to the norm of support for parents; at the same time, older parents generally do not believe such support should be expected. Only 19% of respondents aged 18–34 and 28% of those aged 35–44 agree with the statement, "Grown children should *not* be expected to support their parents." In contrast, 51% of respondents aged 45–64 and 55% of those aged 65 and over agree with the statement. Adult children strongly support intergenerational responsibility toward their parents, even though there is far less expectation by parents that such support be given.

HIDDEN CONNECTIONS IN FAMILY INTERGENERATIONAL RELATIONSHIPS

In Chapter 3 we examined the multidimensional complexities of family intergenerational relations in a quite different way. Using multivariate data reduction techniques, we discovered a set of dimensions that yielded ten patterns of relationships between adult children and parents in our sample. First, the analysis of the six solidarity dimensions yielded three underlying factors: opportunity for interaction; feelings of closeness or affinity; and helping behavior. Second, we were able to identify ten family interaction types based on respondents' reported levels of solidarity in these dimensions.

The most prevalent type of parent–adult child relationship in our sample is one we call *tight-knit-helping*, in which parent and child exhibit high levels on all three dimensions of intergenerational solidarity: high degrees of contact, feelings of closeness, and helping behaviors. This is true of both older parents' and adult children's perspectives. The second most frequent type reported by older parents is the *tight-knit-independent* (high opportunities for contact and high emotional affinity but low degree of helping behavior). The third most frequent is the *dispersed-independent* type (emotional closeness but low opportunities for interaction and low helping behaviors). (It should be noted that, although we use the term "independent" in describing these types, the survey did not elicit information about whether or not a respondent actually needed help from a parent or a child. Thus, inferences should not be made from these descriptions regarding the degree to which children or parents are fulfilling each others' needs.) These three types characterized 48% of the intergenerational relationships, as reported by the older parents in our survey.

The perceptions of adult children in the survey differed only slightly from those of parents. For children, like parents, the most frequent type is *tight-knit-helping;* but the second most prevalent type of relationship is *alienated-independent* (weak on all three dimensions, indicating both emotional detachment and lack of regular interaction). As with parents, the third most frequent relationship is *dispersed-independent.* These three most prevalent types account for 42% of all the relationships with their parents as reported by adult children.

What factors predict whether a parent–child relationship can be characterized as one type compared to another? First is marital status and parenthood. Being married and having children is more likely to yield a "tight-knit" relationship with parents. Second, gender of parent is also important, with mothers having stronger relationships than fathers with their adult children. For fathers in particular, divorce greatly disrupts and limits relationships with adult children. These data reiterate the important link of marital status and marital stability—in both the parents' and the children's generations—to intergenerational solidarity, and suggest again the heterogeneity of contemporary family intergenerational structures.

A third noteworthy factor in explaining intergenerational patterns is race. African American adult children were less likely than other adult children to report helping their parents. Similarly, African

American parents were more likely than other parents to report low help but high closeness with their adult children.

HIDDEN CONNECTIONS IN COMMUNITY LEVEL GIVING AND RECEIVING

We next sought to examine transfers of help and assistance across age groups that occur in the community: both formal volunteer activity and informal help provided to neighbors, friends, and other nonrelatives. Results reported in Chapter 4 indicate that community involvement is a primary way in which Americans of all ages share their social resources. Young, middle-aged, or old, our survey respondents exhibit a wide range of exchanges with members of their community who are not relatives. As with family relations, these exchanges are an important part of the social bonds that link persons within and across generations in American society.

The data presented in Chapter 4 demonstrate first that the majority of adult Americans (54%) are engaged in some kind of volunteer activities. Second, age can be a factor in various aspects of volunteering: While almost two thirds (65%) of persons aged 35–44 report volunteer activities, about one half of those aged 18–34, 45–64, and 65 and over are volunteers. Within the oldest group, 52% of those aged 65–74 are volunteers, compared to 40% of those aged 75 and over—an indicator of physiological challenges that can be barriers to such activity by the oldest members of society.

A third finding suggests the importance of going beyond such percentages. We asked those who are volunteers to estimate the number of hours per month they volunteer—a measure of *intensity* of volunteering. While older persons have the lowest *rate* of volunteering, they devote the highest average hours per month of all age groups (23 hours, compared to an average of 17 hours for all volunteers in the sample). Volunteers aged 65–74 spend, on average, 26 hours per month in such activity—the highest intensity of any age group. These data reflect a notably high level of commitment among older persons once they become volunteers.

Fourth, religious institutions are the most prevalent context for volunteer activity among our respondents, a finding corroborated in other national surveys. More than 45% of all volunteers offer at least part of their time through a church, synagogue, or other religious organization. This is particularly true of the oldest age group, where 54% report this type of volunteering. Educational activity such as tutoring is the second most prevalent context of volunteering (21%). In this case, the oldest volunteers are the least likely to be involved.

Fifth, the data in Chapter 4 also provide new information about the *intergenerational* context of volunteer activity. How much do volunteer activities by one age group specifically benefit another age group? For this analysis we used three age categories to specify the beneficiary groups: children and teenagers, adults aged 20 to 59, and older persons aged 60 and over.

Of those in the sample who are volunteers, two thirds devote time in programs benefiting children and teenagers; but only 35% of volunteers aged 65 and over report such youth-related activities. Using multivariate analyses, we discerned four factors relating to youth-oriented volunteering: educational attainment, an orientation to needs-based rather than age-based programs, strong ties with an adult child, and younger age of the volunteer.

Intergenerational volunteering that benefits older people, by contrast, is more prevalent among respondents who are older, have contact with and emotional closeness to grandparents, and have contact with an adult child—reflecting links between family ties and community-based exchanges.

A sixth finding is that *informal* assistance to relatives, friends, neighbors, and other nonrelatives remains the norm, with more than 70% of our sample reporting they provide such help. As with formal volunteering, the stronger the individual's emotional bonds to family, and the higher the educational level, the more likely that informal types of assistance will be given to both relatives and nonrelatives. Another interesting finding is that older persons neither provide nor receive as much informal help (from persons outside their households) as do younger persons. Age differences also exist in the *types* of informal assistance provided and received, which indicate life course changes in needs as well as abilities. These data reflect the great diversity among adult Americans and, in particular, persons aged 45 and over.

HIDDEN CONNECTIONS AND INTERGENERATIONAL TRANSFERS: PUBLIC AND PRIVATE

We moved next to the macrosocial level of linkages across age groups in contemporary American society, addressing some popular misconceptions about the distribution of societal resources by age. Chapter 5 analyzed transfers across, as well as within, age groups by providing an estimate of the economic value of the various types of transfers (both given and received) that were reported by our respondents in terms of volunteer activity, informal assistance, shared housing, gifts, and bequests. A principal goal of this analysis was to develop (perhaps for the first time) some monetary estimates of the wide array of private resource flows across generations—transfers that are not readily measured in the usual statistics that cite only federal or government outlays across different age groups.

The data presented in Chapter 5 indicate that these private-resource flows, although largely hidden from view, are a surprisingly large and important part of the intergenerational distribution of societal resources. The estimates we report are approximations of the actual monetary value of each type of cross-age group transfer, using a variety of assumptions and measures to calculate their worth. Three findings stand out from this complex analysis.

First, the value of these "hidden" private cross-generational transfers, according to estimates in Chapter 5, was about $1.14 trillion in 1990. This is an astonishing figure. It is about 1.5 times the $780 billion in total government expenditures—federal, state, and local combined—that directly benefited the elderly and children in 1990 (Gist & Aleksa, 1991; U.S. House of Representatives, 1991). These *intergenerational* private transfers—calculated by using the data on giving and receiving across the same three age groups described above—account for 69% of the monetary value of all private transfers.

Second, our data indicate that the bulk of private intergenerational transfers flows *down* the generational ladder, from elders to middle-aged persons and youth. Moreover, more than three fourths of the value of these transfers occurs within families, primarily from parents to children and grandchildren. Each type of transfer shows a different age (or life cycle stage) pattern of giving and receiving. For example, while the monetary value of personal assistance is relatively constant across generations, the private costs of raising young children are concentrated in the age 25–44 group. Costs of college education and shared housing provided to adult children are borne primarily by those aged 45–54, while the value of gifts and major financial assistance to other generations peaks among those aged 55–64. The total monetary value of volunteer activities is highest among persons aged 65–74.

Third, which age groups are net givers and which are net receivers depends on the type of intergenerational transfer identified. Estimates in Chapter 5 included a set of age-based figures—generational account-ings—that identify specific components of transfers. When transfers are limited to interhousehold private transfers that exclude bequests, those aged 55–64 are the largest net givers. When we use a broader definition that includes both inter- and intrahousehold transfers, those aged 35–44 emerge as the peak givers. When transfers are most broad-ly defined to include both bequests given and inheritances received, the oldest age group (65 and over) shows the greatest increment in net giving. Indeed, our analysis shows that elders as a group give more in private transfers than they receive.

Finally, it is important to note that it is only when *public* transfers are considered that the older population becomes a net recipient of generational transfers. To omit the vast amounts of private transfers from any "generational accounting" is to seriously misrepresent the sit-uation. Yet this is precisely what some econometric models have done; an example is Kotlikoff's (1992) analysis of the inequity between what current Social Security beneficiaries receive compared to 40-year-olds when they retire, as a ratio of federal tax payments to benefits.

Nevertheless, how the public *perceives* such net transfers can influ-ence their attitudes about the relative distribution of resources across generations. Indeed, perceptions of "injustice" in the value of different types of transfers across age groups may create intergenerational stresses and tensions; and this is the topic to which we turned next in our analysis.

HIDDEN CONNECTIONS AND INTERGENERATIONAL TENSIONS

The attitudes and opinions of individuals about members of other age groups represent another important dimension of current intergenera-tional linkages. For more than a decade there have been increasing claims of tensions between age groups in American society (see Marshall, Cook, & Marshall, 1993; Quadagno, 1991), leading some to predict significant intergenerational conflict in the decades to come (Longman, 1987; Preston, 1984).

In Chapter 6 we analyzed opinions and attitudes about the relative well-being of different age groups and the distribution of government benefits among them. We found, contrary to some assertions about substantial age group animosity, that no more than 30% of the survey respondents express attitudes and opinions that reflect *any* type of tensions or frictions about other generations or the government benefits they receive.

To better understand the nature of these perceptions and their relevance to intergenerational relations, we made conceptually important distinctions between "stressors," "tensions," and "frictions" in cross-generational relations. First, we note that many intergenerational *stressors* (defined as demands that impinge on personal well-being and become burdens for members of one age group) exist in society, but that these are unlikely by themselves to lead to more intense feelings of tension or friction. Second, generational *tensions* arise when perceived burdens are also seen to benefit another age group inequitably or unfairly. Third, *friction* occurs when the inequitable distribution of societal resources is attributed to the relative power of one age group compared to another. These intense feelings, in turn, are most likely to lead to intergenerational *conflict:* open disagreements in the public or private realm between age groups or those who represent them.

When we asked respondents their opinions about the relative financial well-being of children and older persons, responses varied widely. While recent media attention has focused on the financial plight of children and youth in current American society, our results indicate that the public is divided in their perceptions; 14% view children as financially the worst-off age group, and 11% think of elders as the worst-off. About one fifth see *both* groups as well-off, while another one fifth see both groups as badly off. Clearly, such diverse perceptions indicate no groundswell of opinion identifying one generation as better off than another, although the differences in perceived well-being may themselves become a source of intergenerational tension.

But we did find stressors in the public's responses about the costs or demands of age-related programs or needs. For example, two thirds believe that the cost of child care is an excessive burden for *families;* one third feel that public education is too expensive for local *communities;* and 30% think that *federal* programs for the elderly are too costly. These data suggest that perceptions of burdens and benefits vary not only by the age groups responding but, more importantly, in terms of the benefit in question—public or private, national or local. And as noted above, these stressors do not necessarily translate into negative attitudes toward age groups per se. For example, of the 30% who express concern about the cost of federal benefits to older people, less than half feel that elders are receiving "more than their fair share" of such benefits. Notably, persons aged 65 and over are themselves as likely as those under age 65 to feel that elders are receiving more than their fair share of benefits. Among all respondents, equal proportions (18%) agree that either elders or children/ youth receive more than their fair share of government benefits. But among this 36% of respondents, one third of each group feel this way about *both* the elderly and the young. The remaining respondents (24%) are therefore equally divided in their opinions about which age group receives more than its fair share of government programs and tax benefits.

On the basis of these and other data presented in Chapter 6, we conclude that "generational warfare" is unlikely in the near future and could occur only if there were widespread evidence of generational *frictions*—perceptions by a significant majority of one age group that their well-being is threatened by the power and intentional actions of another age group. And our data indicate relatively little perception of such generational friction. For example, four out of five respondents of all ages agree that Social Security and Medicare are an "earned right" for older Americans.

It should be noted, however, that one half of respondents favor some type of change in Social Security or Medicare to account for income differences within entitlement groups. For example, 58% of the respondents agree that Medicare premiums should be based on income; over half of those aged 65 and over agree with this policy. Similarly, there is little difference by age among those who agree that Social Security benefits should be highest for those who are poor. More than half of those aged 50 and over feel this way, compared with 48% of those under age 50.

Later, in the section on policy implications of our findings, we describe some current features of Social Security and Medicare that do in fact recognize and account for income differences among either beneficiaries or tax payers. A considerable proportion of the public may be largely unaware of the income-related features of these federal entitlement programs. Yet many of those features are favored by at least half of our survey respondents, regardless of age. Such data show substantial agreement among age groups in attitudes toward age-related public benefits and support our general conclusion of surprisingly moderate intergenerational tension in American society today—"hidden connections" not often noted by journalists or politicians.

THE SOURCES OF INTERGENERATIONAL TENSIONS

Although we found relatively little prevalence of distinct intergenerational tensions, we noted the importance of recognizing where they do exist. In Chapter 7 we explored the origins of intergenerational tensions among the minority of survey respondents who reported them. A three-stage process was hypothesized: First, as noted earlier, people perceive different types of societal *stressors* related to the age-based distribution of societal resources, primarily in terms of their cost and relative burden. Second, these stressors may translate into felt *tensions,* based on perceptions that these costs and burdens are unfairly or inequitably distributed across age groups. Third, these tensions can lead to *friction* when the perceived inequities are attributed to the excess influence, power, or deliberate actions of one age group over another, thereby directly reducing the share of resources received by the disadvantaged group. We hypothesized from this model that generational *conflict* can arise from these frictions especially if advocate groups generate collective movements on behalf of one age group versus another.

The survey data indicate that no age group is perceived as much better off than the other, and that perceptions of burden are as likely to be felt by older as by younger age groups. Further, no age group is notably more likely than another to be perceived as receiving an inequitable share of such benefits. And where this *is* perceived, members of the advantaged age group are as likely to feel this way as others.

These empirical findings are, therefore, a contrast to general assumptions about generational animosity today. Less than 10% of all respondents express attitudes reflecting strong animosity or frictions about another age group. Indeed, such intergenerational friction is as likely to be directed toward the young as toward the old. Contrary to general assumptions, those who are the most financially well-off and who do not express high levels of burden are the *most* likely to express intergenerational friction. The importance of norms concerning equity is reflected in these findings: The greater the perception of unmet needs for one age group, the greater the tension about government benefits received by another age group, regardless of the respondent's age. Put another way, self-interest appears to be largely unrelated to intergenerational tensions, except for a small minority of respondents who are well-off or are pessimistic about their future standard of living.

Finally, our analyses suggest that this complex web of perceptions about societal intergenerational resource allocations appears to be independent of respondents' family interactions across the generations. Further analyses of the specific components of generational stressors, tensions, and frictions will be needed before we can project future trends in intergenerational linkages or conflicts. However, by understanding some of the origins of such tensions as hypothesized in Chapter 6, we may be able to reduce potentially damaging frictions and potential future conflict between age groups.

PUBLIC POLICY: THE IMPORTANCE OF GENERATIONALLY RELEVANT PERSPECTIVES

Although the primary goal of this study has been to describe and explain intergenerational linkages in American society, using concepts of basic research in the social sciences, the findings reviewed above also have relevance to many aspects of current and future public policy. We conclude by discussing several public policy issues that our findings might help to enlighten: policy about families and age groups, age-based versus needs-based eligibility criteria, long-term care in the context of family supports, and elder volunteerism as a community resource.

FAMILIES, GENERATIONS, AND PUBLIC POLICY

First, the importance of family relationships, at all stages of the life cycle, is evident from our data. We have noted the high degree of family solidarity reported by our respondents, while also indicating the less frequent patterns of alienation and limited interaction that characterize a minority of families. The prevalence of strong emotional ties within the majority of families, regardless of constraints such as lack of proximity or opportunity for face-to-face interaction, suggests that policies related to the well-being of family members will continue to be a dominant concern in the United States, as discussed below.

Second, during the next two decades policies related to the aging of the American population are likely to receive even more attention among policy makers, the elderly themselves, and those who care about them. The survey elicited respondents' opinions regarding specific government programs, such as Social Security and Medicare, and their attitudes about the principles or criteria upon which government benefits should be based. Our findings indicate that considerable support exists for four types of government programs or the eligibility criteria they use. These include (a) universal age-based entitlement programs that are considered to be earned rights for older Americans—specifically, Social Security retiree benefits and Medicare coverage; (b) needs-based benefits within an age-based entitlement program, such as Social Security benefits for dependent survivors and disabled persons; (c) means-tested benefits for low-income persons of all ages, such as Aid to Families with Dependent Children (AFDC), Medicaid, and the Food Stamp program; and (d) programs that combine means-tested eligibility criteria (low income and limited assets) with either age-based entitlement (elderly persons) or needs-based criteria (blind or disabled persons of any age), as in the Supplemental Security Income (SSI) program.

Third, such support is due in part to respondents' assessments of the relative value and fairness of those benefits. Our multivariate analyses indicate the importance of the public's perception that such benefits should be more equitably distributed according to need or as an earned right. The more positive the public's attitudes toward those groups who benefit from such programs, the greater the degree of support given for such benefits. Indeed, as noted in our summary of data concerning intergenerational tensions (Chapters 6 and 7) and patterns of volunteering and informal assistance (Chapter 4), altruistic values appear quite prevalent, regardless of individuals' age, income, race, or other characteristics.

However, it should be noted that a significant minority of the American public probably feel that some of these benefits are too costly. Ironically, a notably higher proportion of persons aged 65 and over than those aged 18–49 feel this way about federal benefits for the elderly (35% versus 26%, respectively) as well as for the young (31% versus 22%, respectively). But a smaller minority—no more than 20% in any age group—additionally believe that such benefits, whether targeted to the young or the old, are not only costly but also excessive or unfair as well.

Fourth, these data suggest that self-interest is neither strongly related to feelings of intergenerational tension nor a predictor of support for programs benefiting one's own age group. The majority of Americans—especially those who volunteer, who provide informal assistance in the community, and who support the types of government benefits described above—state their belief in sharing one's "wealth" or advantages with those who are in need.

Finally, our findings provide some insight concerning why recent family policy legislation, such as the Family and Medical Leave Act of 1993 (FMLA), has been enacted after many years of debate. The growing number of dual-earner couples and employed single parents with young children require flexible workplace policies to accommodate their child care needs. In addition, most Americans—regardless of their marital or parental status—are increasingly likely to face challenges of caregiving and other types of help for their aging parents, relatives, or friends. While our data indicate that the need for informal caregiving to elders may not be as high as sometimes suggested, the growing proportion of Americans aged 85 and older increases the *potential* need for elder caregiving in future years.

Heightened public awareness and understanding of the expanding demand for assistance with child care and elder care have created widespread support for the FMLA and other government policies that help family members fulfill their roles. As the United States population continues to age, as the proportion of women in the labor force stabilizes or increases, and as family members remain concerned about one another's well-being, policies that bolster intergenerational caregiving and assistance are likely to receive broad public support.

NEEDS-BASED AND AGE-BASED PUBLIC POLICY PERSPECTIVES

A second major policy debate that will continue into the future is whether policies and programs relevant to generations should be based primarily on economic need, primarily on age, or on some combination of both. The outcome of this debate has considerable import for the future well-being of Americans of all ages.

Our findings show, first, that the major federal programs benefiting older persons, disabled persons, and dependent survivors are generally supported by all age groups (see Cook and Barrett, 1993, for similar results in another nationwide study). But such support is grounded in sometimes paradoxical values and attitudes regarding government's role in the public's well-being. For example, a large majority (76%) of our sample agree that government benefits in general should be based on need instead of age (only 10% disagree). An even larger majority (82%) also believe that Social Security and Medicare benefits specifically are an earned right. These attitudes reflect considerable consensus about the social insurance principles upon which these two major programs are based. It appears that older people—the primary beneficiaries of these programs—are seen as both categorically needy *and* deserving of such benefits as a group. But nonelderly beneficiaries are considered entitled on the basis of need alone.

Second, the social insurance and age-based entitlement aspects of these programs are not universally endorsed by our survey respondents. Economic issues and concerns about equity surface in the specific opinions of some Americans about Social Security and Medicare. One fourth (24%) agree that households headed by someone aged 62 or over with a total income exceeding $35,000 should *not* receive Social Security benefits. As might be expected, the lower the socioeconomic status, the higher the proportion who feel this way. But surprisingly, persons aged 65 and over also are *most* likely (34%) to feel this way, even though 81% of the elderly feel that the benefits are an earned right. This anomaly suggests that a significant portion of the public— older as well as younger—apply somewhat conflicting norms to their evaluations of Social Security and those whom it benefits.

Moreover, a substantial minority feel that some type of income-related *adjustment* to entitlements is appropriate. About one fourth (23%) agree that Social Security benefits should be universal (provided to all who are entitled) but *also* included as taxable income. One third (33%) feel that the dollar value of Medicare benefits should be included as income for federal tax purposes. In neither of these cases do the proportions differ significantly by age group.

Thus, a significant minority of our sample feel that the economic status of beneficiaries is an important factor in how federal entitlement benefits are distributed. Wealthier people are seen as entitled to these benefits, like everyone else, but they are expected to assume a greater burden for receiving them. Norms about equity and fairness thus merge with norms about entitlement, universality, and earned rights in the opinions held by this subgroup of respondents.

A third set of findings reflect the blending of income-based with age-based approaches concerning entitlement programs. In response to a statement about the *funding* of Social Security, almost three fifths (58%) of the respondents believe that workers (and their employers) should pay Social Security (FICA) taxes on their *entire* income instead of the current maximum threshold (adjusted annually)—a policy that currently favors the highest paid workers. Not surprisingly, blue collar workers, persons with low income, and persons with less than a college degree are considerably more likely to feel this way. With little difference across age groups or socioeconomic levels, the majority (58%) of respondents also feel that Medicare premiums should be based on income.

It is therefore important to recognize that social insurance principles and the nature of entitlements are not unequivocally supported in our data. If recent declines in real income for most workers continue and the disparity in the distribution of wealth among American households increases (Mishel & Frankel, 1993), further encroachment in the support for age-based benefits could occur among a larger proportion of the public. Despite strong current support for Social Security and Medicare, these programs could become lightning rods for increased criticism if the strain between needs-based and age-based principles grows. Support could also weaken if a majority of Americans do not recognize the existing income-based features of those entitlements, or if such features are considered inadequate. Entitlements are, therefore, not necessarily sacrosanct. Although the Social Security OASDI Trust Funds are generating annual reserves in anticipation of much greater outlays for the burgeoning numbers of retirees after 2010, the funds are often erroneously viewed as contributing to, rather than ameliorating, the current federal budget deficit. Thus, entitlements such as Social Security could become increasingly challenged if *perceptions* of economic inequities between age groups in their funding or benefit structures become more prevalent.

Such economic pressures on the structure of entitlement programs are reflected in the recently passed Omnibus Budget Reconciliation Act (OBRA) of 1993. As with previous legislation, provisions in the OBRA chip away at the periphery of the Social Security program to increase its income-based sensitivity, while leaving intact its principles of universality and social insurance. First, the OBRA reiterates existing tax law that uses income level and marital status to determine which beneficiaries must report their annual Social Security benefit as income for federal tax purposes. Second, beginning in 1994 the proportion of a Social Security beneficiary's annual receipts subject to federal income tax was raised for higher-income single persons and married couples.

Prior to 1994, single persons and couples with "provisional income" (including one half of their Social Security benefit) above a certain amount paid federal income tax on 50% of the Social Security benefit they received. Taxpayers below these income thresholds did not include the Social Security amount for income tax purposes. In January 1994 the OBRA added a second income threshold that subjects the highest-income beneficiaries to taxes on up to 85% of their Social Security receipts. Single persons with income between $25,000 and $34,000 and married couples with income between $32,000 and $44,000 still have up to 50% of their Social Security benefit taxed. But for single persons with income of $34,000 or more, and married couples with joint income of $44,000 or more, up to 85% of their Social Security benefit amount is now subject to federal tax.

These changes in the OBRA reflect another step in the indirect merging of income-related characteristics of beneficiaries with the age-based entitlement features of the Social Security program. While all Americans aged 62 and over who have the minimum quarters of coverage (and their dependent survivors, or those who are disabled) are entitled to receive Social Security benefits, recent legislation has increased the likelihood that moderate- and high-income beneficiaries will "return" some of their benefit through federal income taxes.

As noted earlier, income differences are also partly accounted for by the benefit formula for Social Security. The formula is heavily weighted toward low-wage retirees, whose benefit amount represents a notably higher *proportion* (replacement rate) of their average earnings than the benefit for middle- and upper-income retirees. While the latter groups receive higher *dollar amounts* in benefits, their lifetime FICA tax payments are also higher. This occurs even though workers pay the Social Security portion of the FICA tax only on wages up to $60,000 (for 1994). Those earning more than the maximum are not taxed beyond that level, thus contributing a smaller proportion of their annual income (but a higher amount) than workers earning less than $60,000. As currently designed, however, Social Security will not provide more in retirement benefits, on average, than the value of payroll taxes paid, plus interest, for higher-income retirees who contributed near the maximum in FICA taxes. And many of these retirees are also required to pay federal income taxes on most of their benefit amount, as described above.

Changes to some features of the Medicare program also have made it more income sensitive while retaining its age-based entitlement. On the funding side, all eligible persons receive the same benefits, regardless of payroll taxes contributed. And most Medicare enrollees have the same cost sharing and monthly premiums. Only those with incomes below 120% of the federal poverty level receive subsidies for their cost sharing and premium expenses (through the Qualified Medicare Beneficiary Program).

It is clear, therefore, that universal entitlement programs are being amended with needs-based or income-based components, indicative of a general movement of federal policy toward needs-based criteria for eligibility (Torres-Gil, 1993). These policy trends appear to reflect a growing sensitivity by the public concerning needs-based and age-based approaches to government benefits. The survey data discussed above suggest that many Americans would support additional income sensitive or needs-related modifications to existing age-based entitlement programs.

Some observers suggest that the future will bring growing recognition and agreement that old age per se is no longer an appropriate categorical substitute for other characteristics that describe groups of people who are in need (for example, health status, functional ability, and income level). Some indicate that race is a strong predictor or categorical indicator of risk for poverty, illness, and other disadvantages (Jaynes & Williams, 1989). Indeed, the most recent amendments to the Older Americans Act (OAA) added more specific language in targeting services to persons aged 60 and over. Prior to 1992, the Act emphasized service to older persons with the greatest social and economic need. The Act now also stresses that preference be given to older individuals with the greatest economic or social need, with particular attention to low-income minority individuals (U.S. House of Representatives, 1993).

Although OAA programs are age-based entitlements for anyone aged 60 or over, they have become increasingly targeted on the basis of need. Such distinctions between age-based and needs-based criteria in policies for the elderly were presented more than a decade ago by Neugarten (1979). She predicted the growing irrelevance of age in comparison to measures of need as categorical criteria for government programs and policies; her suggestions centered on the goal of mainstreaming rather than segregating older people in society and in government policy.

Today, the age versus need debate appears to be focused on additional concerns, including those related to the burgeoning long-term costs of entitlement benefits. Many gerontological researchers and policy analysts are now suggesting ways to retain the universal nature of entitlements while increasing the targeting of benefits to those who are most in need or at risk of negative outcomes *within* an entitled group of beneficiaries. For example, Hudson (1993) uses the premise of social contingencies, suggesting that age itself was previously viewed as a contingent status, bringing with it a high likelihood of need (see also

Chapters 1 and 6 in this regard). But the contingency approach focuses on characteristics of need such as low income or poor health—characteristics for which chronological age may no longer be an appropriate categorical indicator. Reflecting the discussion above regarding the changes to Social Security under the OBRA, Hudson and others view the federal retirement income program as the best example of the increased blending of social contingency criteria with universalism. For example, the return rate based on retiree benefit formulas has consistently "favored" lower income workers, while higher income retirees are being required to pay more income tax on a larger proportion of their benefit.

The risk-sensitive or social contingency approach is seen as one way to reduce the dilemmas surrounding the political, ethical, and practical difficulties of eliminating entitlements while also responding to those who call for greater emphasis on needs-based criteria in public policies and benefit programs. These suggestions mirror the mixed feelings expressed by the great majority of our respondents. They, too, juxtapose needs-based criteria with the principle of earned rights in age-based entitlements under Social Security and Medicare. But a dilemma for these programs is that "universal" entitlement applies only to those who reach age 62 or 65 (for the OAA, age 60). Those who are younger are entitled to certain Social Security or Medicare benefits only on the basis of need.

Thus, we are not surprised that some political scientists foresee the eventual elimination of entitlement programs in favor of means-tested or needs-based criteria for Social Security retiree benefits (Binstock, 1993). Such dramatic change will be difficult if not impossible to achieve, because it eliminates the fundamental premise of social insurance that is so strongly supported by our survey respondents. Concerns for equity and parity do not translate into the rejection of universalism, age-based entitlements, or earned rights as elements of public policy.

But the general concern about fairness in the distribution of societal resources may continue to be reflected in incremental changes to current policy. For example, along with the changes noted above, the 1993 OBRA also made it more difficult for wealthy Americans to transfer their assets in order to meet the stringent *means-tested* eligibility standards for Medicaid long-term care coverage (primarily for nursing home care). At the same time, the OBRA increased the income and asset levels that can be retained by the spouses of eligible Medicaid beneficiaries. These changes, like those for entitlement programs, reflect increased attention to issues of equity and fairness in the allocation of public benefits in the United States.

LONG-TERM CARE AND FAMILY SUPPORTS

Other areas of public policy also have differential impacts on families and age groups. The most relevant programs are those providing either direct or indirect benefits for long-term care in institutions or in the home, but they form a patchwork quilt with vastly different approaches, eligibility criteria, and benefits that are confusing. Federal/state Medicaid benefits for long-term care are means-tested, and strongly favor nursing home over community- or home-based care. The Department of Veterans Affairs provides health and long-term care services only to veterans, and funds and regional allocations are limited. The Medicare entitlement provides limited coverage for certain needs-based long-term care: limited post-hospital stays in skilled nursing homes, rehabilitative services, and medically-required home-based care.

Each program—whether means-tested, needs-based, age-based, categorical, or mixed—has limitations that threaten the security of potential beneficiaries, as well as of those who care about them and care for them. The growing sense of insecurity about the costs and availability of health and long-term care benefits have spurred the current debate about health care reform. Indeed, a majority (57%) of our respondents agree that coverage of nursing home and home health care should be increased in the Medicare program, even if it requires higher federal taxes for everyone. Although this support varies somewhat by age (54% of those under age 50 compared to 66% of those 65 and over), a majority in each age group would welcome an expansion of these long-term care benefits.

Our data further indicate that most Americans support government policies that assist not only those in need, but also family members who are their caregivers—spouses or other relatives. Increased attention to community-based services for those in need of assistance would have multigenerational impact. Respite services, adult day care, and other community-based services would not only help those in need, but provide indirect assistance to those who provide informal care to these persons. These programs also relieve the stress and respond to the concerns of many family members who are unable to provide such assistance to elderly relatives. For example, our data indicate that despite the geographic dispersion of such families, the emotional bonds and concerns about each other's well-being remain strong. Public policies that help fill the gaps in caregiving and other types of family supports created by such dispersion are highly likely to be supported by most Americans.

The 1993 passage of the FMLA, mentioned above, is an example of public support for policies that respond to caregiver needs—in this case, in the private sector, namely, the workplace. We suggest that similar family-oriented motivations would engender support for public programs that assist caregivers. Along with direct benefits such as respite services and adult day care, policies providing *indirect* assistance would respond to the family and cross-generational orientations evident in our survey results.

Most studies show that the greatest needs expressed by family caregivers are for supportive services through programs such as home health care, respite services, and adult day care. Second to these are programs that provide emotional supports. Another form of assistance might be financial, such as a dependent tax credit for those who are full-time caregivers. Eligibility for the dependent tax credit to those who provide continuous care in their home to dependent family members would relieve some of the financial burden assumed by these caregivers, especially those who are less well-off. Such credits would be inversely related to the household income of the caregivers, thereby responding to public concerns about equity and income sensitivity in government benefit programs.

These components of a long-term care program would reflect the combined and complex emphases of a majority of our survey respondents on family well-being, altruism, universal entitlement, and income-sensitive policies. A national long-term care policy would be most strongly supported if it is a broad-based program that serves people of all ages (Hudson, 1993). In contrast, this study shows that current or future age-based entitlement programs may be increasingly challenged if *perceptions* of inequity overcome perceptions that they are earned rights for older Americans as a group. The importance of public perceptions about age groups and the relative share of societal resources each receives cannot be overemphasized.

Promoting Elder Volunteerism as a Community Resource

While many public policies are oriented toward serving older Americans, some focus on promoting their contributions to the community.

Although persons aged 65 and over are less likely to volunteer than other age groups, the level of activity among elders who *do* volunteer is higher than any other age group. Thus, policies that promote elder volunteerism are likely to be good public investments. Recent legislation that supports community service by all Americans includes programs specifically targeted to older participants.

The National Service Trust Act of 1993 provides funds for programs that support volunteer work by persons of all ages. But the Act has various age-targeted components. It incorporated the former Older Americans Volunteer Program into the new National Senior Volunteer Corps (NSVC), which includes programs that are needs-based and others that are only age-based. The Foster Grandparent Program (FGP) and the Senior Companion Program (SCP) combine both types of criteria for participation—they are open only to low-income persons aged 60 and over. Eligible participants receive stipends of $2.45 per hour for their volunteer work. Moreover, the programs are targeted to beneficiaries in specific age groups who have certain needs. FGP volunteers (numbering more than 27,000 in 1992) serve as surrogate grandparents to children with special needs, filling an intergenerational gap in the lives of many youngsters. An additional 12,000 SCP volunteers in 1992 helped adults with special needs, especially frail older persons living in the community.

These two programs exemplify public policies that benefit multiple clients across age groups: first, the elderly low-income participants who become volunteers; second, the children and adults with special needs who are served by these participants; and third, the families of those served. In addition to these age- and needs-based programs, the largest component of the NSVC is the Retired and Senior Volunteer Program (RSVP). The RSVP is now open to all persons aged 55 and over and accounts for more than 450,000 elderly volunteers who assist persons of all ages. Included under the umbrella of the 1993 Act are special projects that focus on volunteer assistance to school-age youth—some are part of the RSVP. Increased recruitment of older persons into these programs would promote greater intergenerational volunteering in the community.

Our data indicate that public investments in volunteerism are supported by the majority of Americans, who favor a combination of needs-based and age-based approaches in government programs. Such support also seems evident in the recent growth of *private* sector efforts that promote elder volunteerism, including nonprofit programs that focus on corporate support of volunteer activities by retired employees. Increased funding for programs at all levels of government, when combined with the multitude of nonprofit and private programs, could yield not only greater levels of volunteerism by elders in general but more intergenerational volunteering in particular.

CONCLUSION

The data reported in this volume suggest the following conclusions: (a) despite the unprecedented concern over possible generational conflicts today, strong connections between generations—in families as well as in the community—do create bridges between age groups in contemporary society; (b) many of these bridges are unrecognized by the media or given little political attention by policymakers; (c) the prevalence, scope, and value of private intergenerational transfers are much greater than generally assumed; and (d) the future of intergenerational relationships is not as pessimistic as some observers predict. Moreover, these results are relevant to some important policy discussions concerning relations between age groups, as reviewed in this chapter.

In future decades will we be able to realize the goal that Thomas Jefferson urged upon the founders of the American republic—that each generation should leave its successor no worse off than the preceding generation? Circumstances may have changed in the ensuing two centuries; but if the opinions, values, and behaviors reflected in our survey are any indication, this is a goal that is likely to still guide the behaviors of Americans for decades to come. And that is because the "hidden connections" between generations will continue to be an important aspect of social structure in the future, as they are now, and have been for many decades.

APPENDIX A

Appendix to Chapter 1
Methods and Procedures
of the Survey

The data on which the analyses in this volume are based were collected in 1990 from a nationwide probability sample of 1,500 Americans, aged 18 and above. DataStat, Inc., of Ann Arbor, Michigan, fielded the survey and developed the computerized database. Below are details concerning the methods and procedures of the survey.

The Survey Sample

The sampling frame consisted of all possible telephone numbers within the coterminous United States, capturing 95% of all households in the 48 contiguous states. The sampling method involved contacting households through computer-generated random-digit dialing until 1,500 complete interviews were obtained, yielding a simple random sample at that stage. To assure adherence to equal probability of selection methods ("epsem") and to minimize nonresponse, the system repeated the same telephone number on four different occasions (Kalton, 1983). The contact attempt was ended after four unsuccessful callbacks to the same number (699 cases fell into this category). An additional 659 calls that reached a nonhousehold (e.g., office, telephone pay station, college dormitory, nursing home, or boat) were excluded. Once interviews were begun, 142 respondents broke off the interview; an additional 107 were ineligible because of English language problems; and another 142 were ineligible due to severe hearing problems or other incapacity that prevented participation by telephone.

After a sample household was reached by telephone, one adult aged 18 or older was randomly selected as the designated respondent, based on which adult in the household had the most recent birthday. If that person was not available at the time of selection, an appointment was made for a recall. If the designated respondent was still not available at the appointed time, or the full sample was reached before the callback time, then that respondent was listed as not contacted (82 potential respondents fell into this category). The interviews were conducted during July and August, 1990. This timing increased the chances that college students who might otherwise have been excluded during the nonsummer months (i.e., in group quarters) were included in the random sample of adults aged 18+.

Survey Response Rate

To determine the response rate for the survey we followed the standard approach in most survey method guidelines (Fowler, 1984). When using a random telephone survey, telephone numbers that do not serve a residential unit (e.g., businesses, group quarters) and households with no eligible respondent are omitted in calculating response rates. Potential respondents who were reached but determined to be ineligible (e.g., due to language, hearing, or other problems) are usually included in the calculation, along with those who broke off an interview after it began. Thus, the best approximation of the survey response rate is 79% (1,500/1,891).

As Fowler suggests, however, a telephone survey response rate is uncertain if some units are never reached. In these cases both conservative and liberal calculations are made to indicate a range of response rates. Assuming that the same proportion of nonhouseholds existed among the 699 units that were never reached as were in the 2,550 that were reached, 74% of the unreached units (i.e., 517) would have had a possible respondent. Adding this group to the total of potential respondents yields a very conservative response rate of 62% (1,500/2,408). In contrast, if only persons who broke off an interview are included in the denominator, a very liberal response rate of 91% (1,500/1,642) is reached. Thus, the general response rate of 79% is a good estimate.

Weighting of the Sample

The data that are analyzed in this study are weighted to reflect a nationally representative sample of the United States population at the

time of the survey (U.S. Bureau of the Census, 1988a). Representativeness of the sample was deemed more important for the purposes of
this study than the potential inferential shortcomings of using weighted data in statistical analyses. These possible shortcomings are largely
avoided by use of poststratification fractional weighting for the entire
sample (Henry, 1990). Using this method, the sample size of 1,500 was
retained for integrity of the statistical tests and inferences.

Because each household in the survey had an equal probability of
selection, a self-weighting sample was achieved at that level (Lee,
Forthofer, & Lorimor, 1989). But the survey data were weighted to adjust
for differences in probability of a respondent's selection *within* a household. This inequality in selection probability was corrected by weighting
the data by the number of adults in the respondent's household.

The sample population was then poststratified on the basis of the
gender, age, and educational attainment of the United States population at the time of the survey. The weights were based on the most
recent census data on educational attainment. Table A.1 shows the differences in educational attainment of the sample before and after
weighting. As expected in a telephone survey, the sampling method
overrepresented persons with the highest levels of educational attainment compared to the national population and underrepresented persons with the lowest levels of education. The latter group is most likely
to be poor or to live in rural areas and group quarters, making them
least likely to have a private telephone line and thereby reducing their
probability of selection in the sample. The data in Table A.1 show that
the largest discrepancies between the weighted and unweighted samples were for both males and females who had less than a high school
education or who were college graduates.

Thus, the survey sample was weighted to increase the representation of the least educated and decrease the representation of the most
educated. As noted by some experts, such biases in self-weighted survey samples are well addressed by poststratification weighting methods (Holt & Smith, 1979). Because educational attainment, income, and
occupation are positively correlated, the weighted sample based on
educational attainment provides protection against any moderate or
extreme sample configurations for the socioeconomic characteristics
of this survey sample. Educational attainment data were obtained for
all 1,500 respondents, while information on occupation was given for
only 1,263 respondents. Because household income rather than
respondent's income was elicited, income data could not be used in
the weighting procedure.

TABLE A.1 Educational Attainment by Age and Gender for the Unweighted (U) and Weighted (W) Sample

| Educational attainment | Total | | Age | | | | | | Gender | | | |
| | | | 18-49 | | 50-64 | | 65 + | | Male | | Female | |
	U %	W %	U %	W %	U %	W %	U %	W %	U %	W %	U %	W %
Less than high school	13	24	8	16	25	30	31	49	14	24	13	24
High school graduate	37	39	38	41	42	41	31	30	33	36	40	42
Some college	23	19	25	22	15	14	19	10	23	18	22	19
College grad or higher	26	18	30	20	18	16	18	10	29	21	25	15

Poststratification not only improves the precision of the sample estimates of the United States population but also can reduce nonresponse and respondent refusal biases that are related to population composition. Using the weighted sample thus improves the inferential power of the analyses in this study. We feel that this methodology has permitted an accurate assessment of intergenerational linkages within the American population.

The distribution of the sample before and after weighting, by age, gender, race, ethnicity, and socioeconomic status, is shown in Table 1.1 (in Chapter 1). All results reported in this volume are based on the weighted sample.

The Interview

Interviews were conducted using Computer Assisted Telephone Interviewing (CATI). The CATI system is programmed to select appropriate questions automatically on the basis of preceding responses, thus eliminating inconsistencies due to complex skip patterns. The intergenerational survey required a large number of skip patterns, dependent upon factors such as marital status; the existence of one or more living parents, adult children, grandparent(s), or grandchildren; whether the respondent did volunteer work or gave large gifts to others; and numerous other characteristics. The CATI system is designed to produce a smooth flowing interview and reduce the likelihood of respondent breakoffs. The average interview required 35 minutes to complete. An abbreviated version of the survey instrument is shown in Appendix G.

Because of the CATI system's automatic skip patterns and its direct entry of interviewee's responses, data cleaning and editing were minimal. The system included automatic "fills," using responses to previous questions to logically answer an ensuing one. (For example, if both parents are alive and living together, the respondent is not asked if s/he has a stepparent and the CATI system automatically fills in the answer "no" for that question.)

Measurement of Variables

Race. In analyzing the survey data on the basis of race, the category "African Americans" is used in comparison to the category "others," which refers to all other respondents. The latter group includes whites and all other respondents who gave any response other than African American to the question on race.

Other measures—including those discussed in Chapter 1 regarding the use of age cohort, generation, or policy age group—are described in the chapters in which they are featured.

Analysis of the Data

All results reported in this volume, unless otherwise noted, are statistically significant at least at the .05 level of probability. In Chapters 2 and 3 significance testing was done in the regression analyses, as explained in Appendixes B and C.

Two basic kinds of analysis are reported in this study. In the first, simple bivariate percentage distributions are presented, either in figure or tabular form. In the second, the results of multivariate regression analyses are discussed in the text, with tables of complete results included in the Appendix to each chapter. Regression comprises a set of various analytic techniques that are used to indicate the strength of relationship between a factor (the dependent variable) and one or more other factors (independent variables), while holding other factors constant. Several forms of regression analysis are conducted, as appropriate to the particular variables being analyzed, and are described in each chapter.

APPENDIX B

Appendix to Chapter 2

$\mathbf{A}$ part of the analysis and discussion in Chapter 2 is based on simple percentage distributions. Another part is based on a series of multiple regression and logistic regression models. The tables for the coefficients from these regressions are presented in this Appendix (Tables B.1–B.9). In discussing the six dimensions of intergenerational solidarity, we first describe the profile of the sample on the relevant solidarity dimension (percentages). Then we discuss the family and individual characteristics that influence the strength and weakness of that dimension (multivariate analysis). It should be noted that regression analysis indicates that the percentage differences reported in the text are statistically significant *after* other factors are taken into account. It is possible that simple percentage differences between groups appear to be narrow or nonexistent when there are statistically significant differences between those same groups in regression equations. This can happen because other important factors are held constant when assessing differences in regression analysis.

Regression Analysis

The ordinary least squares regressions were used for the continuous, ordered dependent variables. Associational solidarity (frequency of contact) was measured by the number of visits and phone calls reported such that 10 was daily or more and 0 was never. Consensual solidarity was measured by a 4-point scale of similarity of opinions between two generations.

The logistic regressions were computed with an SAS proc logistic program, and the variables are dichotomous, taking on values 1 when the characteristic measured is present, and 0 if the characteristic is

241

absent. For example, respondents living with parents are coded 1, those not living with parents are 0. Logistic regressions were used in the structural solidarity model (coresidence, living within one hour) and in the model for affectual solidarity (close feelings).

Independent Variables

The sets of independent variables used in the models test for individual, family, and social structural variables. Some of the categorical variables are relatively straightforward (reference category in parentheses): males (females); African Americans (others); and home owners (not home owners).

There are several variations on the measure for marital status. When the respondent is the child in the parent–child dyad and grandchild in the grandchild–grandparent dyad, the categories are never married and separated/divorced, with the married (and the very few widowed) as the reference category. When the respondent is the parent, the categories are separated/divorced and widowed (married). Grandparents' marital status is denoted by widowed (married). When the parent is the respondent, the oldest child's marital status is married (not married). Finally, when the child is the respondent, the parents' marital status is no longer married, or unmarried and remarried (married). In some variations for functional solidarity when the child is the respondent, the parents' marital status is widowed, divorced/separated, and remarried (married).

Age.   The respondent's age is based on age groups; values were recoded according to the midpoints: 21, 29.5, 39.5, 47.5, 52.5, 57.5, 62.5, 67.5, 72.5. The oldest child's age is simply the stated age.

Marital Status.   The parent's marital status is derived somewhat indirectly. If parents are still living together, they are considered married. If not, the parent is considered unmarried, unless there is a stepparent of the opposite sex, in which case the parent is considered remarried.

Income.   Income is household income and is based on income groups, recoded by midpoints, and then logged.

Education.   Education is by groups, and is coded 10 for less than high school diploma, 12 for high school diploma, 13 for some college and/or technical school, and 16 for college degree or more.

Grandparents' Influence.   The measure for the influence of grandparents when the respondent was growing up is a 5-point scale, with 1 having a good deal of influence and 5 having little or no influence.

Measurement of Normative Solidarity

Normative solidarity, unlike other dimensions of solidarity such as distance and frequency of contact, does not have a standard scale of measurement. Instead it is derived from a set of directly measurable items, namely, agreement/disagreement to the statements identified as Items 1–5 in Table 2.11. A test of internal reliability demonstrates that the four observable indicators of parent responsibility for children are consistent.

Responses to the four statements measuring responsibility of parent for adult child are summed and divided by 4, yielding an average of 3.0. The item measuring norm of responsibility of children for parents is measured by only one item. In regression analyses the coding of this last item is reversed so that agreement indicates endorsement of children's responsibility for parents.

TABLE B.1 Logistic Regression of Structural Solidarity: Coresidence

	Coresiding with another generation (coefficient)		
Independent variables	With mother	With father	With oldest child
Parent remarried	−1.172**	−3.298**	
Parent unmarried	−.096	−2.156**	
R. separated/divorced	1.961**	2.742**	−.971*
R. never married	3.498**	3.469**	
R. widowed			.536
Age oldest child			−.068**
Oldest child married			−3.435**
Number of children	−.278*	−.156	−.114
Age	−.020	−.087**	
Males	−.288	−.030	−.826**
African American	.827*	.722	.008
Homeowner	.541*	.613*	.070
Household income (log)	.687**	.982**	−.099
Education	−.303**	−.332**	−.050
Grandparent influence	.199	.303*	.298**
Intercept	−1.514	−.913	3.798**
−2Loglikelihood χ^2	409.01	353.21	169.98
df	12	12	11
Cases	1,018	809	550

*$p \le .05$; **$p \le .01$.

TABLE B.2 Logistic Regression of Structural Solidarity: Living Nearby

Independent variables	From mother	From father	From oldest child	From grandparent	From grandchild
			Living within one hour from the other generation (coefficient)		
Parent remarried	-.445*	-.894**			
Parent unmarried	.008	-.627**			
R. separated/divorced	-.052	-.343	-.332	.062	
R. never married	-.189	.138		.329	
R. widowed			-.000		.559
Age oldest child			-.005		
Oldest child married			-.227		
Number of children	.081	.116	.036	.038	.030
Age	-.020*	-.024*		-.034*	-.003
Males	.382*	.191	-.223	.369	.100
African American	.057	-.252	-.138	-.317	-.343
Homeowner	.781**	.808**	.198	.533*	-.219
Household income (log)	-.159	-.110	.212	-.142	.235
Education	-.157**	-.161**	-.232**	-.190**	-.237**
Grandparent influence	.022	.162	-.135	.214	.001
Intercept	3.108**	2.708**	3.079**	2.787**	3.297
-2Loglikelihood χ^2	54.333	63.581	36.354	42.665	10.002
df	12	12	11	10	9
Cases	872	712	489	528	146

*$p \le .05$; **$p \le .01$.

TABLE B.3 Ordinary Least Squares of Associational Solidarity

Independent variables	To mother	To father	To oldest child	To grandparent	To grandchild
			Frequency of contact (coefficient)		
Parent remarried	-.511*	-1.732**			
Parent unmarried	-.004	-3.108**			
R. separated/divorced	.035	-.031	-.771*	-.129	
R. never married	-.371	-.346		.541*	
R. widowed			-.486		-1.642**
Age oldest child			-.019		
Oldest child married			-.224		
Number of children	-.084	-.127	.113	.050	-.074
Age	-.011	-.011	.000	-.088**	-.010
Males	-.252	-.066	-.540*	-.200	-.986
African American	.326	-.488	.930*	-.245	.438
Homeowner	.637**	1.263**	-.161	.536*	-.354
Household income (log)	-.153	-.380**	.387*	.033	.656*
Education	-.104**	.033	-.121*	-.029	-.280*
Grandparent influence	.066	.034	.126	1.119**	.277
Intercept	9.954**	8.523**	7.961**	4.102**	8.007*
Adjusted R^2	.042	.263	.039	.158	.097
Cases	872	712	489	517	144

*$p \leq .05$; **$p \leq .01$.

TABLE B.4 Logistic Regression of Affectual Solidarity

| | Feelings of closeness (coefficient) | | | | |
Independent variables	To mother	To father	To oldest child	To grandparent	To grandchild
Parent remarried	-.238	-1.293**			
Parent unmarried	-.292	-1.553**			
R. separated/divorced	-.080	.149	.219	.112	
R. never married	-.197	-.412		-.111	
R. widowed			-.337		-.064
Age oldest child			.039**		
Oldest child married			.539*		
Number of children	-.123	-.095	-.085	.064	-.015
Age	.012	.011		-.033	.015
Males	-.256	.105	-.375	-.345	-.257
African American	1.104**	.522	-.040	.840*	.050
Homeowner	.006	.517**	-.221	-.162	.747
Household income (log)	-.076	-.156	.289	.066	.301
Education	-.017	-.019	-.074	-.089	-.253**
Grandparent influence	.299**	.216**	.127	1.347**	.102
Intercept	.539	.366	.041	-2.912**	1.297
-2loglikelihood χ^2	43.58	108.73	33.63	118.08	12.87
df	12	12	11	10	9
Cases	1,018	809	550	528	147

*$p \leq .05$; **$p \leq .01$.

TABLE B.5 Ordinary Least Squares Regression of Consensual Solidarity

Independent variables	Similarity of opinions between the generations (coefficient)			
	To mother	to father	To oldest child	To grandparent
Parent remarried	.062	−.221*		
Parent unmarried	−.047	−.384**		
R. separated/divorced	−.159	.061	.088	−.184
R. never married	−.110	−.062		−.354**
R. widowed			−.126	
Age oldest child			.002	
Oldest child married			.346**	
Number of children	−.046	−.014	.027	.029
Age	.002	−.001		−.017**
Males	.022	.147*	.032	−.062
African American	.185	.097	−.289*	.233*
Homeowner	.101	.338**	−.036	.072
Household income (log)	.005	−.002	.053	−.045
Education	−.006	.022	.017	.026
Grandparent influence	.137**	.047	.068*	.436**
Intercept	2.601**	2.883**	2.915**	3.693**
Adjusted R^2	.027	.062	.036	.195
Cases	1,018	809	550	528

*$p \le .05$; **$p \le .01$.

TABLE B.6 Logistic Regression of Functional Solidarity: Providing Help to Parent and Receiving Help from Parent (Reported by Adult Child)

Independent variables	Child provides help to parent (coefficient)		Child receives help from parent (coefficient)	
	Mother	Father	Mother	Father
Son	-.188	.582**	-.373	.155
African American	-1.017**	-.799	.039	-.389
Owns home	-.417*	-.164	.126	.171
Age	.016	-.002	-.051***	-.066***
Household income (log)	-.198	.027	-.148	-.088
Education	-.016	-.019	.118*	.045
Parent remarried	-.065	-.333	.315	-.092
Parent divorced	.387	.489	.207	.053
Parent widowed	.105	-.798	-.440	-.371
R. never married	-.241	-.303	-.214	-.330
R. separated/divorced	-.547	-.400	-.041	-.085
Frequency of contact with parent	.380***	.248***	.390***	.281***
Affection for parent	.365	.508*	.005	.222
Does not work for pay	-.886***	-.722*	.139	.013
Youngest child ≤ 10 years	-.612*	-.383	.600*	.062
Youngest child 11-17 years	-.750*	-.715	.170	-.118
Youngest child 18 + years	-.909*	-.389	-.980	-.651
Intercept	2.352*	1.276	.855	2.041*
–2Loglikelihood	864	628	734	599
Cases	869	710	869	710

*$p \leq .05$; **$p \leq .01$; ***$p \leq .001$.

TABLE B.7 Logistic Regression of Providing Help to Any Adult Child or Receiving Help from Any Adult Child (Reported by Parent)

Independent variable	Parent provides help to child	Parent receives help from child
Father	−.834***	−.211
African American	−1.514**	−.392
Owns home	.504	.248
Total number of children	.317***	.332***
Age	.005	.041**
Does not work for pay	−.072	.238
Household income (log)	.176	.486**
Education	.064	.099
Any child is married	.852**	.681*
Widowed	−.145	.430
Divorced/separated	.130	1.157**
Contact with children	.098*	.117*
Affection for children	.500	.192
Intercept	−3.178**	−7.736***
−2Loglikelihood	613	565

Note. $N = 483$.

*$p \leq .05$; **$p \leq .01$; ***$p \leq .001$.

TABLE B.8   Multiple Regression of Normative Solidarity

Variable	Responsibility of	
	Parent for child	Child for parent
Age	−.039***	−.007
African American	.066	.201
Owns home	−.195**	−.063
Divorced/separated	−.169	.032
Never married	.248**	.143
Widowed	−.040	.185
Female	−.088	.010
Education	−.077**	.120***
Household income (log)	.001	.000
Parent of dependent child <18	.295**	.054
Parent of adult child 18 +	.543***	−.632***
Only mother is alive	.052	.124
Only father is alive	.278*	−.515**
Mother and father are married	.047	.023
Mother and father are divorced	.005	−.130
Age-squared	.0005***	NS
Intercept	3.758***	2.681***
Adjusted R^2	.077	.118

Note. $N = 1,487$.

*$p \le .05$; **$p \le .01$; ***$p \le .001$.

TABLE B.9 Correlations of Norms of Intergenerational Responsibility with Aspects of Intergenerational Relationships

Relationship	Parent responsibility for child Correlation	(N)	Child responsibility for parent Correlation	(N)
Parent's relation with oldest adult child				
Geographic distance	−.06	(530)	.05	(542)
Frequency of contact	−.01	(531)	.01	(543)
Emotional closeness	.11**	(526)	.01	(538)
Consensus of opinions	.04	(518)	.03	(527)
Gives help (excludes co-residing)	−.01	(469)	.01	(482)
Gets help (excludes co-residing)	.03	(469)	−.06	(482)
Child's relation with mother				
Geographic distance	.09**	(1,011)	.04	(1,014)
Frequency of contact	.08**	(1,009)	.03	(1,012)
Emotional closeness	−.05	(1,009)	.10**	(1,012)
Consensus of opinions	−.03	(1,004)	.06*	(1,007)
Gives help (excludes co-residing)	−.03	(866)	.01	(869)
Gets help (excludes co-residing)	.03	(866)	.09**	(869)
Child's relation with father				
Geographic distance	.10**	(806)	.01	(807)
Frequency of contact	.04	(804)	.04	(805)
Emotional closeness	−.04	(806)	.05	(806)
Consensus of opinions	−.13***	(796)	.02	(797)
Gives help (excludes co-residing)	−.01	(709)	.04	(710)
Gets help (excludes co-residing)	.01	(709)	.07	(710)

*$p \leq .05$; **$p \leq .01$; ***$p \leq .001$.

APPENDIX C

Appendix to Chapter 3

Dimensions of Solidarity

In Chapter 3 we consider only five of the six dimensions of intergenerational solidarity that are discussed in Chapter 2. Normative solidarity is excluded from the typology of relationships because the questions used to measure norms reflect *general* attitudes about intergenerational responsibility and not *personal* attitudes about responsibility felt toward one's parents. Consequently, normative solidarity, as measured, cannot be considered a formal property of family relationships. Functional solidarity is represented by two separate measures in Chapter 3, giving help and getting help, which are thus the fifth and sixth dimensions of solidarity. Separating functional solidarity in this way reflects the possibility that assistance may flow in either direction.

Factor Analysis

Factor analysis is a statistical method that transforms a set of correlated variables into a smaller set of variables that captures most of the shared information in the original set. The goal of the technique is to combine redundant information into *composite* variables. Each composite variable represents an essential component, or underlying dimension, of the data. Factor analysis is particularly useful when there are multiple indicators of the same underlying phenomenon and when the goal of the researcher is to summarize the key aspects of the construct being measured.

In Chapter 3, factor analysis reduced the six indicators of solidarity to three factors (opportunity, closeness, and helping behavior). The summary index for each dimension consists of factor scores computed as an additive scale of the standardized solidarity variables weighted by derived factor coefficients.

Since the factor analyses of the six solidarity items when performed separately for child–mother and child–father relationships show the same pattern, it is possible to pool these relationships into a grand factor analysis performed on all child–parent dyads (as shown in the third column of Table 3.1, in Chapter 3). Thus, when types of parental relations from the perspective of the child are discussed, the results refer collectively to relationships with mothers and fathers.

The same analysis was carried out for grandparent–grandchild dyads, with consistent results (shown in the fifth and sixth columns of Table 3.1). These dyads were analyzed for verification of the overall factor analysis results, but are not included in any of the further analysis in Chapter 3.

Separate types of family relationships were established for child–parent pairs who live apart and for those who live together. In order to maintain the same metric on the closeness factor scores for the two categories, we apply the factor coefficients for affect and consensus variables that were derived from the subsample of respondents who live apart.

Multinomial Logistic Regression Analysis

In the analysis of types of family relationships by individual and family characteristics, multinomial logistic regression is used to identify characteristics that predict to which of the eight family types (excluding the two coresident types) an individual is likely to belong. While the results are presented in summary form as percentage differences, it should be noted that they are all statistically significant predictors of group membership, with other factors taken into account. Due to the small number of dyads who live together, we do not perform this statistical test on coresident family types.

Multinomial logistic regression provides maximum likelihood estimators that describe how much of a change in the probability (transformed into log-odds) of being a member of one group is associated with a one-unit change in an independent variable. For each independent variable there are as many estimated coefficients as there are contrasts (N of groups–1; in this instance, 7 contrasts). Due to the large number of generated coefficients, we report only an omnibus maximum likelihood analysis of variance test for group differences (Tables C.1 and C.2). These results summarize the power of each variable to explain overall differences in the distribution of individuals across the eight family types. Multinomial regression analysis is used for testing statistical significance for both child perspective and parent perspective sections.

Percentage Distributions in Figures 3.2–3.10 and 3.12–3.15

The percentage distributions of types of relationships, shown in Figures 3.2–3.10 and 3.12–3.15, are given in Tables C.3–C.15.

TABLE C.1   Maximum Likelihood Analysis of Variance for Differentiating Eight Types of Child–Parent Relations (Not Co-Residing) from Perspective of Adult Child

Variable	Chi-square (DF = 7)
Age	15.03*
Age squared	12.29
African American	23.75**
Owns home	53.89***
No work for pay	11.41
Divorced/separated	5.11
Never married	11.22
Female (daughter)	7.72
Has children	19.67**
Years of education	47.03***
Log of household income	6.86
Parent is divorced/separated	57.67***
Parent is widowed	24.03**
Parent is mother	3.12
Mother x mother divorced	22.79**
Mother x mother widowed	19.59**
Mother x daughter	14.93*
Intercept	30.41***
Likelihood ratio	4307 (DF = 8568)

Note. N = 1,564 parent–child dyads.

*$p \le$ .05; **$p \le$ .01; ***$p \le$ .001.

TABLE C.2   Maximum Likelihood Analysis of Variance for Differentiating Eight Types of Parent–Child Relations (Not Co-Residing) from Perspective of Parent

Variable	Chi-square (DF=7)
Age	26.27***
African American	[a]
Owns home	6.98
Divorced/separated	6.42
Widowed	6.30
Female (mother)	21.49**
Years of education	37.80***
Log of household income	17.79*
Number of children	44.08***
Oldest child is married	12.50
Intercept	47.63***
Likelihood ratio	1872 (DF = 2983)

Note. N = 467 parent–child dyads.

[a]Empty cells preclude global chi-square test; however, some individual parameter estimates are significant.

*$p \le$ .05; **$p \le$ .01; ***$p \le$ .001.

TABLE C.3   Types of Child–Parent Relations as Reported by Adult Child, by Gender of Parent (Figure 3.2)

Type	Father %	Mother %
Tight-knit-helping	16	23
Ritualized-helping	12	14
Dispersed-helping	4	7
Alienated-helping	6	4
Total helping	38	48
Tight-knit independent	14	14
Ritualized-independent	13	11
Dispersed-independent	13	15
Alienated-independent	22	12
Total independent	62	52
Total %	100	100
Total *N*	604	751

Note.   Percentages may not total to 100% because of rounding.

TABLE C.4 Types of Child–Parent Relations as Reported by Adult Child, by Gender of Child and Parent (Figure 3.3)

Type	Son–father %	Daughter–father %	Son–mother %	Daughter–mother %
Tight-knit-helping	17	14	20	26
Ritualized-helping	15	10	15	14
Dispersed-helping	4	5	5	8
Alienated-helping	5	6	3	4
Total helping	41	35	43	52
Tight-knit-independent	14	14	17	10
Ritualized-independent	10	16	13	9
Dispersed-independent	13	13	15	15
Alienated-independent	22	23	12	13
Total independent	59	66	57	47
Total %	100	101	100	99
Total N	292	312	357	393

Note. Percentages may not total to 100% because of rounding.

TABLE C.5   Types of Mother–Child Relations as Reported by Adult Child, by Marital Status of Mother (Figure 3.4)

Type	Married %	Divorced/separated %	Widowed %
Tight-knit-helping	26	23	18
Ritualized-helping	12	18	14
Dispersed-helping	8	8	4
Alienated-helping	4	8	2
Total helping	48	57	38
Tight-knit-independent	14	11	15
Ritualized-independent	10	8	16
Dispersed-independent	15	10	19
Alienated-independent	12	15	11
Total independent	51	44	61
Total %	99	101	99
Total N	368	139	235

Note. Percentages may not total to 100% because of rounding.

TOTAL C.6   Types of Father–Child Relations as Reported by Adult Child, by Marital Status of Father (Figure 3.5)

Type	Married %	Divorced/separated %	Widowed %
Tight-knit-helping	22	7	4
Ritualized-helping	14	11	6
Dispersed-helping	5	2	4
Alienated-helping	4	9	6
Total helping	45	29	20
Tight-knit-independent	16	7	19
Ritualized-independent	11	16	17
Dispersed-independent	15	9	11
Alienated-independent	13	39	34
Total independent	55	71	81
Total %	100	100	101
Total N	369	163	71

Note. Percentages may not total to 100% because of rounding.

TABLE C.7   Types of Child–Parent Relations as Reported by Adult Child, by Age of Child (Figure 3.6)

Type	18-24 %	25-44 %	45 + %
Tight-knit-helping	20	21	16
Ritualized-helping	17	13	13
Dispersed-helping	8	6	2
Alienated-helping	7	5	2
Total helping	52	45	33
Tight-knit-independent	9	13	19
Ritualized-independent	10	12	14
Dispersed-independent	9	14	21
Alienated-independent	20	17	14
Total independent	48	56	68
Total %	100	101	101
Total *N*	207	906	241

Note.   Percentages may not total to 100% because of rounding.

TABLE C.8   Types of Child–Parent Relations as Reported by Adult Child, by Marital Status of Child (Figure 3.7)

Type	Married %	Divorced/separated %	Never married %
Tight-knit-helping	21	16	15
Ritualized-helping	13	15	13
Dispersed-helping	6	5	6
Alienated-helping	4	5	8
Total helping	44	41	42
Tight-knit-independent	16	14	7
Ritualized-independent	12	9	14
Dispersed-independent	14	13	15
Alienated-independent	14	23	22
Total independent	56	59	58
Total %	100	100	100
Total *N*	934	146	260

Note.   Percentages may not total to 100% because of rounding.

TABLE C.9   Types of Child–Parent Relations as Reported by Adult Child, by Parental Status of Child (Figure 3.8)

Type	Parental status of child	
	Has no children %	Has children %
Tight-knit-helping	18	20
Ritualized-helping	12	14
Dispersed-helping	9	4
Alienated-helping	8	3
Total helping	47	41
Tight-knit-independent	8	16
Ritualized-independent	9	13
Dispersed-independent	16	14
Alienated-independent	20	16
Total independent	53	59
Total %	100	100
Total *N*	396	959

Note.   Percentages may not total to 100% because of rounding.

TABLE C.10   Types of Child–Parent Relations as Reported by Adult Child, by Race of Child (Figure 3.9)

Type	Race of child	
	Other %	African American %
Tight-knit-helping	20	19
Ritualized-helping	14	7
Dispersed-helping	6	5
Alienated-helping	5	3
Total helping	45	34
Tight-knit-independent	14	14
Ritualized-independent	12	13
Dispersed-independent	13	25
Alienated-independent	17	14
Total independent	56	66
Total %	101	100
Total *N*	1251	104

Note.   Percentages may not total to 100% because of rounding.

TABLE C.11 Types of Child–Parent Relations as Reported by Adult Child, by Education of Child (Figure 3.10)

Type	<High school %	High school grad %	Some college %	College grad + %
Tight-knit-helping	23	22	20	13
Ritualized-helping	12	14	15	13
Dispersed-helping	2	4	7	9
Alienated-helping	5	3	4	8
Total helping	42	43	46	43
Tight-knit-independent	12	14	16	12
Ritualized-independent	15	14	11	7
Dispersed-independent	10	12	12	22
Alienated-independent	23	16	16	16
Total Independent	60	56	55	57
Total %	102	99	101	100
Total N	215	533	277	330

Note. Percentages may not total to 100% because of rounding.

TABLE C.12   Types of Parent–Oldest Child Relations as Reported by Parent, by Gender of Parent (Figure 3.12)

Type	Father %	Mother %
Tight-knit-helping	16	27
Ritualized-helping	5	6
Dispersed-helping	10	9
Alienated-helping	4	7
Total helping	35	49
Tight-knit-independent	16	18
Ritualized-independent	15	7
Dispersed-independent	20	16
Alienated-independent	15	11
Total independent	66	52
Total %	101	101
Total *N*	249	295

Note. Percentages may not total to 100% because of rounding.

TABLE C.13   Types of Parent–Oldest Child Relations as Reported by Parent, by Age of Parent (Figure 3.13)

Type	<45 %	45-54 %	55-64 %	65 + %
Tight-knit-helping	14	21	30	18
Ritualized-helping	4	5	6	7
Dispersed-helping	2	8	8	14
Alienated-helping	4	2	8	6
Total helping	24	36	52	45
Tight-knit-independent	12	18	16	21
Ritualized-independent	14	20	6	7
Dispersed-independent	28	13	18	17
Alienated-independent	24	13	9	11
Total independent	78	64	49	56
Total %	102	100	101	101
Total *N*	67	131	162	184

Note. Percentages may not total to 100% because of rounding.

TABLE C.14   Types of Parent–Oldest Child Relations as Reported by Parent, by Race of Parent (Figure 3.14)

	Race of parent	
Type	Other %	African American %
Tight-knit-helping	23	8
Ritualized-helping	5	7
Dispersed-helping	10	7
Alienated-helping	6	0
Total helping	44	22
Tight-knit-independent	17	23
Ritualized-independent	10	15
Dispersed-independent	17	18
Alienated-independent	12	22
Total independent	56	78
Total %	100	100
Total N	502	41

Note. Percentages may not total to 100% because of rounding.

TABLE C.15 Types of Parent–Oldest Child Relation as Reported by Parent, by Education of Parent (Figure 3.15)

Type	<High school %	High school grad %	Some college %	College grad + %
Tight-knit-helping	22	27	20	11
Ritualized-helping	5	4	7	7
Dispersed-helping	8	7	9	21
Alienated-helping	4	7	6	5
Total helping	39	45	42	44
Tight-knit-independent	21	16	24	6
Ritualized-independent	15	8	11	5
Dispersed-independent	16	16	15	26
Alienated-independent	9	15	9	20
Total independent	61	55	59	57
Total %	100	100	101	101
Total N	193	199	75	75

Note. Percentages may not total to 100% because of rounding.

APPENDIX D

Appendix to Chapter 4

Statistical methods used in the analysis of data for Chapter 4 included several regression techniques. *Regression* is a set of analytic techniques that are used to explore the relationship between a factor (the dependent variable) and one or more independent variables. It is possible to create models that simulate the influence of many factors on the dependent variable. These models are based on a set of techniques called *multivariate statistics,* which enable us to assess the relative influence of several factors simultaneously and to identify each factor's relative contribution to the dependent variable. In this manner regression analysis shows the specific effect of a particular independent variable on the dependent variable, holding constant all other independent variables (i.e., controlling for their effects). The results of the regression analysis are presented in Tables D.1–D.8.

Multiple Regression

The relative effect of each factor can be identified through a technique called *multiple regression,* which measures the influence that each factor has on a dependent variable. The relative influence of each factor is indicated by a standardized regression weight or Beta coefficient.

Linear Regression

The relationship between the dependent and independent variables may be linear: as the value of the independent variable increases or decreases, the value of the dependent variable increases or decreases consistently. The relationship may also be curvilinear: the value of the dependent variable increases or decreases with increasing or decreasing values of the independent variable up to a point and then changes direction.

Logistic Regression

Logistic regression is a method for determining the odds that a condition will be met from a set of dichotomous variables. In many cases, questions that have many answers can be converted into yes-no responses by creating a series of *dummy variables*.

Tobit Analysis

When a large number of cases in the sample have zero for the value of the dependent variable the relationships of the independent variables to the dependent variable can be distorted because the range of values for the dependent variable is truncated or limited by zero. The Tobit model corrects for this distortion.

Discriminant Analysis

Discriminant analysis is a means of distinguishing between groups on the basis of the values of a set of factors. For example, are there differences in the factors age, race, education, and income between two groups in which we are interested? If so, is any of these factors a better predictor of group membership than the others? Discriminant analysis measures the contributions of each variable to making the group assignments.

TABLE D.1 Discriminant Analysis of Volunteer Activity

Independent variables	Canonical coefficient	Correlation within function
White collar occupation	0.08***	0.32
Male	0.06	0.02
Age group		
35-44	0.25***	0.23
45-64	0.01	−0.06
65 +	−0.00	−0.07
Marital status		
Separated or divorced	−0.08	−0.13
Married	0.01***	0.22
Widowed	−0.02	−0.11
White	−0.20	−0.08
Respondent has children	0.13	0.08
Two earner household	0.04	0.03
Household size	0.11**	0.19
Education		
Less than high school	−0.84***	−0.57
High school graduate	−0.50	−0.06
Some college	−0.16***	0.24
College graduate	−0.11***	0.22
Graduate school or advanced degree	0.05***	0.32
Income		
$10,000-$19,999	0.07***	−0.22
$20,000-$29,999	0.18	−0.01
$30,000-$49,999	0.33***	0.21
$50,000-$74,999	0.19*	0.14
$75,000-$100,000	0.05	
More than $100,000	0.16*	0.14
Employment status		
Full-time	−0.19	0.02
Part-time	0.08	0.12
Retired	0.12	0.04
Attitudinal variables		
Parents should help adult children	−0.03	−0.12
Public benefits should be based on need, not age	−0.01	0.06

TABLE D.1 *continued*

Wealthy should share their advantages	0.27*	0.13
Adult children should not be expected to support parents	−0.08**	−0.20
Can count on parents for emotional support	−0.02	0.08
Received financial help from parents	−0.11	−0.06
Youth and elderly contribute much to the community	0.27***	0.21
Youth and elderly receive unfair share of public benefits	−0.05	−0.10
Childcare and eldercare are burdens for families	−0.14	−0.10
Youth and elderly programs are too costly	−0.04**	−0.18
Perception of relative financial status of one's age group	−0.08	−0.02
Self-rating of one's life at present	0.19***	0.29
Type of family relation		
Alienated-independent	−0.12	−0.09
Alienated-helping	−0.12	−0.08
Dispersed-independent	−0.10	0.07
Dispersed-helping	0.00	0.10
Ritualized-independent	−0.24***	−0.23
Ritualized-helping	0.00	0.04
Tight-knit-independent	−0.15	−0.04
Tight-knit-helping	−0.05	0.02
Eigenvalue	−0.183	
Canonical correlation	−0.394	
Group centroids		
Volunteers	0.396	
Nonvolunteers	−0.463	

$^*p \le .05; ^{**}p \le .01; ^{***}p \le .001.$

TABLE D.2   Tobit Estimation of Hours Devoted to Volunteer Activity

Independent variables	Coefficient	S.E.
Constant	−10.49	11.72
Male	−0.59	2.04
Age group		
35-44	2.26	2.46
45-64	0.27	3.38
65 +	−2.33	5.05
Marital status		
Separated or divorced	−5.57	3.77
Married	2.55	3.81
Widowed	5.85	5.78
White	−7.80**	2.76
Respondent has children	8.34**	2.91
Two earner household	−7.51*	3.15
Household size	0.74	0.81
Education		
Less than high school	−23.04***	6.78
High school graduate	−9.05	6.20
Some college	−6.15	6.28
College graduate	−4.45	6.45
Graduate school or advanced degree	1.22	6.67
Income		
$10,000-$19,999	2.37	3.87
$20,000-$29,999	4.07	3.94
$30,000-$49,999	1.94	3.87
$50,000-$74,999	4.38	4.40
$75,000-$100,000	5.86	5.72
More than $100,000	5.18	6.17
Employment status		
Full-time	−2.39	3.26
Part-time	4.86	3.86
Retired	2.48	4.56
Attitudinal variables		
Parents should help adult children	0.00	1.01
Public benefits should be based on need, not age	−0.12	0.87
Wealthy should share their advantages	1.92**	0.68

TABLE D.2 *continued*

Adult children should not be expected to support parents	−0.57	0.71
Can count on parents for emotional support	−1.35	0.75
Received financial help from parents	0.01	0.60
Youth and elderly contribute much to the community	4.52***	1.12
Youth and elderly receive unfair share of public benefits	−0.59	1.02
Childcare and eldercare are burdens for families	−1.29	0.93
Youth and elderly programs are too costly	0.49	0.83
Perception of relative financial status of one's age group	−0.29	0.94
Self-rating of one's life at present	1.08*	0.55
Type of family relation		
Alienated-independent	−2.35	2.66
Alienated-helping	−5.72	3.66
Dispersed-independent	0.38	2.63
Dispersed-helping	1.98	2.94
Ritualized-independent	−6.12*	2.09
Ritualized-helping	−0.11	2.86
Tight-knit-independent	−1.44	2.61
Tight-knit-helping	−0.48	2.62
Σ^2		0.083

$*p \le .05; **p \le .01; ***p \le .001.$

TABLE D.3   Multiple Regression Analysis of Proportion of Volunteer Activity that Benefits Children and Teens by Volunteers Age 65 and Older

Independent variables	Beta weight	
Education	.568***	
Youth programs are too costly	−.533***	
Programs should be based on need, not age	.389**	
Rating of financial status of children	.380***	
Young receive an excess share of government benefits	−.286*	
Constant	4.461	
Adjusted R^2		.617

*$p \le .05$; **$p \le .01$; ***$p \le .001$.

TABLE D.4   Multiple Regression Analysis of Proportion of Volunteer Activity that Benefits Children and Teens by All Volunteers

Independent variables	Beta weight	
Education	.593***	
Frequency of contact with oldest adult child	.497***	
Age	−.313***	
Programs should be based on need, not age	.302***	
Constant	4.197	
Adjusted R^2		.539

***$p \le .001$.

TABLE D.5   Multiple Regression Analysis of Proportion of Volunteer Activity that Benefits Adults Aged 60 and Older, by All Volunteers

Independent variables	Beta weight	
Age	.242***	
Perceived closeness to grandparents	.179**	
Frequency of contact with grandparents	.152*	
Frequency of contact with oldest adult child	.151*	
Constant	2.933	
Adjusted R^2		.117

Note. $N = 802$.
[a]Base population = all volunteers.
*$p \le .01$; **$p \le .05$; ***$p \le .001$.

TABLE D.6   Tobit Estimation of Hours of Help Given to Nonrelatives

Independent variables	Coefficient	S.E.
Constant	2.68	6.60
Male	−1.13	1.15
Age group		
35-44	−0.36	1.37
45-64	−1.67	1.90
65 +	−4.19	2.85
Marital status		
Separated or divorced	1.10	2.04
Married	0.24	2.10
Widowed	3.60	3.05
White	−0.63	1.57
Respondent has children	−0.26	1.59
Two earner household	−2.80	1.78
Household size	1.21**	0.46
Education		
Less than high school	2.62	3.91
High school graduate	0.59	3.68
Some college	0.53	3.73
College graduate	0.004	3.82
Graduate school or advanced degree	1.12	3.96
Income		
$10,000-$19,999	−1.77	2.11
$20,000-$29,999	−0.003	2.15
$30,000-$49,999	−0.009	2.11
$50,000-$74,999	0.95	2.43
$75,000-$100,000	−4.98	3.24
More than $100,000	−0.14	3.52
Employment status		
Full-time	0.45	1.82
Part-time	2.64	2.17
Retired	7.50**	2.59
Attitudinal variables		
Parents should help adult children	−0.53	0.57
Public benefits should be based on need, not age	0.001	0.48
Wealthy should share their advantages	0.79*	0.38

TABLE D.6 *continued*

Adult children should not be expected to support parents	−0.86*	0.40
Can count on parents for emotional support	−0.34	0.43
Received financial help from parents	0.008	0.33
Youth and elderly contribute much to the community	0.87	0.62
Youth and elderly receive unfair share of public benefits	−0.18	0.58
Childcare and eldercare are burdens for families	−0.96	0.52
Youth and elderly programs are too costly	0.002	0.47
Perception of relative financial status of one's age group	0.92	0.53
Self-rating of one's life at present	−0.31	0.31
Type of family relation		
Alienated-independent	0.29	1.48
Alienated-helping	−1.52	2.01
Dispersed-independent	3.03*	1.48
Dispersed-helping	−1.19	1.65
Ritualized-independent	−1.04	1.26
Ritualized-helping	−2.41	1.62
Tight-knit-independent	−0.46	1.47
Tight-knit-helping	0.13	1.46
Σ^2		28.2

$*p \leq .05;$ $**p \leq .01;$ $***p \leq .001.$

TABLE D.7   Discriminant Analysis of Giving Gifts to Adult Children

Independent variables	Canonical coefficient	Correlation within function
White collar occupation	0.12**	0.27
Male	0.05	0.123
Age group		
35-44	−0.90**	0.26
45-64	−1.30	−0.06
65 +	−1.18*	−0.20
Marital status		
Separated or divorced	0.48	−0.07
Married	0.68*	0.18
Widowed	0.46	−0.16
White	0.01	0.04
Two earner household	−0.10	−0.09
Household size	−0.16	0.12
Education		
Less than high school	−0.16***	−0.34
High school graduate	−0.15	0.05
Some college	−0.03	0.12
College graduate	0.09*	0.19
Graduate school or advanced degree	0.03*	0.17
Income		
$10,000-$19,999	0.12**	0.26
$20,000-$29,999	0.43	0.06
$30,000-$49,999	0.60**	0.32
$50,000-$74,999	0.38	0.15
$75,000-$100,000	0.29**	0.23
More than $100,000	0.19	0.12
Employment status		
Full-time	−0.08*	0.22
Part-time	−0.13	0.07
Retired	0.15	0.02
Attitudinal variables		
Parents should help adult children	0.19	0.03
Public benefits should be based on need, not age	0.19	0.09
Wealthy should share their advantages	0.02	0.02

TABLE D.7   *continued*

Adult children should not be expected to support parents	−0.23**	−0.22
Can count on parents for emotional support	−0.15	−0.00
Received financial help from parents	−0.01	−0.08
Youth and elderly contribute much to the community	−0.21*	−0.17
Youth and elderly receive unfair share of public benefits	−0.09	−0.10
Childcare and eldercare are burdens for families	−0.23*	−0.18
Youth and elderly programs are too costly	0.00*	−0.17
Perception of relative financial status of one's age group	−0.10	−0.03
Self-rating of one's life at present	0.14	0.11
Type of family relation		
Alienated-independent	0.30*	0.20
Alienated-helping	0.34*	0.18
Dispersed-independent	0.01	−0.12
Dispersed-helping	0.30	0.09
Ritualized-independent	0.17	0.00
Ritualized-helping	0.08	0.01
Tight-knit-independent	0.15	0.07
Tight-knit-helping	0.57**	0.26
Eigenvalue	0.231	
Canonical correlation	0.433	
Group centroids		
Gives gifts	0.485	
Does not give gifts	−0.473	

$*p \leq .05$; $**p \leq .01$; $***p \leq .001$.

TABLE D.8   Discriminant Analysis of Making Bequest Plans

Independent variables	Canonical coefficient	Correlation within function
White collar occupation	0.15**	0.19
Male	0.02	0.06
Age group		
35-44	−0.09***	−0.24
45-64	−0.01	−0.09
65 +	−0.01	−0.01
Marital status		
Separated or divorced	0.14***	0.29
Married	−0.70***	−0.73
Widowed	0.06*	0.16
White	0.08	−0.01
Respondent has children	−0.22***	−0.48
Two earner household	−0.14	0.06
Household size	−0.02*	−0.16
Education		
Less than high school	0.31	−0.02
High school graduate	0.22	−0.09
Some college	0.28	0.10
College graduate	0.22	0.06
Graduate school or advanced degree	0.17	0.01
Income		
$10,000-$19,999	0.27	0.03
$20,000-$29,999	0.18	−0.10
$30,000-$49,999	0.47	0.07
$50,000-$74,999	0.42	0.09
$75,000-$100,000	0.26*	0.13
More than $100,000	0.10	0.01
Employment status		
Full-time	0.09*	0.16
Part-time	−0.05	−0.04
Retired	0.06	−0.01
Attitudinal variables		
Parents should help adult children	0.33***	0.26
Public benefits should be based on need, not age	−0.01	0.03

TABLE D.8 *continued*

Wealthy should share their advantages	0.03	0.06
Adult children should not be expected to support parents	0.10	−0.05
Can count on parents for emotional support	0.11*	0.14
Received financial help from parents	0.04***	0.21
Youth and elderly contribute much to the community	0.03	0.01
Youth and elderly receive unfair share of public benefits	0.16	−0.09
Childcare and eldercare are burdens for families	0.04	−0.04
Youth and elderly programs are too costly	0.08	0.01
Perception of relative financial status of one's age group	−0.13*	−0.13
Self-rating of one's life at present	0.05	0.03
Type of family relation		
Alienated-independent	0.06	−0.02
Alienated-helping	−0.03	0.01
Dispersed-independent	−0.01	0.05
Dispersed-helping	0.13	0.09
Ritualized-independent	0.02	0.02
Ritualized-helping	0.07	0.08
Tight-knit-independent	0.03	0.02
Tight-knit-helping	0.00	−0.06
Eigenvalue	0.173	
Canonical correlation	0.385	
Group centroids		
Has specific bequest plans	0.331	
Has no bequest plans	−0.525	

*$p \leq .05$; **$p \leq .01$; ***$p \leq .001$.

APPENDIX E

Appendix to Chapter 5

This appendix details the major assumptions and data sources used for creating our estimates of the magnitude of private and public transfers. This discussion is organized by the three steps of the analysis: identifying generations, allocating resources, and creating monetary equivalents. At the end we discuss special issues related to estimating the value of government benefits.

Classifying Family Generations

Most of the family relationships identified in the survey can be combined into the five family generations (grandchildren's, children's, own, parents', and grandparents' generations); examples are daughter and niece into children's generation; sister into own; and aunt into parents' generation. The family generations index uses only those relationships that are included in the general definition of family, including "cousin" and "family/relatives," although for these the generational allocation is ambiguous. These ambiguous responses are allocated to the five family generations in the same proportion as the allocation of the other family members.

Classifying Policy Age Groups

Since the policy age groups reflect societal groupings, not family generations, we include here the relationships excluded from the family index: friend, neighbor, co-worker, and church member. For the policy age group index, unlike the family generations, classification depends on the *age* of the givers and recipients.

Allocation of family relationships to policy age groups therefore requires estimation of the age of the giver or recipient. In some cases

278

age can be determined directly from the survey. For gifts or help from adult children to the respondent, the ages of the respondent's children are known. Although we do not know which specific child provided the gift, we can estimate the age of the giver by using the ages of all of the children.

If the respondent gave help to a parent, the parent's age is not known. For these cases, we estimate the parent's age using information from the sample on the average age gap between parents and their adult children, adding this to the age of the respondent. The age gap is estimated using the midpoint of each age range, and 85 for those aged 80+.

Some family relationships are assigned to policy age groups on the basis of the age of the respondent and/or the likely age group of the other individual. For example, if the respondent is over 60, a sibling is considered an elder; grandparents are considered elders, since all respondents are 18 or older.

The policy age group index includes all the family relationships identified above plus a number of social relationships. For some responses, the policy age group is clear, such as "other adult," which is allocated to adult under 60. For others, assumptions are made in order to allocate people to a particular age group, such as co-workers to the adult (under 60) group.

Types of Transfers

The types of private intergenerational transfers measured in the survey are available for both giver and receiver, with a few exceptions: bequests for givers; and benefits of formal volunteering and charitable contributions for receivers. Methods of estimating and allocating these transfers are described below.

Allocation of Resources

It is necessary to translate the survey responses, which may indicate transfers to and from more than one person, into generational allocations of resources. This requires allocating total time and monetary transfers among the different recipient generations, for both definitions of generation (family generation and policy age group). For instance, if the respondent mentions only one type of relationship, for example, "daughter," when asked whom he/she helped, then the generational allocation is clear: 100% of the value is allocated to the appropriate generation. Two or more relationships might be mentioned, for example, "daughter" and "son," but the relationships are all in the same family generation or policy age group, and the allocation is again clear. Complications arise when the relationships mentioned belong to different family generations or policy age groups. Unfortunately, the survey did not determine what proportion of each transfer type was associated with the different relationship categories, or even the number of people in that relationship category who provided help or gifts.

Help and Gifts. We allocate help and gifts based on the proportion of all mentioned relationships that correspond to the various family generations and policy age groups. For example, a respondent reports that she helps her mother and her son and gives a total of 5 hours of informal help. Each generation is allocated 2.5 hours. Because of limitations in the survey, only gifts given to a child have a clear generational assignment. Gifts received, however, can be assigned to both a family generation and a policy age group.

Housing. Shared housing presents special difficulties in allocation. The survey asked whether the respondent was living with his or her oldest or youngest adult child or with his or her parent(s). The survey also determined if the respondent ever gave or received housing from a parent or child. But the survey did not probe to determine the direction of the current transfer, by ascertaining who owned the housing unit, or the nature of the financial arrangements between the generations, such as payment of rent.

To make the various indices of intergenerational transfers comparable, we focus on only those who are *currently* giving or receiving housing. If the respondent indicated that he or she was currently living with either a parent or an adult child, we first checked the response to the questions concerning owning or renting. Some respondents volunteered the answer "live with someone else." These respondents were allocated as receiving housing. For the remaining respondents, we used answers to the question on whether they had ever given or received housing in the past from the relative (parent, child) in question. If the respondent had only received, but not given, then we assigned that respondent as currently receiving. We assigned the respondents who reported both giving and receiving using the ratio of months given to months received, assigning them probabilistically.

For a respondent living with grandparents, the allocation depended on whether the respondent was giving or receiving from the parents' generation. If he or she was considered to be giving housing to a parent, then we assumed that he or she was also giving to a grandparent. Similarly, if the respondent was receiving from parents, then it was assumed that the parents were giving to the respondent's grand-parent. For housing situations in which grandchildren were living with grandparents with no intervening generation, we allocated 37% of the cases as giving by the grandchild, and 63% as receiving, based on the ratio of giving to receiving for children with respect to their parents.

To allocate these transfers to the policy age groups, giving or receiving housing from grandparents is assumed to be giving or receiving from elders. For parents and children, the age of the parent or child is estimated using the average age gap between parents and adult children.

Volunteer Time.   For volunteer time, the survey determined whether "all," "most," "some," or "none" of the respondent's volunteer activities benefited youth, adults, elders, or all ages. If all volunteer time benefits one policy age group, the value of the total number of volunteer hours is allocated to that policy age group. We generally interpret the "most" response as indicating 2/3 of volunteer hours and "some" as 1/3 of hours for the relevant policy age group, with minor modifications to eliminate double counting of volunteer hours.

Contributions.   To allocate charitable contributions by policy age group, we assume that the age distribution of the beneficiaries of a respondent's contributions is the same as the beneficiaries of the respondent's volunteering. For respondents who give money but do not volunteer at all, we use the average allocation for those who both volunteer and give financial contributions.

The survey did not ascertain whether respondents benefited from volunteer organizations or charities. To compute the aggregate receiving and the net transfer indices, we impute the value of volunteering and charitable contributions by age group, assuming that all in that age group benefit equally.

Bequests.   Because this survey gathered information about living persons, we could not assess the value of estates bequeathed, although we did have information about inheritances received. To correct this asymmetry of giving and receiving, we obtained data on the magnitude of estates by the age of the decedent (Munnell & Ernsberger, 1988). These data are presented as an average for all those still alive in a given age group. We separated the value of estates bequeathed to surviving spouses (defined as intrahousehold) from that bequeathed to nonspouses (interhousehold) on the basis of the probabilities that people dying at specified ages have surviving spouses.

Creating Monetary Equivalents

Housing. For the value of housing given and received, we use the median gross rent for the county where each respondent lives. A monetary equivalent for housing provided is the number of months of housing times the value per month. This does not take account of other shared living expenses, such as food and transportation, and so will understate the value of this transfer.

Time. For time transfers, we value the time devoted to each type of assistance at the national median weekly wage rate for an analogous occupation (U.S. Department of Labor, 1991, Table 56). For example, if the help given was "providing transportation," the value of this time is computed using the average earnings for taxi drivers, $308 per week, or $8.80 an hour for a 35-hour work week. Examples of hourly wages for other services are $3.77 for baby/adult care, and $10.91 for repairs/maintenance. In effect, these figures represent the cost of employing paid workers to provide each particular service.

This is better than the usual method of valuing time at a person's own wage rate, termed by economists as the *opportunity cost* of time, since the market places no value on the time of people who are not in the formal labor force, including homemakers and the retired.

We then convert the amounts of giving or receiving into annual equivalents, since the questions in the survey asked about transfers over different time periods—hours of help per month, housing provided at the moment of the survey, gifts and major financial assistance over the last three years, and inheritances over the last five years.

Child-Rearing Time and Money. Espenshade (1984) computed the additional household spending associated with having children of different ages for three broad socioeconomic statuses, which he labeled high, medium, and low. For each socioeconomic status, he estimated average child-rearing expenses, distinguishing couples on the basis of the employment status of the wife. We classified all survey respondents with children into Espenshade's three socioeconomic statuses, using information on their occupations and education, and then assigned to them Espenshade's estimates of typical child-rearing costs.

To compute the time devoted to raising children, we used information on the number of hours devoted to household activities (Morgan, 1986). Morgan found that this increases with the number of children. For example, households with children under the age of two devote an extra 337 hours per year to household activities. We converted these hour figures into dollars by using the wage rate of $6.70 per hour, which is an average of the wage rate for household chores, repairs/ maintenance, and baby/adult care.

College Education. The value of parental support of college education was estimated in several steps. Because the survey does not directly provide information on whether a son or daughter is attending college, we were forced to rely on population averages. McPherson and Schapiro provide information on the average student and parental contribution expected for students attending private 4-year colleges, public 4-year colleges, and public 2-year colleges, stratified by family income level (1991, p. 61).

We combined data on the number of students, by age, in each of these types of schools (U.S. Department of Education, 1990, Table 161) and population statistics (U.S. Bureau of the Census, 1990) to estimate the probability of attending these different types of institutions. We could then combine the distribution of household income for families with children aged 18–25 (from the survey) with these probabilities of attendance and the distribution of cost to derive the expected cost of college for families, stratified by income and age of student. We decreased these figures for students aged 23, 24, and 25 by 25% per year, assuming their increasing financial independence from their parents. In addition, we computed the expected costs separately for those living away from home (by including room and board costs) and those living at home. These expected costs, based on income, child's age, and whether the child lives at home, were then allocated to each respondent from the survey who had one or more children aged 18–25.

Government Benefits

Our estimates include non-means-tested benefits, means-tested benefits, government retiree benefits, and the general benefits of government. Shoven, Topper, and Wise (1991) compiled data on receipt of cash transfers in 1986 from the Survey of Income and Program Participation, and, separately, the benefits of Medicare and Medicaid, using data on total government spending on these programs. Both were reported by the age of household head. From their list of government benefits we included the following:

- Means-tested benefits: Aid to Families with Dependent Children, Supplemental Security Income, general assistance, other welfare, Medicaid, food stamps, and Women, Infants, and Children Supplemental Food Program (WIC);

- Non-means-tested benefits: Social Security, Medicare, foster child care, and unemployment and workers' compensation;
- Government retirement benefits: military retirement, veterans' compensation, GI bill benefits, federal civil service pensions, and state and local government pensions.

We supplemented these estimates with information on government spending for elementary, secondary, and higher education (which is largely non-means-tested) and spending on public housing and rent subsidies (which are means-tested benefits). Finally, we also estimated the value of the general benefits of government.

Education.   The value of publicly provided primary and secondary education was estimated as equal to educational spending. For the 1989-1990 school year, the expenditure per pupil in average daily attendance was $4,896 (National Education Association, 1989). To compute averages that could be applied to every parent in the survey who has children aged 6 to 17, we reduced this by the probability that a child would be attending a private school, and for children aged 16–17, by the probability that a child has dropped out of school (U.S. Bureau of the Census, 1988b). (We assumed that children aged 18–25 are college age.) This yields an average value of education of $4,357 for each child aged 6–15, and $3,991 for each child aged 16–17.

Higher education is subsidized by state appropriations to fund public colleges and universities, federal financial aid for students, and government research contracts for university overhead. Using the Higher Education General Information Survey, McPherson and Schapiro (1991) computed estimates of these subsidies to the total revenue per student. The total benefit per student of the three forms of government aid amount to $795 for 4-year private colleges, $6,362 for 4-year public colleges, and $4,294 for 2-year public colleges. Depending on who is paying the bills for college, both parents and their college-age children benefit from this subsidy. We divided these benefits between parents and their college-age children by using the probability of college attendance and the fractions of college expenses paid by parents and by students, with an adjustment for increasing financial independence for students aged 23–25.

Housing.   Housing is subsidized by the deductibility of mortgage interest and property taxes in the computation of federal and state income taxes. But because we have obtained a direct measure of taxes actually paid, it is unnecessary to compute this subsidy in order to determine the net of taxes and government benefits. Because of data limitations, we were unable to obtain information on the benefits of other home purchase assistance programs operated by states and localities.

Certain low-income renters are subsidized, either because they rent publicly-owned apartments or participate in rental voucher programs. William Apgar, from the Joint Center for Housing Studies, Harvard University, computed for us the age distribution of rental subsidies using data from the American Housing Survey. These estimates include *rental* subsidies only, and exclude federal, state, and local expenditures that subsidize house purchases, either directly, or indirectly through mortgage guarantee programs. We estimate that the subsidy value received by each subsidized household amounts to $300 per unit per month (W. Apgar, personal communication, November 8, 1991).

General Benefits. The remainder of government programs provide general benefits that do not have particular recipients; examples are national defense, highway spending, and police and fire departments. We valued these as equal to the dollar expenditures reported in the National Income Accounts (U.S. Department of Commerce, 1991). Because most of these benefits are in the nature of "public goods," the allocation of the benefits to individuals or households is somewhat arbitrary. In the absence of government, many of these services would be purchased. Some, such as fire protection, would probably be priced per household; others, such as the use of parks, would probably be priced per individual user.

We computed the spending accounted for by these two types of programs and applied the resulting proportion to all programs that could not be specifically allocated between the household basis and the individual basis. We allocated government spending for health and hospitals, highways, and natural resources by person. We allocated spending on police, fire, corrections, sewage and sanitation, housing and community development, and utilities by household. The remainder of government spending (government administration, interest payments, and other spending) was allocated in the same ratio as the categories that could be specifically allocated. In all, per person spending amounted to 55% of government spending, per household amounted to 45%.

Taxes. Total government revenue includes taxes paid by individuals, households, and businesses. We obtained the total level of revenue paid to all levels of government and allocated this total by age group on the basis of the relative proportion of taxes and retirement contributions reported by the Consumer Expenditure Survey (U.S. Department of Labor, 1987).

Net Public-Private Transfers. To be consistent with government tax and spending data, which were based on households, we used households as the basis for the net flow of public and private transfers. This required us to divide private transfers into those that occur within households and those between households. Many of the questions in the survey, such as those concerning personal assistance and financial assistance, were limited to between-household transfers. Other transfers, such as volunteering and charitable contributions, are by definition between households. Shared housing and college expenses for children still living at home are within household, and were thus excluded from the interhousehold index. Inheritances can be either between or within households. Within-household inheritances usually occur with the death of a spouse. We computed the fraction of deaths of those still married at the time of death (National Center for Health Statistics (1992), and excluded this fraction of inheritances from the interhousehold category.

APPENDIX F

Appendix to Chapter 7

Measurements

Opinion questions asked respondents to indicate agreement/disagreement on a 5-point scale. The results reported in the text are the combined "1" and "2" for agree and the combined "4" and "5" for disagree, unless otherwise noted. The variables are included in the statistical analyses in the 5-point version. When we refer in the text to percentage increases in the prevalence of perceived burdens or tensions, we are referring to increases in the sense of this scale.

The question measuring financial well-being was designed so that each age group would be ranked on a 5-point scale from "worst-off" (1) to "best-off" (5), with only one age group at each extreme. Respondents were not, however, always consistent in their answers. In other words, they may have ranked several groups as "worst-off" and none as "best-off." To adjust for this inconsistency, we rescaled responses so that each age group is ranked relative to the average answer given by each respondent. In other words, if a respondent indicated that all age groups but one were "worse-off than average," with the remaining group "worst-off," then the group designated as worst-off was scored a 4 rather than a 5, since they were only one category worse than the "average" group for that respondent.

Regressions

Four separate multivariate regression models are presented in Tables F.1–F.4. Each of these regressions was estimated using ordinary least squares. One should also be aware of the limitations in the statistical methods that underlay these results. In any multivariate statistical model, one can accurately identify the influence of a particular factor only if one has measured all the other factors that might plausibly be influencing tensions. Given the complexity of intergenerational perceptions, norms of equity, and relationships, it is almost certain that some relevant factors have been omitted, and their omission may have biased the results that are reported here.

TABLE F.1   Multiple Regression of Sociodemographic Characteristics on Reported Burdens and Tensions for Age-Targeted Public Programs for Children

	Attitudes toward benefits for children			
	Burdens: Benefits too costly		Tensions: Children get more than their fair share	
Explanatory variables	Coefficient	t-statistic	Coefficient	t-statistic
Education	−0.127	(4.26)*	−0.057	(2.07)*
Unemployed	0.351	(2.10)*	0.144	(0.94)
African American	0.042	(0.33)	0.108	(0.93)
Hispanic	0.194	(1.25)	0.106	(0.75)
Age				
25-44	−0.037	(0.35)	0.042	(0.44)
45-64	−0.080	(0.67)	0.146	(1.35)
65-69	0.332	(1.83)	0.299	(1.78)
70-74	−0.075	(0.36)	0.099	(0.51)
75-79	−0.015	(0.06)	0.508	(2.26)*
80 +	0.167	(0.65)	0.523	(2.10)*
Annual income				
$10,000-19,999	0.186	(1.39)	−0.067	(0.55)
$20,000-29,999	0.129	(0.97)	0.075	(0.62)
$30,000-49,999	0.037	(0.29)	−0.039	(0.34)
$50,000-74,999	0.037	(0.25)	0.004	(0.03)
$75,000-99,999	0.022	(0.11)	0.045	(0.27)
$100,000 +	0.652	(2.87)*	0.062	(0.29)
R^2	0.035		0.017	
F-statistic for regression	3.018		1.42	
Observations	1,355		1,346	

Note.   Education in six categories, ranging from less than high school to postgraduate training. African Americans and Hispanics compared to non-Hispanic whites. Age groups compared to those 24 and younger. Income groups compared to those with annual household incomes of under $10,000.

*$p \leq .05$.

TABLE F.2   Multiple Regression of Sociodemographic Characteristics on Reported Burdens and Tensions for Age-Targeted Public Programs for Elders

Explanatory variables	Attitudes toward benefits for elders			
	Burdens: Benefits too costly		Tensions: Elders get more than their fair share	
	Coefficient	t-statistic	Coefficient	t-statistic
Education	−0.097	(3.15)*	−0.011	(0.40)
Unemployed	0.270	(1.55)	0.091	(0.58)
African American	−0.162	(1.25)	−0.339	(2.84)*
Hispanic	0.145	(0.91)	−0.026	(0.18)
Age				
25-44	−0.154	(1.42)	−0.196	(1.98)*
45-64	−0.096	(0.78)	−0.129	(1.16)
65-69	0.015	(0.08)	−0.115	(0.66)
70-74	0.181	(0.82)	−0.103	(0.52)
75-79	−0.610	(2.40)*	0.342	(1.47)
80 +	−0.135	(0.89)	0.047	(0.19)
Annual income				
$10,000-19,999	0.064	(0.47)	0.112	(0.89)
$20,000-29,999	0.047	(0.34)	0.117	(0.93)
$30,000-49,999	−0.040	(0.30)	0.040	(0.34)
$50,000-74,999	−0.064	(0.42)	0.264	(1.89)
$75,000-99,999	−0.171	(0.80)	0.416	(2.12)*
$100,000 +	0.250	(1.07)	0.274	(1.28)
R^2	0.026		0.021	
F-statistic for regression	2.254		1.789	
Observations	1,355		1,361	

Note.   Education in six categories, ranging from less than high school to postgraduate training. African Americans and Hispanics compared to non-Hispanic whites. Age groups compared to those 24 and younger. Income groups compared to those with annual household incomes of under $10,000.

*$p \leq .05$.

TABLE F.3 Multiple Regression of Attitudes and Perceptions on Reported Burdens from Costs of Age-Targeted Federal Public Programs

| | Attitudes toward costs of federal benefits | | | |
| | Elders' benefits too costly | | Children's benefits too costly | |
Explanatory variables	Coefficient	t-statistic	Coefficient	t-statistic
Emotional bonds				
Close to mother	0.001	(0.01)		
Close to father	−0.050	(1.10)		
Close to oldest child			0.111	(1.77)*
Parents were emotionally supportive in the past	−0.049	(1.76)*		
Obligations				
Children owe to parents	−0.033	(1.54)		
Parents owe to children			0.026	(1.36)
Personal circumstances				
Female	−0.018	(0.26)	0.013	(0.19)
Two-earner household	0.065	(0.68)	−0.037	(0.40)
Married	−0.020	(0.22)	0.012	(0.14)
Competing needs				
Child care burdens families	0.058	(2.14)**	0.082	(3.28)**
Elder care burdens families	0.175	(7.01)**	0.135	(5.51)**
Education burdens communities	0.103	(3.84)**	0.080	(3.04)**
Health costs burden employers				
Personal resources				
Own age group well-off	−0.337	(2.85)**	−0.258	(2.19)**
Own life getting better	−0.019	(1.26)	−0.002	(0.11)
Unemployed	0.185	(1.12)	0.253	(1.56)

TABLE F.3 *continued*

Self-interest		
Over 65		
Has young children	−0.091 (0.75)	−0.087 (0.96)
Has school-aged children		−0.045 (0.50)
Size of recipient groups		
Percent of poor in community who are elders	0.014 (1.97)**	
Percent of poor in community who are children		0.015 (2.25)**
R^2	0.081	0.062
F-statistic for regression	8.179	6.591
Observations	1,409	1,406

*$p \leq .10$; **$p \leq .05$.

TABLE F.4 Multiple Regression of Attitudes and Perceptions Associated on Reported Tensions from Distribution of Federal Benefit Programs

Explanatory variables	The distribution of federal benefits			
	Elders get more than their fair share		Children get more than their fair share	
	Coefficient	t-statistic	Coefficient	t-statistic
Burdens from benefits				
For elders: too costly	0.131	(5.49)**		
For children: too costly			0.139	(5.73)**
Social Equity				
Parent's generation better off	0.025	(1.18)	0.072	(3.39)**
Intergenerational sharing				
Parents obligated to help	0.048	(1.89)*		
Helped by parents in past	−0.000	(0.08)		
Gifts from parents in past	0.000	(0.37)		
Adult children obligated to help parents			0.024	(0.87)
Helped by children in past			−0.007	(1.28)
Gifts from children in past			−0.000	(0.45)
Contribution to community				
Elders contribute a lot	−0.097	(3.08)**		
Young people contribute a lot			−0.077	(2.90)**
Relative needs				
Age group receiving benefits is financially well-off	0.466	(4.52)**	0.200	(2.01)**

TABLE F.4 continued

Age group receiving benefits is burden to most families	0.019	(0.80)	−0.082	(3.35)**
Elders earned special treatment	−0.164	(5.59)**		
Self-interest				
Age 65 +	0.236	(1.92)**	−0.114	(1.48)
Age 45 to 64	0.123	(1.41)	−0.142	(1.11)
Age 18 to 44			−0.094	(0.83)
Has young children			0.102	(1.41)
Has school-aged children			−0.022	(1.38)
Is or was divorced	−0.202	(2.77)**		
Own life will get better	0.010	(0.60)		
Programmatic/political equity				
Programs should be means-tested	0.046	(2.03)**	0.051	(2.26)**
Elders have more political voice	0.184	(6.23)**	0.002	(0.07)
R^2	0.141		0.068	
F-statistic for regression	13.488		6.078	
Observations	1,330		1,351	

$*p \leq .10;\ **p \leq .05.$

APPENDIX G

Survey Instrument

$\mathbf{T}$he following is an abbreviated version of the instrument used in the 1990 AARP Intergenerational Linkages Survey. Most instructions to the interviewer, response categories, and skip patterns have been omitted. Thus, this version does not indicate logical sequencing of items. Some question numbers are missing but all questions that were asked have been included.

(Make sure you are talking to an adult 18 years or older.)

Hello, my name is _____. I am calling from Ann Arbor, Michigan. Is this (XXX) XXX-XXXX? I am calling from DataStat, a national research firm. We are conducting a study about today's families and the relationships between different generations. **(If needed:** "This is purely a scientific study, we are not trying to sell anything or conduct any sort of business with you.") **(If needed:** "Your household was randomly selected to represent people in your area.") **(If R asks what is the study for:** "We are doing this research for a national nonprofit organization. It will help them develop better programs to serve families and individuals.") **(If needed:** "Your responses will be kept strictly confidential—only summaries of the answers from all respondents will be reported.") **(If they want to call and verify that this is genuine survey, give them Mr. . . .'s number at Datastat, (XXX) XXX-XXXX. They can call collect.)**

A1.   To choose one member of your household to interview, I need to know how many people 18 years of age or over, **including yourself,** are currently living in your household.
A2.   And who in your household, 18 years of age or older, had the most recent birthday?

A3.   Hello, my name is _____. [Same as above.]

1.   First, would you please tell me your age?

Intro.Q2 Now, I'd like to read you some statements about different groups of people.*
Rotate Q2, Q3, Q4, Q5

(2–5).   (How much do you agree or disagree that/How about)

> "Older people contribute a lot to their communities."
> "Younger people contribute a lot to their communities."
> "If the government cut back spending on programs for older people, we would all be hurt."
> "Senior citizen discounts—for instance, at movie theaters and on buses—are fair because older people deserve special treatment."

Intro.Q8 We are interested in looking at the relationships within families. Our definition of family includes: parents, stepparents, grandparents, in-laws, children, brothers and sisters, and grandchildren. We would like you first to think about when you were growing up.

8.   Before you reached age 18, did you **always** live with **both** of your parents?

(If R asks: This includes biological parents and adopted parents, but not stepparents or foster parents) (If R asks: This does not include leaving for college)

9.   Was that because your parents were divorced or one of them died or for some other reason? **Note: If R says both divorced and died, ask:** "Which happened first?"
10.   And how old were you when [your parents got their divorce/that happened (one/both of them died)]?

Intro.Q12 Now, **focusing on the present,** we would like to discuss how family members interact. We are interested in the size of your family and whether the relatives I mention live near you or far away from you.

12.   Is your mother still living?

(If R asks: This includes biological parents and adopted parents, but not stepparents or foster parents)

13.   Does she live with you?
14.   Does she live within one hour driving time from you?
15.   Is your father still living?

(If R asks: This includes biological parents and adopted parents, but not stepparents or foster parents)

16.   Does he live with you?
17.   Does he live within one hour driving time from you?
18.   Do your parents live together?
19.   Do you have a stepmother?
20.   Does she live with you?
21.   Does she live within one hour (driving time) from you?
22.   Do you have a stepfather?
23.   Does he live with you?
24.   Does he live within one hour (driving time) from you?
25.   Are any of your grandparents still living?
26.   Do any of your grandparents live with you?
27.   Do any [of your/other] grandparents live within one hour (driving time) from you?
28.   How many children do you have?
29–48.   Could you please give me the age of each one of your children and for each one tell me if they are currently married.
49.   Does your [**(age of oldest child)** year old child/oldest child 18 or over] live with you?
50.   Does your [**(age of oldest child)** year old child/oldest child 18 or over] live within one hour driving time from you?
51.   Does your [**(age of youngest adult child)** year old child/youngest child 18 or over] live with you?
52.   Does your [**(age of youngest adult child)** year old child/youngest child 18 or over] live within one hour (driving time) from you?
53.   Do you have any grandchildren 18 years of age or older?
54.   How many grandchildren 18 or over do you have?
55.   Do any of these adult grandchildren live with you?
56.   Does your oldest grandchild live with you?
57.   Do any of your adult grandchildren live within one hour (driving time) from you?

61. Today, how often do you see or have contact with your mother?
62. Today, how often do you see or have contact with your father?
63. In general, how close do you feel to your mother?**
64. In general, how close do you feel to your father?**
65. Now think about your childhood and the grandparent or grand-parents that you **saw and had contact with most often as a child.** How often did you see or have contact with this grandparent or set of grandparents? **(Interviewer: If R says "every day" probe with: "Did you live with them?")**
66. In general, would you say these grandparents' influence on you was very important, somewhat important, not very important, or not at all important?
67. Now think about the grandparents with whom you have the most contact **today.** How often do you **now** see or have contact with your grandparents?
68. In general, how close do you feel to these grandparents **today?**

Intro.Q69 Now, let's think about your [**adult** children/**adult child**], age 18 or older.

69. Although you can probably make distinctions among them, in general, how close do you feel to your **adult** children?**
70. **Today,** how often do you **see or have contact with** your [oldest] adult child?
70a. In general, how close do you feel to your oldest adult child?**
71. Is there one adult child that you feel closer to than the others?
72. How old is that child?
73. Is that child a son or a daughter?

Intro.Q74 Now let's think about your [**adult** grandchildren/**adult** grandchild], age 18 or older.

74. Although you can probably make distinctions among them, how close do you feel to your adult grandchildren?**
75. **Today,** how often do you **see or have contact with** your [oldest] adult grandchild?
76. How close do you feel to your oldest adult grandchild?**

Intro.Q77 Now, I'd like to read you some statements about programs and policies that benefit different generations.*
Rotate Q77, Q78

Rotate Q80, Q82
Rotate Q83, Q84, Q85

(How much do you agree or disagree that/How about)
(77, 78).

> "Persons aged 65 and over get more than their fair share of government programs and tax benefits."
> "Children and youth get more than their fair share of government programs and tax benefits."

(80, 82).

> "Advocates for older Americans have been more successful than those representing children and youth."
> "If choices must be made, government benefits should be given on the basis of need instead of age."

(83, 84, 85).

> "People who are wealthy should share their advantages with people who are not wealthy."
> "There's still plenty of opportunity for young people to achieve a better life than their parents."
> "My parents' generation had a better standard of living than my generation has."

Intro.Q88 Now we'd like to know how similar you think your values and opinions are to those of your different relatives.

88.   How similar are your opinions to those of your mother?***
89.   How similar are your opinions to those of your father?***
90.   How similar are your opinions to those of your [oldest] child?***
91.   How similar are your opinions to those of your grandparents?***
92.   How similar are your opinions to those of your [oldest] grandchild?***

Intro.Q93 I am now going to read you some statements about the cost of educational, social service, and income support programs.*
Rotate Q93, Q94, Q95, Q96, Q97, Q98, Q99, Q100, Q101

(93-101).   (How much do you agree or disagree that/How about)

"Child-care costs are too much of a burden for many families."
"Providing care for older parents is too much of a burden for their families."
"Many employers are not able to finance pension and health benefits for their **retirees.**"
"Many employers are unable to finance health care insurance for employees and their families."
"Communities cannot afford to provide quality public education."
"Federal programs that provide benefits to older persons are too costly."
"Federal programs for children and youth are too costly."
"College students whose family income is over $35,000 should not be eligible for government loans."
"The federal government has a responsibility to assure that everyone gets the health care they need."

103. Now, using a scale from 0 to 10, thinking of "0" as representing the worst possible life you could imagine and "10" as the best possible life you could imagine, what number from "0" to "10" would you use to rate your life **at the present time?**
104. Where on a scale of "0" to "10" do you think you were **five years ago?** (Where "0" represents the worst possible life you could imagine and "10" the best possible life you could imagine.)
105. Where on a scale of "0" to "10" do you think you will be **five years from now?** (Where "0" represents the worst possible life you could imagine and "10" the best possible life you could imagine.)

Intro.Q106 Now, I'd like you to compare some different age groups in terms of how well off they are financially. Use a "5" if you feel that the age group is the best off financially, a "1" if you feel that the age group is the worst off financially, or a number anywhere in between.

(106–109). (How well off are/How about)

"Children under 18 years?"
"Young adults—18 to 34 years old?"
"Adults 35 to 59 years old?"
"Older adults—aged 60 and over?"

Intro.Q112 The next few questions are about the role that volunteer activities may play in your life. Please think of **formal volunteering** as help you provide for free to organizations such as charities, schools, religious organizations, and civic groups. This formal volunteering does **not** include help you provide to your own family members, friends, or neighbors.

112.   Do you **ever** volunteer any of your time to these types of activities or organizations?
113.   For what needs or types of programs do you volunteer your time?

(Select all that apply.) (If R says "charity," probe: "What type of organization would that be?") **(Probe for specific kinds of programs.)**

01.   Arts, culture and humanities; 02. Civic organizations and fraternal associations/foundations; 03. Community/neighborhood action; 04. Disease-related causes/organizations; 05. Education/tutoring; 06. Environment/animals/conservation; 07. Health care; 08. Housing/homeless; 09. International; 10. Political/legislative/advocacy; 11. Recreation/sports; 12. Religious; 13. Senior citizen organizations; 14. Social services and welfare; 15. Youth groups; other _____ (specify)

Intro.Q114 Some volunteer programs benefit people of all ages; others benefit people in particular age groups, such as children and teenagers, or adults ages 20–59, or older people 60 and over.

114.   How much of your volunteer time is spent on activities that benefit people of **all** ages?****
115.   How much of your volunteer time is spent on activities that benefit children and teenagers?****
116.   How much of your volunteer time is spent on activities that benefit adults aged 20 through 59?****
117.   How much of your volunteer time is spent on activities that benefit older persons aged 60 and over?****
118.   On average, approximately how many **hours per month** do you spend doing **formal** volunteer activities?

Intro.Q119 Now we would like to ask about **financial contributions** you may have made to voluntary and charitable organizations, including religious institutions. Sometimes people give money, or they donate items, or spend their own money in supporting voluntary or charitable programs.

119.   Thinking about all of these types of support, approximately how much did you spend in the past year? Please stop me when I reach the total dollar value of money and **items** you gave last year to support voluntary and charitable activities. Was it . . . **(read list) 1. $50.00 or less; 2. $51.00–$100.00; 3. $101.00–$300.00; 4. $301.00–$500.00; 5. $501.00–$1,000.00; 6. $1,001.00–$5,000.00; or was it 7. More than $5,000.00?**

Intro.Q120 Now, please think about **help that you provide for free** to neighbors, friends, and family members who don't live with you. This might include doing things like baby-sitting, running errands for a friend, or helping a neighbor with repairs. This does **not** include help you give to dependent children under age 18 who live with you.

120.   Do you **ever provide this type of** help to neighbors, friends, or family members?
121.   What types of activities are you likely to do? **(Do not read list) (Select all that apply) 01. House/animal sitting; 02. Gardening/lawn care; 03. Household chores (e.g., cleaning, laundry, and cooking); 04. Repairs/maintenance; 05. Running errands; 06. Transportation; 07. Personal care (e.g., dressing, bathing); 08. Baby-sitting/adult caregiving; 09. Entertainment/recreation; 10. Tutoring; 11. Other _____ (Specify)**
122.   Who do you help in this way? **(If R says family, probe:** "Which members of your family would that be?")
123.   On average, approximately how many **hours per month** do you spend helping people in this way?

Intro.Q124 Now, please think about help **you receive,** that you don't pay for, from neighbors, friends, and family members who don't live with you. This includes free help you receive for things like baby-sitting, household chores, home repairs, shopping, and transportation. This does not include the help you receive from dependent children under age 18 who live with you.

124.   Do you ever receive this type of help from neighbors, friends, or family members?
125.   What type of help do you receive?
126.   Who are the people who help you?
127.   On average, approximately how many **hours** of help **per month** do you **receive?**

128. Are you familiar with the Social Security program?

Def.Q128 Social security is a national social program that provides income when workers retire or are disabled and provides benefits to dependent survivors when a worker dies. Retirement payments are based on workers' earnings during employment.

Intro.Q129 Now I'm going to read you some statements about Social Security.*
Rotate Q129, Q130, Q131, Q132, Q133

(129–133). (How much do you agree or disagree that/How about)

> "Social Security and Medicare are an earned right for persons aged 62 and over."
> "Social Security benefits should be highest for those who are poor."
> "Households headed by persons over age 62 with a joint income greater than $35,000.00 should not receive Social Security benefits."
> "Everyone should receive Social Security **benefits,** but they should be subject to federal income taxes."
> "All workers should pay Social Security **taxes** on their entire income."

134. Are you familiar with the Medicare program?

Def.Q134 Medicare is a national health insurance plan for people over 65 and for some people under 65 who are disabled. It includes two parts: part A covers hospital costs and some skilled nursing care, and part B is the supplemental portion covering a portion of the physician's fee as well as various types of therapy.

Intro.Q135 Now I'm going to read you some statements about the Medicare program.*
Rotate Q135, Q136, Q137, Q138

(135–138). (How much do you agree or disagree that/How about)

> "Medicare premiums should be based on income."
> "The government should add coverage of nursing home care and home health care to Medicare, even if it means higher federal

taxes for everyone."
"The dollar value of Medicare benefits should be included in federal income tax calculations."
"All people over age 65 should pay a larger share of their medical costs than they do today."

Intro.Q139 People often give gifts for special occasions, such as birthdays, anniversaries, graduations, and religious holidays.

139. Do you regularly give these types of gifts to family members and friends?

Intro.Q140 Sometimes individuals also give **special assistance** or **large gifts** to family members or friends. These may be in the form of money or gifts of major items. These may include large gifts for birthdays, graduations, weddings, births, or religious holidays.

140. Have you **ever** given any of these large gifts or major types of financial assistance to your **adult** [child/children]?
141. What types of gifts did you give your adult [child/children]? **(Do not read.) (Select all that apply.) 01. Major appliance/audio visual equipment/furniture; 02. Automobile; 03. Vacation trip; 04. Down payment for purchasing a home; 05. Real estate (land, house, apartment, condo); 06. Other housing costs (rent, major repairs, etc.); 07. Insurance policy; 08. Stock, bonds; 09. Certificate of deposit; 10. Savings account; 11. Educational expenses; 12. Travel expenses; 13. Loan of money without interest; 14. Cash; 15. Other _____ (specify)**
142. What would you estimate to be the total value of these gifts and financial assistance that you have given to your adult [child/children]?
143. **In the past three years,** have you given anyone [other than your [child/children]] this type of financial assistance or large gift?
144. What types of gifts were they?
145. What would you estimate to be the total value of these gifts and financial assistance?
146. Now, thinking about yourself, in the past three years, have you **received** this type of major financial assistance or gift?
147. What types of gifts have you received?
148. Who gave you the financial assistance or gifts? **(If R says "family," probe:** "Which members of your family would that be?")
149. What would you estimate to be the total value of these gifts and financial assistance?
150. What is your current marital status? Are you . . . **1. married, 2.**

separated, 3. divorced, 4. widowed, or 5. have you never been married?

151.   Some people inherit gifts or money from family members or friends who die. In **the last five years,** have you **received such an inheritance** from a relative or friend?

152.   As best as you can estimate, what was the total dollar value of the **noncash items** you inherited?

153.   What was the dollar amount of any **cash** you received?

154.   Now, please think about what you might leave to others in the future. Do you have plans to **leave an inheritance** to your family [other than your spouse], to your friends, or to charitable organizations?

155.   Are you planning to leave an inheritance to . . . **(Read list.) (Select all that apply.) 1. Your family? 2. Friends? 3. Charitable organizations? 4. Any place else? (Specify)**

Intro.Q156 Another way that people assist one another is to provide housing when needed.

156.   Have you ever **provided housing in your own home** for [your adult child/any of your adult children] [or] [your adult grandchild/any of your adult grandchildren]? **(If R says they have provided part-time housing, probe:** "Would that be for more than half of the year?" **If "yes," enter "yes.")**

157.   For how many years was that?

158.   Have you ever provided housing **in your own home** for a parent or grandparent? **(If R says they have provided part-time housing, probe:** "Would that be for more than half of the year?" **If "yes," enter "yes.")**

159.   For how many years was that?

160.   Have you ever **lived in the home** of [your adult child/any of your adult children] [or] [your adult grandchild/any of your adult grandchildren]? **(If R says they lived there part-time, probe:** "Would that be for more than half of the year?" **If "yes," enter "yes.")**

161.   For how many years did you live there?

162.   As an adult, have you ever **lived in the home** of your parent or grandparent? **(If R says they lived there part-time, probe:** "Would that be for more than half of the year?" **If "yes," enter "yes.")**

163.   For how many years did you live there?

Intro.Q164 I am now going to read you some statements about family relationships.*

Rotate Q164, Q165, Q166, Q167, Q168

(164–168).   (How much do you agree or disagree that/How about)

> "Grown children should not be expected to support their parents."
> "Parents whose adult children have financial problems should assist them with housing costs."
> "Parents should save money or property to leave as an inheritance for their children."
> "Parents should assist adult children in paying for health care, if those children cannot do it themselves."
> "Parents should assist adult children with their child care if needed."

Intro.Q170 For each of the following statements I read, please tell me how well that statement describes **you personally.** Use a "5" if it describes you perfectly, a "1" if it does not describe you at all, or a number anywhere in between.
Rotate Q170, Q171, Q172

(170–172).   (How well does this statement describe you?/How about)

> "I've always known I could count on my parents for emotional support when I needed it."
> "If I were ever in financial trouble, I'd rather get help from the government than from my family."
> "Without financial help from my parents when I was starting out, I would never have gotten this far."

Intro.Q182 Now I have a few final questions for classification purposes only.

182.   **(Interviewer record gender)**
183.   How many times have you been married?
184.   How many of your previous marriages ended in divorce?
185.   Have you ever been the single parent in a household with children aged 17 and under?
186.   For how many years were you a single parent with children aged 17 and under at home?
187.   Do you own or rent your current residence?
188.   Are you working in a job for pay full-time, part-time, or not at all?
189.   As I read the following list, please tell me which ones describe

your current employment situation: **(Read list.) (Select all that apply.)**
1. Looking for paid work? 2. Retired? 3. A homemaker? 4. A full-time
student? 5. Disabled? 6. Something I haven't mentioned? _____
(Specify)
190.   What [is/was] your occupation? Please be as specific as you can.
(If R gives area they work in, such as "real estate or "manufactur-
ing," probe: "Can you tell what you personally [do/did] in that field?")
191.   What [is/was] your spouse's **occupation?**
192.   Including yourself, all children, and other adults, how many people live in your household?
193.   What is the last grade of school you completed?
195.   Are you, yourself, of Hispanic origin or descent, such as
Mexican, Puerto Rican, Cuban, or some other Spanish background?
196.   Do you consider yourself to be white, black, or of some other race?

[Q194 shown in order asked]

194.   Please stop me when I read the category that describes your
household's total annual income in 1989 from all sources before taxes?
197.   Finally, for statistical purposes only, may I please have your zip
code?
199.   That's the last question that I have, but in case my supervisor
wants to make sure I did this interview, could I have your first name?
(Our supervisors verify about ten percent of all interviews completed
just to make sure that the interviewers are being polite and friendly to
the people that they talk to.)

Thanks.

Thank you very much for your time. The information you have given
us will be very helpful. Have a pleasant day/evening.

NOTES

*Please tell me how strongly you agree or disagree with the statement
using a 5-point scale where a "5" means you strongly agree, and a "1"
means you strongly disagree. You may use any number from "5" to "1."
**Do you feel very close, somewhat close, or not at all close to [her,
him, them]?

***Are they very similar, somewhat similar, somewhat different, or very different?

****Would you say all of your volunteer time, most of it, some of it, or none of your volunteer time?

REFERENCES

Achenbaum, W. A. (1993). Generational relations in historical context. In V. L. Bengtson & W. A. Achenbaum (Eds.), *The changing contract across generations* (pp. 25–42). Hawthorne, NY: Aldine de Gruyter.

ACTION. (1975). *Americans volunteer—1974.* Washington, DC: U.S. Government Printing Office.

Alderfer, C. (1972). *Existence, relatedness, and growth.* New York: The Free Press.

Aldous, J. (1987). New views on the family life of the elderly and near elderly. *Journal of Marriage and the Family, 49,* 227–234.

Altergott, K. (1985). Marriage, gender, and social relations in later life. In W. B. Peterson & J. Quadagno (Eds.), *Social bonds in later life* (pp. 51–70). Newbury Park, CA: Sage.

Alves, W., & Rossi, P. (1978). Who should get what? Fairness judgements of the distribution of income. *American Journal of Sociology, 84*(3), 541–564.

American Association of Retired Persons. (1987). *Intergenerational tension in 1987: Real or imagined?* Washington, DC: Public Policy Institute, American Association of Retired Persons.

Aquilino, W., & Supple, K. (1991). Parent–child relations and parent's satisfaction with living arrangements. *Journal of Marriage and the Family, 53,* 13–27.

Bane, M. J., & Ellwood, D. (1989). One fifth of the nation's children: Why are they poor? *Science, 245,* 1047–1053.

Bar-Tal, D. (1984). American study of helping behavior. In E. Staub, D. Bar-Tal, J. Karylowski, & J. Rykowski (Eds.), *Development of prosocial behavior* (pp. 5–27). New York: Plenum Press.

Baybrooke, D. (1987). *Meeting needs.* Princeton, NJ: Princeton University Press.

Bengtson, V. L. (1990). Toward understanding health in older families impacted by Alzheimer's Disease. In T. Brubaker (Ed.), *Family relationships in later life* (2nd ed.), pp. 245–266. Newbury Park, CA: Sage.

Bengtson, V. L., & Allen, K. R. (1993). The life course perspective applied to families over time. In P. Boss, W. Doherty, R. LaRossa, W. Schumm, & S. Steinmetz (Eds.), *Sourcebook of family theories and methods: A contextual approach* (pp. 469–498). New York: Plenum Press.

Bengtson, V. L., Cutler, N. E., Mangen, D. J., & Marshall, V. W. (1985). Generations, cohorts, and relations between age groups. In R. H. Binstock & E. Shanas (Eds.), *Handbook of aging and the social sciences* (2nd ed., pp. 304–338). New York: Van Nostrand.

Bengtson, V. L., & Kuypers, J. A. (1971). Generational differences and the developmental stake. *Aging and Human Development, 2,* 249–260.

Bengtson, V. L., & Kuypers, J. A. (1985). The family support cycle: Psychosocial issues in the aging family. In J. M. A. Munnichs, P. Mussen, & E. Olbrich (Eds.), *Life span and change in a gerontological perspective* (pp. 61–77). New York: Academic Press.

Bengtson, V. L., Mangen, D. J., & Landry, P. J. (1984). The multi-generation family: Concepts and findings. In V. Garms-Homolova, E. M. Hoerning, & D. Schaeffer (Eds.), *Intergenerational relationships* (pp. 63–80). Lewiston, NY: C. J. Hogrefe.

Bengtson, V. L., Marti, G., & Roberts, R. E. L. (1991). Age group relations: Generational equity and inequity. In K. Pillemer & K. McCartney (Eds.), *Parent–child relations across the lifespan* (pp. 253–278). Hillsdale, NJ: Lawrence Erlbaum Associates.

Bengtson, V. L., & Murray, T. M. (1993). Justice across generations (and cohorts): Sociological perspectives on the life course and reciprocities over time. In L. Cohen (Ed.), *Justice across generations: What does it mean?* (pp. 111–138). Washington, DC: American Association of Retired Persons.

Bengtson, V. L., Rosenthal, C., & Burton, L. M. (1990). Families and aging: Diversity and heterogeneity. In R. H. Binstock & L. K. George (Eds.), *Handbook of aging and the social sciences* (3rd ed., pp. 263–287). New York: Academic Press.

Bengtson, V. L., & Schrader, S. S. (1982). Parent–child relations. In D. Mangen & W. Peterson (Eds.), *Handbook of research instruments in social gerontology* (Vol. 2, 115–185). Minneapolis: University of Minnesota Press.

Binney, E. A., & Estes, C. L. (1988). The retreat of the state and its transfer of responsibility: The intergenerational war. *International Journal of Health Services, 18,* 83–96.

Binstock, R. H. (1983). The aged as scapegoat. *The Gerontologist, 23,* 136–143.

Binstock, R. H. (1990). Aging and the politics of health-care reform. In C. Eisdorfer, D. Kessler, & A. Spector (Eds.), *Caring for the elderly:*

Reshaping health policy (pp. 422–447). Baltimore, MD: Johns Hopkins.

Binstock, R. H. (1992). Older voters and the 1992 presidential election. *The Gerontologist, 32,* 601–606.

Binstock, R. H. (1993, November). *A decade of balancing age and need as eligibility criteria.* Paper presented at the meeting of the Gerontological Society of America, New Orleans, LA.

Blau, Z. (1961). Structural constraints on friendship in old age. *American Sociological Review, 26,* 429–438.

Blumenthal, D., Schlesinger, M., & Brown-Drumheller, P. (1988). *Renewing the promise: Medicare and its reform.* New York: Oxford University Press.

Brody, E. M. (1985). Parent care as a normative family stress. *The Gerontologist, 25,* 19–29.

Brubaker, T. H. (1990). Families in later life: A burgeoning research area. *Journal of Marriage and the Family, 52,* 959–981.

Burton, L. (in press). Intergenerational support within African American families. In V. L. Bengtson, K. W. Schaie, & L. M. Burton (Eds.), *Intergenerational issues in aging.* New York: Springer.

Chambré, S. M. (1987). *Good deeds in old age: Volunteering by the new leisure class.* Lexington, MA: D. C. Heath and Company.

Chen, Y-P. (1989). Low confidence in Social Security is not warranted. *Journal of Aging and Social Policy, 1,* 103–130.

Committee on an Aging Society. (1986). Summary. In Institute of Medicine, *Productive roles in an older society* (pp. 1–22). Washington, DC: National Academy Press.

Cook, F., & Barrett, E. (1993). *Support for the American welfare state.* New York: Columbia University Press.

Cooney, T., & Uhlenberg, P. (1990). The role of divorce in men's relations with their adult children after mid-life. *Journal of Marriage and the Family, 52,* 677–688.

Coughlin, R. (1980). *Ideology, public opinion and welfare policy: Attitudes toward taxes and spending in industrialized societies.* Berkeley, CA: University of California at Berkeley Institute of International Studies.

Cox, D., & Raines, F. (1985). Interfamily transfers and income redistribution. In M. David & T. Smeeding (Eds.), *Horizontal equity, uncertainty, and economic well-being* (pp. 393–425). Chicago, IL: University of Chicago Press.

Daniels, N. (1989). Justice and transfers between generations. In P. Johnson, C. Conrad, & D. Thomson (Eds.), *Workers versus pension-*

ers: Intergenerational justice in an ageing world (pp. 57–79). Manchester, UK: Manchester University Press.

Dewit, D., Wister, A., & Burch, T. (1988). Physical distance and social contact between elders and their adult children. *Research on Aging, 10,* 56–80.

Doty, P. (1986). Family care of the elderly: The role of public policy. *The Milbank Quarterly, 64,* 34–75.

Dougherty, C. (1988). *American health care: Realities, rights, and reforms.* New York: Oxford University Press.

Dychtwald, K., & Flowers, J. (1989). *Age wave.* Los Angeles: Tarcher.

Easterlin, R. A. (1987). The new age structure of poverty in America: Permanent or transient? *Population and Development Review, 13*(2), 195–208.

Eggebeen, D. J., & Hogan, D. P. (1990). Giving between generations in American families. *Human Nature, 1,* 211–232.

Elder, G. H., Rudkin, L., & Conger R. D. (in press). Intergenerational continuity and change in rural America. In V. L. Bengtson, K. W. Schaie, & L. M. Burton (Eds.), *Intergenerational issues in aging.* New York: Springer.

Espenshade, T. (1984). *Investing in children: New estimates of parental expenditures.* Washington, DC: Urban Institute Press.

Fischer, C. S. (1982). *To dwell among friends: Personal networks in town and city.* Chicago: University of Chicago Press.

Foner, A. (1974). Age stratification and age conflict in political life. *American Sociological Review, 39,* 187–196.

Fowler, F. J., Jr. (1984). *Survey research methods.* Beverly Hills, CA: Sage.

Gans, H. (1962). *The urban villagers.* New York: The Free Press.

Gerber, J., Wolff, J., Klores, W., & Brown, G. (1989). *Lifetrends: The future of baby boomers and other aging Americans.* New York: Macmillan.

Gibbs, N. (February 22, 1988). Grays on the go: America's seniors are more numerous, active and powerful, but their clout comes at a cost. *Time,* 66–75.

Gibbs, N. (October 6, 1990). Shameful bequests to the next generation. *Time,* 42–46.

Gist, J., & Aleksa, K. (1993). *Entitlements and the federal budget deficit: Setting the record straight.* Washington, DC: Public Policy Institute, American Association of Retired Persons.

Gold, D. T., Woodbury, M. A., & George, L. K. (1990). Relationship classification using grade of membership analysis: A typology of sibling relationships in later life. *Journal of Gerontology: Social Sciences, 45,* S43–51.

Gurin, P., Miller, A., & Gurin, G. (1980). Stratum identification and consciousness. *Social Psychology Quarterly, 43,* 30–47.

Hagestad, G. O. (1986). The family: Women and grandparents as kinkeepers. In A. Pifer & L. Bronte (Eds.), *Our aging society: Paradox and promise* (pp. 141–160). New York: W. W. Norton.

Hagestad, G. O. (1987). Parent–child relations in later life: Trends and gaps in past research. In J. Lancaster, J. Altmann, A. Rossi, & L. Sherrod (Eds.), *Parenting across the life span: Biosocial dimensions* (pp. 405–534). New York: Aldine De Gruyter.

Harootyan, R. A. (1981). Interest groups and the development of federal legislation affecting older Americans. In R. B. Hudson (Ed.), *The aging in politics: Process and policy* (pp. 74–85). Springfield, IL: Charles C. Thomas.

Harris, L. (1981). *Aging in the eighties: America in transition.* Washington, DC: National Council on the Aging.

Hayes-Batista, D., Schink, W., & Chapa, J. (1988). *The burden of support: Young Latinos in an aging society.* Stanford, CA: Stanford University Press.

Heclo, H. (1988). Generational politics. In J. Palmer, T. Smeeding, & B. B. Torrey (Eds.), *The vulnerable* (pp. 381–411). Washington, DC: The Urban Institute Press.

Henry, G. T. (1990). *Practical sampling.* Newbury Park, CA: Sage.

Herzog, A. R., Kahn, R. L., Morgan, J. N., Jackson, J. S., & Antonucci, T. C. (1989). Age differences in productive activities. *Journal of Gerontology, 44,* 129–138.

Hing, E. (1987). *Use of nursing homes by the elderly: Preliminary data from the 1985 national nursing home survey* (Advance Data from Vital and Health Statistics, No. 135). Hyattsville, MD: National Center for Health Statistics.

Hochschild, J. (1981). *What's fair? American beliefs about distributive justice.* Cambridge, MA: Harvard University Press.

Holt, D., & Smith, T. M. (1979). Post stratification. *Journal of the Royal Statistical Society, 142* (Series A), 33–46.

Howe, N. (1990). *Entitlements and the aging of America.* Washington, DC: National Taxpayers Union Foundation.

Hudson, R. B. (1978). The "graying" of the federal budget and its consequences for old-age policy. *The Gerontologist, 18,* 428–440.

Hudson, R. B. (1993). Social contingencies, the aged, and public policy. *The Milbank Quarterly, 71,* 253–277.

Hurd, M. (1989). The economic status of the elderly. *Science, 244,* 659–664.

Independent Sector. (1985). *Volunteer Statistics.* Paper presented at the annual meeting of The Independent Sector, Washington, DC.

Independent Sector. (1986). *Americans volunteer 1985.* Washington, DC: Author.

Independent Sector. (1990). *Giving and volunteering in the United States.* Washington, DC: Author.

Independent Sector. (1992). *Giving and volunteering in the United States: Findings from a national survey.* Washington, DC: Author.

Jackson, J. S. (1980). *Minorities and aging.* Belmont, CA: Wadsworth.

Jackson, T. (1991). Volunteerism: Developing an agenda for the future. In American Association of Retired Persons and Cornell University (Eds.), *Resourceful aging: Today and tomorrow* (pp. 95–97). Washington, DC: American Association of Retired Persons.

Jaynes, G. D., & Williams, R. M., Jr. (1989). *A common destiny: Blacks and American society.* Washington, DC: National Academy Press.

Johnson, P., Conrad, C., & Thomson, D. (1989). Workers versus pensioners: Intergenerational justice in an ageing world. London: Centre for Economic Policy Research.

Kalton, G. (1983). *Introduction to survey sampling.* Newbury Park, CA: Sage.

Kennickell, A., & Shack-Marquez, J. (1992). Changes in family finances from 1983 to 1989: Evidence from the survey of consumer finances. *Federal Reserve Bulletin, 78*(1), 1–18.

Kieffer, J. A. (1986). The older volunteer resource. In Committee on an Aging Society (Ed.), *Productive roles in an older society* (pp. 51–72). Washington, DC: National Academy Press.

Kingson, E. R. (1988). Generational equity: An unexpected opportunity to broaden the politics of aging. *The Gerontologist, 28,* 765–772.

Kingson, E. R., Hirshorn, B. A., & Cornman, J. M. (1986). *Ties that bind: The interdependence of generations.* Washington, DC: Seven Locks Press.

Kluegel, J., & Smith, E. (1986). *Beliefs about inequality: Americans' views of what is and what ought to be.* New York: Aldine De Gruyter.

Kotlikoff, L. (1992). *Generational accounting: Knowing who pays, and when, for what we spend.* New York: The Free Press.

Kreps, J. (1977). Intergenerational transfers and the bureaucracy. In E. Shanas & M. Sussman (Eds.), *Family, bureaucracy and the elderly* (pp. 21–34). Durham, NC: Duke University Press.

Kriegel, A. (1978). Generational difference: The history of an idea. *Daedalus, 107*(4), 23–38.

Laslett, P. (1992). Is there a generational contract? In P. Laslett & J. S. Fishkin (Eds.), *Justice between age groups and generations* (pp. 24–47). New Haven: Yale University Press.

Lawton, L. (1990a, May). *The quality of the parent/adult-child relationship and family structure.* Paper presented at the Annual Meeting of the Population Association of America, Toronto.

Lawton, L. (1990b, November). *The effect of marital disruption on the parent/adult-child relationship.* Paper presented at the Annual Meeting of the Gerontological Society of America, Boston.

Lazear, E., & Michael, R. (1980). Family size and the distribution of real per capita income. *American Economic Review, 70,* 91–107.

Lee, E. S., Forthofer, R. N., & Lorimor, R. J. (1989). *Analyzing complex survey data.* Newbury Park, CA: Sage.

Lillydahl, J., & Singell, L. (1982). The scope of the grants economy and income distribution: An examination of intergenerational transfers of income. *American Journal of Economics and Sociology, 41,* 125–139.

Litwak, E. (1985). *Helping the elderly: The complementary roles of informal networks and formal systems.* New York: Guilford Press.

Litwak, E., & Longino, C. F. (1987). Migration patterns among the elderly: A developmental perspective. *The Gerontologist, 27,* 266–272.

Longman, P. (1986). Age wars: The coming battle between young and old. *The Futurist, 20,* 8–11.

Longman, P. (1987). *Born to pay: The new politics of aging in America.* Boston, MA: Houghton Mifflin.

Maddox, G. L., & Lawton, M. P. (1993). *Annual review of gerontology and geriatrics, Vol. 13: Kinship, aging, and social change.* New York: Springer.

Mangen, D. J., Bengtson, V. L., & Landry, P. H., Jr. (Eds.). (1988). *Measurement of intergenerational relations.* Newbury Park, CA: Sage.

Mannheim, K. (1952). The problem of generations. In P. Kecskemeti (Ed. and Trans.), *Essays on the sociology of knowledge* (pp. 276–320). London: Routledge & Kegan Paul. (Original work published 1928)

Marshall, V. W., Cook, F. L., & Marshall, J. G. (1993). Conflict over intergenerational equity: Rhetoric and reality in a comparative context. In V. L. Bengtson & W. A. Achenbaum (Eds.), *The changing contract across generations* (pp. 119–140). Hawthorne, NY: Aldine de Gruyter.

McCormick, J. (Fall/Winter, 1991). Where are the parents? *Newsweek,* Special Issue, 55–58.

McPherson, M. S., & Schapiro, M. O. (1991). *Keeping college affordable: Government and educational opportunity.* Washington, DC: Brookings Institution.

Meyers, C., & Wolff, N. (1992). *Social Security and individual equity.* Westport, CT: Greenwood Press.

Mindel, C. (1983). The elderly in minority families. In T. Brubaker (Ed.), *Family relationships in later life* (pp. 193–208). Newbury Park, CA: Sage.

Minkler, M. (1986). "Generational equity" and the new victim blaming: An emerging public policy issue. *International Journal of Health Services, 16*(4), 539–551.

Minkler, M., & Robertson, A. (1991, Autumn). Generational equity and public health policy: A critique of "age/race war" thinking. *Journal of Public Health Policy,* 322–341.

Minow, M., & Weisbourd, R. (1993, Winter). Social movements for children. *Daedalus, 122*(1), 1–30.

Mishel, L., & Bernstein, J. (1992). *The state of working America: 1992-93.* Washington, DC: Economic Policy Institute.

Mishel, L., & Frankel, D. M. (1993). *The state of working America: 1992-1993.* Armonk, NY: M. E. Sharpe.

Moore, L. F. (Ed.). (1985). *Motivating volunteers: How the rewards of unpaid work can meet people's needs.* Vancouver, B.C.: Vancouver Volunteer Centre.

Morgan, J. (1978). Intra-family transfers revisited: The support of dependents inside the family. In G. Duncan & J. Morgan (Eds.), *Five thousand American families—Patterns of economic progress* (Vol. 6, pp. 347–365). Ann Arbor, MI: Institute for Social Research.

Morgan, J. (1983). The redistribution of income by families and institutions and emergency help patterns. In G. Duncan & J. Morgan (Eds.), *Five thousand American families—Patterns of economic progress* (Vol. 10, pp. 1–59). Ann Arbor, MI: Institute for Social Research.

Morgan, J. (1984). The role of time in the measurement of transfers and well-being. In M. Moon (Ed.), *Economic transfers in the U.S.* (pp. 199–238). Chicago, IL: University of Chicago Press.

Morgan, J. (1986). Unpaid productive activity over the life course. In Committee on an Aging Society, Institute of Medicine and National Research Council (Ed.), *America's aging: Productive roles in an older society* (pp. 73–109). Washington, DC: National Academy Press.

Munnell, A. H., & Ernsberger, C. N. (1988, November/December). Wealth transfer taxation: The relative role for estate and income taxes. *New England Economic Review,* pp. 3–28.

National Center for Health Statistics. (1992). *Vital statistics of the U.S.* Washington, DC: Government Printing Office.

National Education Association. (1989). *Estimates of School Statistics— 1989-1990.* Washington, DC: Author.

Neugarten, B. (1973). Patterns of aging: Past, present and future. *Social Service Review, 47*(4), 571–580.

Neugarten, B. (1979). Policy for the 1980s: Age or need entitlement? In Government Research Corporation, *Aging: Agenda for the eighties,* National Journal Issues Book (pp. 48–52). Washington, D.C.: Government Research Corporation.

Olsen, L. (1982). *The political economy of aging: The states, private power and social welfare.* New York: Columbia University Press.

Olson, D. H., Sprenkle, D. H., & Russell, C. S. (1979). Circumplex model of marital and family systems: I. Cohesion and adaptability dimensions, family type and clinical adaptations. *Family Process, 18,* 3–28.

Palmer, J., Smeeding, T., & Torrey, B. B. (Eds.). (1988). *The vulnerable.* Washington, DC: Urban Institute Press.

Palmore, E. (1988). *The facts on aging quiz.* New York: Springer.

Parsons, T. (1944). The social structure of the family. In R. N. Ashen (Ed.), *The family: Its function and destiny* (pp. 173–201). New York: Harper.

Pearlstein, S. (1993, February 17). The battle over "generational equity": Painful spending, tax choices have the young calling for the old to get less. *The Washington Post,* pp. F1, F5.

Preston, S. H. (1984). Children and the elderly: Divergent paths for America's dependents. *Demography, 21,* 435–437.

Preston, S. H. (1984). Children and the elderly in the U.S. *Scientific American, 251*(6), 44–49.

Quadagno, J. (1989). Generational equity and the politics of the welfare state. *Politics and Society, 17,* 353–376.

Quadagno, J. (1991). Generational equity and the politics of the welfare state. In B. Hess & E. Markson (Eds.), *Growing old in America* (pp. 341–351). New Brunswick, NJ: Transaction Publishers.

Rae, D., Yates, D., Hochschild, J., Morone, J., & Fessler, C. (1981). *Equalities.* Cambridge: Harvard University Press.

Randall, W. S. (1993). *Thomas Jefferson: A life.* New York: Henry Holt.

Richman, H., & Stagner, M. (1986). Children: Treasured resource or forgotten minority? In A. Pifer & L. Bronte (Eds.), *Our aging society: Paradox and promise* (pp. 161–179). New York: W. W. Norton.

Roberts, R. E. L., & Bengtson, V. L. (1990). Is intergenerational solidarity a unidimensional construct? A second test of a formal model. *Journal of Gerontology: Social Sciences, 45,* S12–20.

Roberts, R. E. L., Richards, L. N., & Bengtson, V. L. (1991). Intergenerational solidarity in families: Untangling the ties that bind. In S. K. Pfeifer & M. B. Sussman (Eds.), *Marriage and Family Review* (Vol. 16, no. 1/2, pp. 11–46). Binghamton, NY: Haworth Press.

Rossi, A. S., & Rossi, P. H. (1990). *Of human bonding: Parent–child relations across the life course.* Hawthorne, NY: Aldine De Gruyter.

Russell, E. B. (1982). *The baby boom generation and the economy.* Washington, DC: Brookings Institution.

Ryscavage, P., Green, G., & Welniak, E. (1992). The impact of demographic, social, and economic change on the distribution of income. In U.S. Bureau of the Census, *Current Population Reports,* P60-183, 11–26. Washington, DC: U.S. Government Printing Office.

Samuelson, R. (October 29, 1990). Pampering the elderly. *Newsweek,* 61.

Schlesinger, M., & Brown-Drumheller, P. (1988). Beneficiary cost sharing in the Medicare program. In D. Blumenthal, M. Schlesinger, & P. Brown-Drumheller (Eds.), *Renewing the promise: Medicare and its reform.* New York: Oxford University Press.

Schlesinger, M., & Eisenberg, L. (1990). Little people in a big policy world: Last questions and new directions in health policy for children. In M. Schlesinger & L. Eisenberg (Eds.), *Children in a changing health system* (pp. 325–360). Baltimore: Johns Hopkins Press.

Schram, V. R. (1985). Motivating volunteers to participate. In L. F. Moore (Ed.), *Motivating volunteers: How the rewards of unpaid work can meet people's needs* (pp. 13–29). Vancouver, B.C.: Vancouver Volunteer Centre.

Schulz, J. (1988). *The economics of aging.* Dover, MA: Auburn House.

Seelback, W., & Sauer, W. (1977). Filial responsibility expectations and morale among the aged. *The Gerontologist, 17,* 492–499.

Shanas, E. (1978). *A national survey of the aging, 1975: Report to the Administration on Aging.* Washington, DC: Administration on Aging.

Shanas, E. (1979). Social myth as hypothesis: The case of family relations of older people. *The Gerontologist, 19,* 3–9.

Short, P., & Leon, J. (1990). *Use of home and community services by persons ages 65 and older with functional difficulties* (National Medical Expenditure Survey, Research Findings 5). Rockville, MD: Public Health Service.

Shoven, J., Topper, M., & Wise, D. (1991, July). *The impact of the demographic transition on government spending.* Paper presented at the National Bureau of Economic Research Summer Workshop on the Economics of Aging, Cambridge, MA.

Silverman, C. J. (1986). Neighboring and urbanism. *Urban Affairs Quarterly, 22,* 312–328.

Sindelar, J. (1989, July). *Intergenerational transfers to and from the elderly: Pecuniary and nonpecuniary transfers.* Unpublished paper submitted to the Joint Economic Committee, U.S. Congress.

Sinha, D. (1984). Community as target, a new perspective to research on prosocial behavior. In E. Staub, D. Bar-Tal, J. Karylowski, & J. Rykowski (Eds.), *Development of prosocial behavior* (pp. 445–455). New York: Plenum Press.

Smeeding, T., Torrey, B. B., & Rein, M. (1988). Patterns of income and poverty: The economic status of children and the elderly in eight countries. In J. L. Palmer, T. Smeeding, & B. B. Torrey (Eds.), *The vulnerable* (pp. 89–119). Washington, DC: Urban Institute.

Smith, D. H. (1982). Altruism, volunteers, and volunteerism. In J. D. Harman (Ed.), *Volunteerism in the eighties: Fundamental issues in voluntary action* (pp. 23–44). Washington, DC: University Press of America.

Smith, J. M. (1993). Function and supportive roles of church and religion. In J. S. Jackson, L. M. Chatters, & R. J. Taylor (Eds.), *Aging in black America* (pp. 124–147). Newbury Park, CA: Sage.

Smith, L. (1992, January 13). The tyranny of America's old. *Fortune,* pp. 68–72.

Soldo, B. J., & Manton, K. G. (1985). Health status and service needs of the oldest old: Current patterns and future trends. *Milbank Memorial Fund Quarterly, 63,* 286–319.

Stack, C. B. (1974). *All our kin: Strategies for survival in a black community.* New York: Harper and Row.

Stone, R., Cafferata, G. L., & Sangl, J. (1987). Caregivers of the frail elderly: A national profile. *The Gerontologist, 27,* 616–626.

Strauss, W., & Howe, N. (1991). *Generations: The history of America's future, 1584–2069.* New York: Morrow.

Suitor, J. J., & Pillemer, K. (1988). Explaining intergenerational conflict when adult children and elderly parents live together. *Journal of Marriage and the Family, 50,* 1037–1047.

Taylor, R. J., & Chatters, L. M. (1986). Church-based informal support among elderly blacks. *The Gerontologist, 26,* 637–642.

Thomson, D. W. (1993). A lifetime of privilege? Aging and generations at century's end. In V. L. Bengtson & W. A. Achenbaum (Eds.), *The changing contract across generations* (pp. 215–237). New York: Aldine de Gruyter.

Torres-Gil, F. M. (1993, November). *Public policies on aging: Reconsidering the old-age eligibility criteria.* Discussion presented at the meeting of the Gerontological Society of America, New Orleans.

Treas, J., & Bengtson, V. L. (1987). Family in later years. In M. Sussman & S. Steinmetz (Eds.), *Handbook on marriage and the family* (pp. 625–648). New York: Plenum.

Troll, L. (1987). Gender differences in cross-generation networks. *Sex Roles, 17,* 751–766.

Troll, L. (1988). New thoughts on old families. *The Gerontologist, 28*(5), 588–592.

U.S. Bureau of the Census. (1988a). *Educational attainment in the United States, March 1987* (Current Population Reports, Series P-20, No. 428). Washington, DC: U.S. Government Printing Office.

U.S. Bureau of the Census. (1988b). *Statistical abstract of the United States.* Washington, DC: U.S. Government Printing Office.

U.S. Bureau of the Census. (1989). *Changes in American family life* (Current Population Reports, P-23, No. 163). Washington, DC: U.S. Government Printing Office.

U.S. Bureau of the Census. (1990, January). *United States population estimates, by age, sex, race and Hispanic origin: 1980 to 1988* (Current Population Reports, Series P-25, No. 1045). Washington, DC: Government Printing Office.

U.S. Bureau of the Census. (1992a). *Educational attainment in the United States: March 1991 and 1990* (Current Population Reports, P-20). Washington, DC: U.S. Government Printing Office.

U.S. Bureau of the Census. (1992b). *Households, families, and children: A 30-year perspective* (Current Population Reports, P23-181). Washington, DC: U.S. Government Printing Office.

U.S. Bureau of the Census. (1992c). *Studies in the distribution of income* (Current Population Reports, P60-183). Washington, DC: U.S. Government Printing Office.

U.S. Department of Commerce. (1991). *Statistical Abstract.* Washington, DC: U.S. Government Printing Office.

U.S. Department of Commerce, Bureau of Economic Analysis. (1991). *Survey of current business, 71*(11), 12-13.

U.S. Department of Education, National Center for Education Statistics. (1990). *Digest of education statistics.* Washington, DC: U.S. Government Printing Office.

U.S. Department of Labor, Bureau of Labor Statistics. (1987). *Consumer Expenditure Survey.* Washington, DC: U.S. Government Printing Office.

U.S. Department of Labor, Bureau of Labor Statistics. (1991, January). *Employment and earnings.* Washington, DC: U.S. Government Printing Office.

U.S. House of Representatives, Committee on Ways and Means. (1991). Appendix L: Federal spending on children and the elderly. In *Overview of entitlement programs: 1991 green book* (Committee Print, WMPC: 102-9, pp. 1342–1352). Washington, DC: U.S. Government Printing Office.

U.S. House of Representatives, Committees on Education and Labor and on Labor and Human Resources. (1993). *Compilation of the Older Americans Act of 1965 and the Native American Programs Act of 1974 as amended through December 31, 1992* (Committee Print, Serial No. 103-E). Washington, DC: U.S. Government Printing Office.

U.S. Senate, Special Committee on Aging. (1991). *Aging America: Trends and projections, 1991 edition.* Washington, DC: U.S. Department of Health and Human Services.

Vaux, A. (1985). Variations in social support associated with gender, ethnicity, and age. *Journal of Social Issues, 41,* 89–110.

Vogel, R. (1988). An analysis of the welfare component and intergenerational transfers under the Medicare program. In M. Pauly & W. Kissick (Eds.), *Lessons from the first twenty years of Medicare* (pp. 73–115). Philadelphia: University of Pennsylvania Press.

Wellman, B., & Hall, A. (1986). Social networks and social support: Implications for later life. In V. Marshall (Ed.), *Later life: The social psychology of aging* (pp. 191–231). Beverly Hills, CA: Sage Publications.

Wolff, N. (1987). Women and the equity of the Social Security program. *Journal of Aging Studies, 2,* 357–377.

INDEX

Activities of daily living (ADLs), 97, 99
Adult children and parents, 22–38
   adult children's obligations to
     parents, 36–38
   affectual solidarity, 26–27, 28t
   associational solidarity, 25–26
   consensual solidarity, 27–29
   functional solidarity, 29–31, 32t,
     33t, 34t
   getting help from children, 33–34
   giving help to children, 33
   giving help to parents, 31–32
   intergenerational norms and other
     dimensions of solidarity, 38
   normative solidarity, 35–36, 37t
   parents' obligation to children, 36
   receiving help from parents, 32–33
   structural solidarity, 22–25
Affectual solidarity, 26–27, 28t
   of grandparents and grandchildren,
     39–40
   logistic regression of, 246t
     (Appendix B)
African Americans. *See also* Race
   optimism about future, 178–179
   perceptions of political influence,
     179
   relationships with parents, 214–215
Age, and intergenerational tensions,
   192–193
Age-based government programs,
   224–230. *See also* Entitlements,
   Social Security, *and* Medicare
Age group(s)
   generational relations across, 11
   as term, 12
Age-related needs, 177–179
"Age wars," 153, 154
Aid to Families with Dependent
   Children (AFDC), 203, 223
Alienated–independent relationship, 214
Altruistic values, 86, 223

"American" collective will, xi
"American dream," 203
Associational solidarity, 25–26, 39
   ordinary least squares of, 245t
   (Appendix B)

Bequests. *See also* Gifts and bequests
   allocating, 281 (Appendix E)
Burdens, 155, 188–190, 219–220. *See
   also* Intergenerational burdens
   and stressors

Caregiving, 98
   within household, 101
Child–parent relations, 49–65. *See
   also* Adult children and parents;
   Parent–child relations
   age of adult child, 57–59
   closeness of, by personal
     characteristics, 53t
   distribution of types of, 50f
   education of adult child, 61–65
   gender of children, 52
   gender of parents, 50–52
   marital and parental status of adult
     child, 59–61
   marital status and gender of parent,
     52–57
   race of adult child, 61
   relation types
     by age of child, 58f
     by education of child, 64f
     by gender of child and parent, 54f
     by gender of parent, 51f
     by marital status of child, 60f
     by marital status of father, 56f
     by marital status of mother, 55f
     by parental status of child, 62f
     by race of child, 63f
Child-rearing time and money,
   monetary equivalent of, 282–283
   (Appendix E)

Children
  child-care costs as burden, 177–178
  economic need of, 163–164
  elders' perception of well-being of,
    176–177
  getting help from, 33–34
  giving help to, 33
  government spending on, 115–116
  nonfederal government expendi-
    tures for, 162–163
  parents' obligation to, 36
  perceived financial well-being of,
    165f
  political advocates for, 168–170
  poverty rates for, 115, 163–164
  unequal spending on, 166–168
  volunteering and, 84–85, 91–93
Computer Assisted Telephone
    Interviewing (CATI), 239
Conflict, intergenerational, 170–171,
    219, 221
Consensual solidarity, 27–29
  of grandparents and grandchildren,
    41
  ordinary least squares regression
    of, 247t (Appendix B)

Democratic egalitarianism, xii
"Dependency ratios," 150–151
de Tocqueville, Alexis, xi–xii
Discriminant analysis, 86
  of giving gifts, 274–275t (Appendix D)
  of making bequests, 276–277t
    (Appendix D)
  of volunteer activity, 266, 267–268t
    (Appendix D)
Dispersed-independent relationship,
    214
Dissonance, 160–161
  intergenerational burdens and, 163
  intergenerational frictions and,
    168–171
Duty of beneficence, 158

Earned benefits, 159, 172–173
Earned rights, 223–224
Economic abundance, x
Education
  family solidarity and, 41

importance of, 110
intergenerational tensions or
    burdens and, 192
monetary equivalent of, 284
    (Appendix E)
volunteering and, 81–82, 86–88,
    91–93
Elderly
  as burdens, 177–178
  caregiving to, 224
  costs of programs for, 187
  federal policy toward, 171–173,
    222–230
  government spending on, 115–116,
    217
  perceived financial well-being of,
    165f, 219
  political influence of, 168–171
  poverty rates of, 115, 163–164
  taxing federal benefits for, 173–174,
    225–227
  unequal spending on, 166–168
Emerson, Ralph Waldo, xi
Entitlements, 223–230. See also
    Federal entitlement programs
Equal opportunity, 158
Equal outcome, 158
Equality, 158
Equity, as term, 7

Factor analysis, 252–253
Family
  hidden connections and intergener-
    ational solidarity, 212–213
  hidden connections in intergenera-
    tional typologies, 213–215
  importance of, 110
  societal-level tensions and, 157
  as source of financial support, 118
Family and Medical Leave Act of 1993,
    224, 231
Family caregivers, 231
Family characteristics, 21
Family generations, 119
  classifying, 278 (Appendix E)
Family intergenerational solidarity, 15
Family members, individual charac-
    teristics of, 20–21
Family relationships, 9–10, 41–49

factor analysis of components of solidarity, 44–47
typology of, 47–49
Family safety valve hypothesis, 187–188, 205
Family types, 15
Federal entitlement programs, 5, 223, 225–230. *See also* Entitlements
Foster Grandparent Program (FGP), 232
"Fragment" thesis, of Hartz, x
Frictions, 17, 156, 172f, 219, 221. *See also* Intergenerational frictions
Frontier thesis, of Turner, ix–x
Functional solidarity, 29–31, 32t, 33t, 34t
   logistic regression of, 248t (Appendix B)

General government transfers, 145
Generation
   defining, 119–120
   in family solidarity, 41
   as term, 10–12
"Generation gap," 161
Generational linkages, 210–233
   hidden connections in community, 215–216
   hidden connections and family intergenerational solidarity, 212–213
   hidden connections in family inter-generational typologies, 213–215
   hidden connections and intergener-ational transfers, 216–218
"Generational stake" hypothesis, 136
"Generational symmetry," 117
"Generational warfare," 220
"Generations," 10–11
   kinship lineages, 11
   other age groupings, 12
   views about equity across, 151
Gifts and bequests, 78, 105–109, 123–127
   allocating, 280 (Appendix E)
   bequests and inheritances, 108–109
   discriminant analysis of, 106
   discriminant analysis of giving, 274–275t (Appendix B)

discriminant analysis of making bequests, 276–277t (Appendix D)
gender differences in source of gifts, 108
gift giving, 105–107, 111
magnitude of giving, 124
magnitude of receiving, 124–127
receiving gifts, 107–108
regression model in, 109
socioeconomic characteristics and family relationships, 106
Government-based transfers, 116, 145
   to elderly and children, 115–116
   government revenue and benefits, per household, 147f
   per household, by age of household head and type of benefit, 146f
   private transfers and, 116
Government benefits, 283–286 (Appendix E)
   net public-private transfers, 286 (Appendix E)
Government programs, as source of intergenerational tensions, 198–206
Grandparent–grandchild solidarity, 40t
Grandparents, relationship between, 42
Grandparents and grandchildren, 38–41
   affectual solidarity, 39–40
   associational solidarity, 39
   consensual solidarity, 41
   grandparent–grandchild solidarity, 40t
   structural solidarity, 39

Hartz, Louis, x, xii
Help, giving and receiving. *See also* Informal assistance
   logistic regression of, 249t
Hidden connections, 2
   in American society, 211
   in community, 215–216
   and family intergenerational solidarity, 212–213
   in family intergenerational typologies, 213–215

Hidden connections *(continued)*
   intergenerational tensions and,
      218–220
   intergenerational transfers and,
      216–218
Historical generation, as term, 12
Housing
   as government benefit, 284–285
      (Appendix E)
   monetary equivalents of, 282
      (Appendix E)
   sharing, 280 (Appendix E)

Income, and intergenerational
      tensions or burdens, 191–192
Income-based government programs,
      224–230. *See also* Needs-based
      government programs
Income inequality, in 1980s, 4–5
Independent variables, in models
      test, 242 (Appendix B)
"Individualism," xi
Informal assistance, 78, 94–105, 216
   activities of daily living (ADLs), 97, 99
   age differences in, 95–96
   Area Agencies on Aging, 99
   assistance in community, 101–103
   assistance to relatives, 100–101
   baby sitting, 98
   caregiving, 96, 98
   community involvement and, 102
   employment status and, 102
   formal services compared with, 99
   giving versus receiving, 95–98
   hours of help given in community,
      103–105
   household size, 104–105
   instrumental activities of daily
      living (IADLs), 96–97, 99
   intensity of community-based
      helping, 105
   for older persons, 99–100
   opportunity to provide help,
      102–103
   rates of assistance received from
      relatives and nonrelatives, 97t
   rates and average hours of assis-
      tance provided to nonrelatives,
      102t

rates and hours of assistance
      provided to relatives, 100t
   regression analysis on, 104
   regression model for, 103
   types of assistance, 96–100
   types of assistance provided to
      neighbors, friends, and relatives,
      95t, 96t
Inheritances. *See* Gifts and bequests
Instrumental activities of daily living
      (IADLs), 96–97, 99
Intensity, as measure of volunteer
      effort, 81–85, 88–89, 110. *See also*
      Informal assistance
Intergenerational bonds, 211
   educational attainment and, 110
Intergenerational burdens. *See also*
      Burdens *and* Stressors, *and*
      Intergenerational tensions
   competing needs, 195–196
   costs of programs, 194
   dissonance and, 163
   emotional bonds, 196–197
   factors that exacerbate, 194–196
   factors that reduce, 196–198
   family obligations, 197
   family solidarity, 109–110
   personal circumstances and
      resources, 197
   sources of, from federal programs,
      194–198
Intergenerational conflict, 3–7
   income inequality in 1980s, 4–5
   intergenerational equity and public
      resources, 5–6
Intergenerational dissonance, 17, 161
   contemporary tensions and,
      168–171
   public attitudes and, 162–166
Intergenerational equity, 3–4, 115,
      117, 162–163
   assessments of, 158–159
   assumptions in debate about,
      186–188
   bequests and, 144
   paradoxical nature of, 152–153
   and public resources, 5–6
   tension in, 160
   as term, 152

Intergenerational family relation-
    ships, dispersed-independent,
    103–104
Intergenerational flows, between
    family generations, 140f
Intergenerational frictions. *See also*
    Frictions
    dissonance and, 168–171
    perceptions of political influence
        and, 179
Intergenerational linkages, 1–18
    design of intergenerational linkages
        survey, 12–15
    economic well-being across age
        groups, 1
    "generation," 10–11
    "generations," "cohorts," and "age
        groups," 10–12
    goals of research, 2–3
    intergenerational solidarity, 42–43
    overview of book, 16–18
    policy debate on intergenerational
        conflict, 3–7
    relationships between grandpar-
        ents and grandchildren, 38–41
    rotated factor pattern for those
        living apart, 46t
    social contexts of, 9–10
    societal resources and their distrib-
        ution across age groups, 7–9
Intergenerational linkages survey,
    12–15
    distribution of sample before and
        after weighting, 14t
    family types, 15
    major topic areas covered by, 13
Intergenerational norms, 38t
Intergenerational patterns, factors in,
    214–215
Intergenerational resource flows,
    137–148
    aggregate magnitude of private
        transfers, 137–141
Intergenerational responsibility,
    norms of, 35t, 251t (Appendix B)
Intergenerational solidarity, 41–43
Intergenerational stressors, 154–157,
    219
Intergenerational tensions, 152–184,

    185–209, 219
    age groups and cohorts, 207–208
    assessments of programs providing
        age-targeted benefits, 201–202
    assessments of societal institu-
        tions, 202–203
    assumptions in intergenerational
        equity debate, 186–188
    in contemporary society, 154–162
    creating, 181
    "deservingness" of particular age
        groups, 199–201
    dissonance and, 163–166
    distribution of, among American
        public, 182
    explanatory variables in regression
        models, 190–193
    from government programs,
        198–206
    hidden connections and, 218–220
    indirect benefits through intra-
        family transfers, 205–206
    measuring, 188–190
    and norms of societal equity,
        158–160, 199, 208
    perceived burdens, 199
    personal expectations, 204–205
    personal prospects, 206
    personal self-interest, 207
    prevalence of, 181–182
    public attitudes and, 162–181
    regression models for measuring, 190
    sources and categories of, 160–162,
        221–222
    types of, 160f
Intergenerational transfers, 16, 79,
    112–151, 216–218
    alternative definitions of transfers,
        142–144
    assessing intergenerational
        resource flows, 137–141
    between-household transfers, 118
    creating monetary equivalents, 123
    defining generation, 119–120
    family generations, 122f
    "generational symmetry," 117
    gifts and, 108
    government spending and, 113,
        115–116

Intergenerational transfers *(continued)*
  living arrangements and shared
    resources, 120
  measuring transfers, 123
  methods in study of, 118–123
  policy age groups, 121f
  private transfers between genera-
    tions, 123–137
  private transfers relative to
    income, 141–142
  public and private transfers,
    144–147
  resource flows, 113
  significance of, 114–118
Intergenerational volunteering, 89–94,
    216
Isolated family, definition of, 72–74

Jefferson, Thomas, 1

Kinship lineages
  generational relations in, 11
  as term, 11

Lineage, 11
Linear regression, 265–266 (Appendix
    D)
Logistic regression, 22, 266 (Appendix
    D)
Long-term care, and family supports,
    230–231

Mannheim, Karl, 12
Marital status, family solidarity and, 41
Measurements, in study, 287
    (Appendix F)
Medicaid, 223
Medicare, 5, 171–173, 187, 203, 220,
    224, 225. *See also* Federal entitle-
    ment programs
  changes in, 227
  nursing home and home health
    care, 230
  premiums, 226
  Qualified Medicare Beneficiary
    Program, 227
Models test, independent variables
    in, 242 (Appendix B)
Modified-extended family, 74

Monetary equivalents, creating,
    282–283 (Appendix E)
Multinomial logistic regression analy-
    sis, 253–254 (Appendix C)
Multiple regression, 22, 265
    (Appendix D)
  of attitudes and perceptions on
    reported burdens, 291–292t
    (Appendix F)
  of attitudes and perceptions on
    reported tensions, 293–294t
    (Appendix F)
  of sociodemographic characteris-
    tics on reported burdens and
    tensions, 289t, 290t (Appendix F)
  of volunteer activity, 271t
    (Appendix D)
Multivariate statistics, 265

National Senior Volunteer Corps
    (NSVC), 232
National Service Trust Act of 1993,
    232
Needs-based government programs,
    224–230. *See also* Income-based
    government programs
Net public transfers, 144, 147
  interhousehold transfers only, 149f
  net government revenue minus
    benefits, 148t
Normative solidarity, 35–36, 42, 213
  measurement of, 243 (Appendix B)
  multiple regression of, 150t
    (Appendix B)
Normative tensions, 161–162
  public attitudes and, 171–175
Norms, 158
Norms of contribution, 158, 159

Old Age, Survivors and Disability
    Insurance (OASDI), 173
Older Americans Act (OAA), 120, 228
Omnibus Budget Reconciliation Act
    (OBRA) of 1993, 226
"Option value," 135

Paradox of age-related salience, 183
Paradox of displaced compassion,
    182–183

Paradox of ill-defined social contract, 183
Parent–child relations (parent's perspective), 65–72; *See also* Child–parent relations
  age of parent, 67–70
  distribution of types of, 66f
  education of parent, 70–72
  gender of parents, 65–67
  marital status of parent, 67
  race of parent, 70, 71f
  relation types by age of parent, 69f
  relation types by education of parent, 73f
  relation types by gender of parent, 68f
  types of, 258t, 262t, 263t, 264t (Appendix C)
Parents
  adult children's obligations to, 36–38
  giving help to, 31–32
  obligation to children, 36
  receiving help from, 32–33
Policy age groups
  classifying, 278–279 (Appendix E)
  Older Americans Act, 120
  as term, 12
Political influence, perceptions of, 179–181
Political process, perceptions of inequality in, 202
Potter, David, x, xii
Poverty rates, 115
Private Intergenerational transfers, 217
Private transfers. *See also* Intergenerational transfers
  aggregate magnitude of, 137–141
  importance of, 117
  intergenerational flows between policy age groups, 138f
  interhousehold transfers only, by age of household head, 149f
  intra- and interhousehold transfers, by age of household head, 150f
  relative to income, 141–142, 142f
  as "safety valves," 116
Private transfers between generations, 123–137

  assessing potential limitations, 132–137
  beneficiaries of, 127
  characteristic age patterns of, 137
  giving to family, by age of giver and generation receiving, 128f
  giving to policy age groups, 130f
  magnitude of, 124–127
  net giving minus receiving, family generations, 133f
  net giving minus receiving, policy age groups, 134f
  net transfer flows, 127–132
  private transfers given, 125f
  private transfers received, 126f
  receiving from family, by age of recipient and generation giving, 129f
  receiving from policy age groups, 131f
  reported giving and receiving, 135–137
Productivity, 79
Public attitudes
  and intergenerational dissonance, 162–166
  and intergenerational tensions, 162–181
  and normative tensions, 171–175
  on opportunity, 178–179
  perceived well-being of different age groups, 175–177
  perceptions of age-related needs, 177–179
  and perceptual tensions, 175–181
Public policy, 222–233
  age-based, 224–230
  families and, 222–224
  generations and, 222–224
  long-term care and family supports, 230–231
  needs-based, 224–230
  promoting elder volunteerism as community resource, 231–233
Public transfers, 145, 218. *See also* Net public transfers

Race. *See also* African Americans
  and coresidence, 24

Race *(continued)*
  family solidarity and, 41
  giving help to parents, 31–32
  in intergenerational tensions, 191
  living close to other generation, 25
  of parent, in parent–child relations, 71f
  of parents, 70
  volunteering and, 85, 89
Regression analysis, 221, 241–242 (Appendix B)
Regression model of volunteerism, 88–89
Regressions, 287–288 (Appendix F)
Resources, allocation of, 279–281 (Appendix E)
Retired and Senior Volunteer Program (RSVP), 232
"Retirement migration," 70

Self-interest hypothesis, 176, 186–187
Senior Companion Program (SCP), 232
Social adequacy principle, 158
Social context, 79
Social networks, 78
Social Security, 5, 171–173, 187, 205, 218, 220, 224, 225, 233. *See also* Entitlements *and* Federal entitlement programs
  benefit formula for, 227
  benefits, 161
  funding of, 225
  means-testing, 202
  OASDI Trust Funds, 226
  OBRA, 229
  taxation of, 226–227
Social structural characteristics, 21
Societal resources, and distribution, 7–9
Solidarity
  dimensions of, 252
  interdependent dimensions of, 20
  as term, 20
Solidarity between generations in families, 19–42
  family characteristics, 21
  individual characteristics of family members, 20–21
  relationships between adult

children and parents, 22–38
  social structural characteristics, 21
Stressors, 17, 156, 172f, 219, 221. *See also* Burdens
  in broader social context, 156–157
  definition of, 155
Structural solidarity, 39
  coresidence, 22–24
  living close to other generation, 24–25
  logistic regression of, 243
Supplemental Security Income (SSI), 223
Survey instrument, 295–308 (Appendix G)
Survey methods and procedures, 235–240 (Appendix A)
  analysis of data, 240
  educational attainment by age and gender, 238t
  interviews, 239
  measurement of variables, 239–240
  race in, 239
  response rate, 236
  survey sample, 235–236
  weighting of sample, 236–239

Taxes, 285–286 (Appendix E)
Tensions, 17, 172f, 219, 221. *See also* Intergenerational tensions
  as term, 155–156
Tight-knit-helping relationship, 214
Time, monetary equivalent of, 282 (Appendix E)
Tobit model, 266t (Appendix D)
  estimation of hours of help given to nonrelatives, 272–273t (Appendix D)
  estimation of hours of volunteer activity, 269–270t (Appendix D)
Traditional family, 74
Transfers. *See also* Intergenerational transfers, Private transfers, *and* Private transfers between generations
  alternative definitions of, 142–144
  intra- and interhousehold transfers, 150f
  measuring, 123

net flow of, 127–132
specific age patterns of, 149
types of, 279 (Appendix E)
Turner, Frederick Jackson, ix, xii

Unemployed status, and intergenerational burdens or tensions, 191
United States, as liberal society, x

"Value of insurance," 132–135
Volunteer participation rates, 80t
   and average hours of volunteer
      activity, 83t
   by age of volunteer and age of
      benefit group, 91t
   volunteer service to older persons,
      93–94
   volunteer service to youth, 91–93
Volunteering, 78, 80–94
   age and, 82
   age-related patterns in, 110–111
   allocating time for, 281 (Appendix E)
   characteristics of volunteers, 81–85
   children and, 84–85
   discriminant analysis of, 267–268t
      (Appendix D)
   educational attainment and, 82, 86,

89, 92, 93
   by elders, as community resource,
      231–233
   employment status and, 84
   factors affecting, 85–88
   family relationships and, 87, 89
   federal programs and, 87
   intergenerational context of, 89–94,
      216
   hours devoted to, 88–89. *See also*
      Intensity
   household income and, 82
   household size and, 87
   income status and, 86
   intensity of, 81–85, 88–89, 110
   intergenerational, 89–94, 216
   marital status and, 82–84, 87
   multiple regression analysis of,
      271t (Appendix D)
   parents of adult children and, 87
   race and, 85, 89
   regression analysis of, 93–94
   regression model of degree of,
      88–89
   self-esteem and, 87
Volunteers, social functions or
   "relatedness needs" of, 78

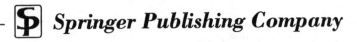

Springer Publishing Company

INTERGENERATIONAL LINKAGES
Hidden Connections in American Society

Vern L. Bengtson, PhD,
Robert A. Harootyan, MS, MA, Editors

Published in cooperation with the American Association of Retired Persons (AARP), this volume contains the results of a national study intended to better our understanding of the many linkages between generations in American society. This study, undertaken by eminent researchers in gerontology, unvieled a complex set of attitudes and behaviors — hidden connections — between different age groups in our society, including relations and conflicts between parents and their children, as well as between entire families and their communities.

Contents:

I.   **Intergenerational Linkages: The Context of the Study.**
     Robert A. Harootyan and Vern L. Bengtson

II. **Solidarity Between Generations in Families.**
     Leora Lawton, Merril Silverstein, and Vern L. Bengtson

III. **Types of Relations Between Parents and Adult Children.**
     Merril Silverstein, Leora Lawton, and Vern L. Bengtson

IV. **Volunteering, Helping, and Gift Giving in Families and Communities.** Robert A. Harootyan and Robert E. Vorek

V.   **Intergenerational Transfers.**
     Karl Kronebusch and Mark Schlesinger

VI. **Intergenerational Tensions and Conflict: Attitudes and Perceptions About Social Justice and Age-Related Needs.** Mark Schlesinger and Karl Kronebusch

VII. **The Sources of Intergenerational Burdens and Tensions.**
     Mark Schlesinger and Karl Kronebusch

VIII. **Generational Linkages for Public Policy.**
     Vern L. Bengtson and Robert A. Harootyan

1994   352pp   0-8261-8670-X   hardcover

536 Broadway, New York, NY 10012-3955 • (212) 431-4370 • Fax (212) 941-7842